The ELLA FITZGERALD Companion

The ELLA FITZGERALD Companion

Seven Decades of Commentary

Edited by
LESLIE GOURSE

SCHIRMER BOOKS
An Imprint of
Simon & Schuster Macmillan
New York

Prentice Hall International
London Mexico City New Delhi Singapore Sydney
Toronto

Schirmer Books
An Imprint of Simon & Schuster Macmillan
1633 Broadway
New York, New York 10019

Printed in the United States of America

Printing Number
10 9 8 7 6 5 4 3 2 1

Library of Congress Cataloging-in-Publication Data

The Ella Fitzgerald companion : seven decades of commentary / edited
  by Leslie Gourse.
        p.   cm.
  Includes discography and index.
  ISBN 0–02–864625–8 (alk. paper)
  1. Fitzgerald, Ella—Criticism and interpretation. I. Gourse, Leslie.
ML420.F52E45 1998
782.42165'092—dc21   97–34301
                                                                 CIP
                                                                 MN

Publisher's Note

This book consists of articles, interviews, and reviews that originally appeared in a variety of publications. Except for silently correcting obvious omissions or spelling errors, no changes have been made in the original texts. Where permission to reprint could not be obtained, all best efforts were made to locate copyright owners. Offensive language used by some writers reflecting racist attitudes has been left as an important part of the historic record.

Contents

Contents

Introduction

"The only thing better than singing is more singing," Ella Fitzgerald told May Okon, author of "She Still Gets Stage Fright," published in the *Sunday News* in New York on September 8, 1957. Ella went on: "What greater honors could come to a gal like me than being invited to sing at the Newport Jazz Festival and the Monte Carlo Gala, as I was this year—and having an Ella Fitzgerald night at the Hollywood Bowl (with Duke Ellington's band) as I did last July 20th?"

Ella Fitzgerald had been winning top honors in the music polls for twenty years by then, beginning with first place as a vocalist in the first *Down Beat* magazine poll in 1937. The next year, 1938, she had her first million-record seller, "A Tisket, a Tasket." Although her career went through ups and downs in the 1940s, she was still referred to as "The First Lady of Song" in several places that decade and in a headline in the *New York Times* by 1951. In the mid-1950s her career took a mighty upward swing. By 1953 she had firmly secured the management of jazz impresario Norman Granz, founder of Jazz at the Philharmonic. He had at first ignored her, considering her to be a pop singer, not a jazz artist, but he revised his opinion, and his eventual alert attention to details of her bookings, her public image, and her private problems and his decision to have her record collections—songbooks—of the country's greatest popular composers beginning in 1956 made her a superstar.

But the hefty singer, who was about one hundred pounds overweight for most of her adult life and who shook visibly and twined her fingers round and round self-consciously when she performed at Royal Albert Hall in London as late as 1954, never really learned to take her stardom and prestige completely for granted. Sometimes she mentioned a nightmarish incident that had happened when she was sixteen years old. She had been competing in an amateur show in Harlem, when she and her accompanist went in different musical directions. The pianist played the wrong chords. Ella started singing out of tune and then fled the stage, while the audience booed and hooted. She always referred to the incident as if it had happened the day before.

Every reporter who met Ella noticed immediately how unprepossessing and innocent she seemed. She asked other celebrities for their autographs—and then wondered if they minded. She marveled when anyone wanted her autograph or when a headwaiter picked up a check in a restaurant for her. She was so shy and complex that it was the rare writer who obtained permission to interview her.

One night in 1954 backstage at Basin Street East, a jazz club where she was performing in New York, she told *New York Post* columnist Murray Kempton: "The other night I was so nervous. This is home. If you flop at home, where do you go after that? Then Benny Goodman came in. You know, with a musician, he will notice something. And Benny is not the kind to come back and say 'Gee Sis, you were crazy' when you know you weren't. And I was hoarse that night." Kempton mumbled that, of course, Benny Goodman wouldn't have noticed. "I don't know," Ella said. "He didn't come back to the dressing room afterward."

Kempton called the resulting column simply "She," describing her as a kid though she was nearly forty and celebrating her nineteenth year in the entertainment field though she had been singing professionally since her teens. "She stands with those great arms, that self-deprecating smile, severely frontal in the Byzantine fashion, the mother, the little sister . . . the hope of us all . . . a cultural force, a permanent tradition, a great river. . . ."

At this time Norman Granz was taking over the helm of Ella's career. Granz had been wanting to sign Ella exclusively to Verve for a long time. He finally acquired the leverage when Decca wanted to release an album including artists under Granz's authority; Granz agreed to let Decca use those artists if Decca would release Ella from her contract before it ran out. Decca did it. Ella signed with Granz in December 1955, and she was poised on the threshold of a great surge forward in her career.

Kempton's article appeared during one of Ella's engagements at Basin Street East in 1954. Gathered to salute Ella were representatives of leading European jazz magazines including *Jazz Hot* of France and *Musica Jazz* of Italy; Ella's fellow singers Pearl Bailey, Eartha Kitt, and Harry Belafonte; trumpeter Dizzy Gillespie; and other stars from Broadway, broadcasting, jazz, and the record industry. Congratulatory telegrams and cablegrams poured in from around the world. Ella received eighteen awards plus a plaque from Decca Records in honor of her 22 million dollars in record sales. Still in her future were the extraordinary years with Verve.

Ella went on to even greater acclaim. She won thirteen Grammies—the most for any jazz singer—and had one of the longest recording careers in history. Among her few rivals were Frank Sinatra and bandleader Benny Carter. She placed first in the critics' and readers' popularity polls of music magazines more often than any other singer. She even won a Grammy for a recording in 1990, when she was seventy-two years old, and her voice quavered, her vibrato quaked, her intonation wobbled uncertainly, and her once peerless sense of time wavered. She won in part because her name was still magical for the judges; no other female jazz singer had ever achieved her international fame. Most pop and jazz singers always say the greatest influences in their lives have been Ella and Louis Armstrong. Even Billie Holiday usually ranks after them.

The people who compile encyclopedias of the most important women and African-American women always select for inclusion Ella, and only Ella, among all the great jazz singers. In 1991 she ranked among the most notable African-American women in a book of that name. In 1993, *Black Women in America: An Historical Encyclopedia* featured her as the "First Lady of Jazz." In the section called "The Visual Arts" in the book *Women of Achievement: Thirty-five Centuries of History*, Ella shows up in the niche between the legendary, inspirational Italian actress Eleonora Duse and Britain's prima ballerina Dame Margot Fonteyn. If it is at least in part true that people are known by the company they keep, then Ella Fitzgerald achieved recognition as an uncontested immortal. In 1996 she was chosen for a profile in the December 19 magazine section of the *New York Times*, which saluted the great people who had died that year.

Yet less was known about her than any other jazz singer. Few celebrities in any part of the entertainment world had more misinformation written about their private lives than Ella Fitzgerald. Perhaps only Thelonious Monk among all the jazz stars seemed as cloaked in mystery as Ella.

In the early years of her career, with her successful 1938 recording of "A Tisket, A Tasket" (three years after her first recording, "Love and Kisses," with bandleader Chick Webb), jazz criticism was a young art. Reporters assigned to write about her tended to poke fun at her and portray her as lacking in intellect. She was overweight, homely, girlishly ebullient, and Negro—all attributes that tended to make her fair game in those days for a writer looking for a way to write a flashily entertaining story. Nobody probed to find out anything definitive or accurate about the childhood struggles of the young woman. Nobody realized that her hardships had forged her character as a loner and thoroughly committed musician in a brilliant and original American art form. Nobody seemed to realize that as a singer she was a genius, and certainly nobody predicted she would develop into a virtual flag of American popular music. Even critic and contributor to *Metronome* magazine George T. Simon, who recognized her as a talented singer and wrote an item about Ella when he first heard her with Chick Webb's band at the Savoy Ballroom in Harlem in the 1930s, said he could never have foretold how great she would become.

Undoubtedly her feelings were hurt by the slights of the 1930s and early 1940s, when reporters depicted her as simple and childlike. They had no idea she had spent some no-doubt terrifying days as a street urchin and that her first marriage and her early romances (and some of her later affairs, too, according to rumor) were with slick hustlers. Her second marriage, to bassist Ray Brown, would last little more than five years, ending in divorce in August 1953; but that alliance was a casualty of their careers and does not reflect on their fine characters.

In 1949, *Ebony* magazine featured her as a star to be reckoned with. Little, however, was written about her private life. Her family history remained shadowy, for Ella divulged little, and what she did reveal, she tinkered with to make the facts more palatable to herself. Her manager, Norman Granz, and his staff, colleagues, and friends tended to shield Ella from interviews. Leonard Feather, whose career as an eminent jazz critic developed as Ella matured into a legendary singer, became her friend; to the degree that any writer established an intimate relationship with her, he was one of the few writers granted the opportunity to write about her with information gleaned in personal interviews. Even Edward R. Murrow, visiting Ella in her home in Los Angeles for his popular CBS show "Person to Person," discovered very little about her life behind the scenes. She had a niece and nephew with her on that show, but their names were not revealed, and neither was the identity of their mother, Ella's half sister, Frances, with whom, until Frances's death in the 1960s, Ella remained close and enjoyed, in the words of Stuart Nicholson, "one of the few enduring relationships" of her life.

Neither Ella nor Norman Granz ever published her memoirs or biography. They seemed to shy away from the very idea of a book or even articles about her life, although Ella once said she had thought about a book. But one day when a writer happened by chance to get Ella on the telephone at her house, she said in a shrill voice, "Call the office," and hung up fast.

When Ella was old and ill, a few tentatively probing articles and book-length biographies were written about her—without her cooperation. For most of her life, the best information came from a handful of critics who knew her fairly well or from musicians who observed her closely when they traveled with her.

Another reason for the lack of books about Ella was that her life lacked controversy, or anyway publicized controversy. It was actually a rather dull life compared with the lives, times, and antics of such stars as Frank Sinatra or Sarah Vaughan or Miles Davis or Rosemary Clooney. Ella never hit a photographer—well, not hard anyway, and not until her later years. And she never had a true nervous breakdown, although she did begin suffering from exhaustion in middle age, when she sometimes sang different concerts in two different cities on the same day. American publishers gauged correctly that the public would never make a run on the bookstores to buy the story of Ella Fitzgerald's life.

Not until Stuart Nicholson published his *Ella Fitzgerald: A Biography of the First Lady of Jazz* in 1994—the first major biography of Ella—did some of the folklore swaddling and obfuscating the facts of Ella's life begin to evaporate. Nicholson included so much documented factual material about her childhood, plus a wonderful discography by jazz historian Phil Schaap, that the book currently stands as the most authoritative biography about her. Nicholson's book is, for the most part, used as a criterion for accuracy, and virtually everything written about Ella before it appeared must be revised.

Ella told columnist Earl Wilson that she had been in the second year of high school—not A.W.O.L. from an orphanage—at the time that bandleader Chick Webb hired her, and Wilson let her claim go at that. About sixty-five years later, Nicholson's biography would reveal that she had been such a truant in high school that the authorities had plucked her out of her aunt's apartment in Harlem and sent her to an orphanage, from which she was indeed A.W.O.L. when she met Chick Webb. She was living by her wits, running numbers, dancing and singing for pennies in the streets of Harlem, wearing rags and men's shoes, and avoiding going back to her aunt's house because she was afraid the authorities might find her and ship her back to the hated "orphanage." And it becomes clear that so much misinformation dogged Ella's footsteps throughout her career because she purposely avoided telling people what really had happened. Perhaps she instinctively understood the old maxim popularized by the legendary African-American baseball player Satchell Paige: "Don't look back, your past may be gaining on you."

She continued to work into her seventies, even though she couldn't see or walk very well, being beset by myriad illnesses. Some people thought she was a pitiful sight, hobbling onto stages, but the majority viewed her as an American heroine. Why did she keep going? As Jimmy Rowles, a pianist and accompanist who worked with her regularly for a while, told me, "I don't know what she would do without music. When she walks down the street, she trails notes." Rowles also recalled amusing tales about the way she concentrated on her repertoire and found new songs to sing wherever she went, even when she was traveling on airplanes. She always kept her road manager, Pete Cavallo, hopping to find sheet music.

Now that Ella has died, and because she was so close-mouthed, it seems unlikely that some details will ever come to light. But it's possible to speculate that Ella sang, with such joyousness in her sound and style, in part because, by singing, she could tame the memories of her early hardships and keep them at bay. The attitude she took in her singing made her a whole person and enriched the rest of us.

Murray Kempton aptly provides the keynote for this book. His writing reflects the reverence that Americans felt for Ella. The much-esteemed journalist and interpreter and commentator on American politics and culture, Kempton had been assigned to Rome, where he had been disturbed by encounters with some American tourists and by their peculiar values and lack of appreciation—or perhaps simply their innocence—of art and culture. Ella Fitzgerald saved the day for him. And so he wrote about her in "The Americans" in the *New York Post* on June 25, 1959:

. . . And yet there is an America to which I shall come home and I am grateful for the hope and memory of it to Ella Fitzgerald. She was here this spring . . .

She sang the cruel and demanding bop songs, and those survivals of the '20s, the most sophisticated work in the book, which she has made her special province. And then, unconscious of trying something more, absolutely unaffected, she put her hands together and sang Bess's part of the "You Is My Woman Now" duet from *Porgy*, which before I had always thought was a man's song.

It is, of course, the song of a loser, or a chippie, who has begun to feel the wonder of possible redemption, the tender of a second chance. I could not believe then that anything Violetta sings in *Traviata* is any wiser and more beautiful; after two months I do not believe it yet.

The lights were of the careless sort one expects at jazz concerts. She lowered her head and barely spoke these lines, and her face between speech and silence had those harsh lights on it; and there was a sudden alteration of all ideas of a peace and beauty. That is the face of America. Grant Wood is already only quaint—a withered newspaper photograph— because he never saw that face. If we had a blessed Angelico, that is the face from which he would have worked. She was a child from the colored schools of Newport News when Chick Webb took her on to sing swing songs; she has no education except what she got there, as cruel a school as Palermo; she has never had a coach except her own interior.

Most of the literature about Ella Fitzgerald consists of reviews and previews of her performances. This book reprints a portion of those pieces and also includes those rarer pieces that address Ella's personal life and views. Sometimes the "facts" about her early life vary from piece to piece. It is my hope that this collection of articles in which she talked freely to her interviewers face-to-face will bring Ella vividly to life for the reader.

PART ONE

Spring Is Here

Early Years

"In emulating Armstrong, Ella's musical subconscious was being shaped by the most important vernacular vocalist of the twentieth century . . . It was Armstrong's concept of improvisatory liberty with lyrics, the way he made them swing, and his variety of attack and inflection that had a profound effect on both jazz and popular singing. . . ."

—Stuart Nicholson

Ella Jane Fitzgerald was born in Newport News, Virginia, on April 25, 1917. Her mother, Tempie (for Temperance) Williams Fitzgerald, a laundress, was abandoned by Ella's father, William Fitzgerald, when Ella was just three years old. Soon after, joining a massive historic migration north, Ella's stepfather, Joseph Da Silva, moved the family into a single room of a red-brick apartment building in the mill town of Yonkers, New York, where in 1923 Frances Da Silva, Ella's half sister, was born.

In *Ella Fitzgerald: A Life Through Jazz*, Jim Haskins describes the Yonkers milieu in which Ella grew up. Haskins explores the first stirrings of Ella's ego and budding self-confidence when she was a schoolgirl nurtured by her mother.

Ella was eleven when she was called "nigger" for the first time. The boy was a newcomer at school, and in response Ella pushed him, knocking him down. But her schoolmates thought she had hit him and were impressed. Ella was a small girl, and her classmates respected her for besting the new kid. . . .

Stuart Nicholson, in his *Ella Fitzgerald: A Biography of the First Lady of Jazz,* has come up with fascinating details. If they are not absolutely correct, most of them will stand as the last word on Ella's childhood and adolescence until an even better source comes along. He gives us memories of Ella's childhood friends and acquaintances and attempts to explain Ella's drive and will to succeed despite the odds against her.

Much of the drama in Ella's life seems to have taken place during her childhood and adolescence, and precious little of her true thoughts and feelings about those years has ever come to light. Even jazz world insiders had only the sketchiest ideas about Ella Fitzgerald's life before she began singing with Chick Webb's band in 1935, when she was eighteen years old. The historic value of the earliest articles reproduced in this book resides in their candid peek at Ella long before anyone knew how accomplished and famous she would become.

Musicians are exquisitely reliable sources of information about their world. If they don't know something absolutely to be a fact, they intuitively know an approximation of the truth—or else they readily admit they don't know. In his book *First Lady of Song*, Geoffrey Fidelman had the courage to include the hearsay passed along by musicians who knew about Ella's romantic life. And Fidelman also came up with tantalizing suggestions about Ella's relationships with friends and relatives. All the biographers have deduced that Ella became completely committed to her career first and foremost, putting it before her personal life. Fidelman suggests that her career engulfed her because she worked hard at it, succeeded so well, and found she could rely upon it when all else failed her.

One of Fidelman's anonymous sources revealed the following:

Ella's recording work throughout this time [1941–1945] had shown a woman still searching for an identity. Her personal life followed a similar pattern. There was little time for her family. . . . Companionship came and went, but her schedule left little time for anything deeper than an evening's entertainment. With little satisfaction from either her relatives or companions, more and more Ella *was* her career.

From studying the lives of the "girl singers," as the women were called in the big band era when Ella began her career, I can readily believe that Ella's experience did not differ much from that of her performing peers. Of the people attracted to the successful singers, some sincerely wanted to befriend the talented women. But many simply wanted to share in the profits—or even to take control of them. It's a testimonial to Ella that she survived and transcended the rugged lifestyle abounding with hustlers.

The early articles I've included in this first part of the book contain the legend and lore and, mostly, the real story of Ella's early years, before she stepped into the spotlight and became a public figure.—*LG*

EARL WILSON

A TISKET, A TASKET, THE WRONG COLORED BASKET

New York Post, 1938

Earl Wilson, a popular and influential columnist writing about the world of celebrities in New York for decades, aimed his sights at presenting an entertaining story about "the Negro gal" who was making a stir with a charming pop song. His piece was one of the first to focus on Ella Fitzgerald as a budding star. His irreverent approach is fascinating for its period flavor and for its depiction of young Ella's candor, playfulness, and apparent trust that she would be presented as a rising star. Wilson gives a faithful report of the attention she was garnering from fans and show business publications. His attitude toward Ella is simultaneously patronizing, appreciative, and affectionate. She allowed him the sort of view that almost nobody would have of her after a few more years passed. Of course, too, she grew older, stouter, and less girlish, relinquishing some of the high, puppyish spirits that characterized her in the 1930s.

This article was not the first to mention Ella in the press, but it was one of the first pieces to focus on her as a budding star. And it has historic value because, while starlets of any race were rarely received seriously, Wilson sheds some light on the way the establishment viewed the young African-American singer in 1938. Here Wilson compliments her voice while revealing the abundant energy that would carry her through electrifying performances for the rest of her life.

It's interesting to note that Ella changed the lyrics to the old nursery rhyme, or rhymed fable, "A Tisket, A Tasket," which originally said that someone sent a letter to his love. Ella substituted lyrics that said she had sent a letter to her "mommy." Tempie

Williams, Ella's mother, had lovingly imparted to Ella the courage and confidence to push herself to succeed against the odds. Ella's voice did the rest of the work.—LG

Ella Fitzgerald, Who Borrowed Nursery Rhyme for Her Song, Says Brown, Not Green

We've got all the news for you today about that new song, "A Tisket, A Tasket."

Ella Fitzgerald, the Negro gal whose voice, somebody said, "has peach fuzz on it," bounced her 170 pounds into a dressing room at the Paramount Theatre yesterday, hauled a pink rayon housecoat tightly around her, and pleaded guilty to writing it.

Ella, who is only twenty, but has shoulders which make you wonder whatever happened to Jim Londos, was further charged with digging-up a centuries-old nursery jingle, rewriting it with much duplication into a swing tune, and driving a lot of people nuts.

"Aw right, aw right," said Ella, grinning to her ears, "but don't say I STOLE it.

"Jes' say I borrowed it.

"I borrowed it from that old drop-the-handkerchief game I played from six-seven years old on up. I played that game at Newport News, where I was born, and at Yonkers, and at that orphanage which some folks say I run away from."

She Invents New Dance

So far, so good, but after that it started getting tougher by the minute to get this information for you. That was because (a) the members of Chick Webb's Negro swing band (for which Ella is vocalist) started ganging in; (b) Ella discovered a telegram from somebody saying she had charm and (c) Ella had to break in every few minutes to show us a new dance she has invented in honor of having her name in lights on Broadway.

Just to show you:

"How did you come to write this song, Ella?" asked the reporter.

Ella answered (we warned you) by hopping up and grabbing a powder box which had three pennies in it and holding it out toward everybody in the dressing room.

"Come a-w-n, everybody give me some pennies!" she said, turning on another grin. She said she had a whole jar of pennies, maybe 400 or so, in her room at the Hotel Braddock, up in Harlem, and why didn't all of us give her a lot more so she'd have a whole lot?

"You ought to give US some pennies," said a newspaper man (whose name we didn't catch) very sourly.

Several other parties present seemed to feel the same way because Ella's new song, or old song, or whatever it is, is selling sheet music and records by the thousands, her tune has been rated as "most plugged on the air" by *Variety*, and every day at the Paramount the jitterbugs swarm out of their seats and make a dash to the stage to shake Ella's hand, or just touch her.

Ella finally settled for one bent penny given her by a spendthrift photographer, then sat down beside Chick Webb, her four-foot-one-inch boss, and didn't interrupt again for fifteen seconds.

Boss Says She Did It

"Now," said the reporter, getting somewhere at last, "who really thought up this song?"

"I did!" said four voices, simultaneously.

Reading from left to right, the voices belonged to a saxophonist, a press agent, Ella, and a porter who sweeps out.

Chick Webb stood up and scowled around the room. "We all sing together, but for God's sake don't you know we can't all talk together?" he said. "Let Ella talk. It's her song."

Boogy-Woogy's Ducky

Ella thought at this point, however, that it would be awfully nice to show everybody her new dance step first. She calls it the boogy-woogy. It's ducky.

"Well," said Ella finally, when there didn't seem to be anything left to do but talk about the song, "we was playin' Boston in April, and I says to Al Feldman, our arranger, 'Look here, I got something terrific! They're swingin' everything else—why not nursery rhymes?'

"I had most of the words wrote out, so we sat down and jammed around till we got the tune, and that's the way it was."

"Did you have to go to a library to get the original words, Ella?"

The reporter added that foolishness to the general foolishness because for several days several very courteous young ladies up at the New York Public Library had been trying to trace the origin of the old nursery song and hadn't been able to find Ella's exact version. They had come to the conclusion that the original song was brought to America by the English colonists, that it was first sung to a game called "Drop the Glove," and that it went like this:

"I tisket, I tasket
A green and yellow basket.
I sent a letter to my love
And on the way I dropped it.
I dropped it, I dropped it.
And on the way I dropped it."

Possibly, states one dusty old tome at the Public Library, this old song may date back to marriage games played in the days of Plutarch.

Got Colors Mixed Up

All this heavy talk about libraries bored Ella and she said "Library" very contemptuously and added, "I remembered all them words I put in my song!"

"Most of them, anyway," spoke up arranger Al Feldman, whose name also appears on the sheet music. "We got the color of that basket wrong. You know, in the old song it's a green and yellow basket. We thought it was brown and yellow. Who are we to go around remembering the colors of baskets?"

"Sure" said Ella, doing a few more turns of the boogy-woogy.

"And—" resumed Mr. Feldman, but never mind. Here are the words to the first sixteen bars of the swing tune, reprinted by permission of the Robbins Music Corporation, the copyright owners, and you can see the similarity for yourself.

"A tisket, a tasket
A brown and yellow basket.
I sent a letter to my mommy.
On the way I dropped it.

I dropped it, I dropped it.
Yes on the way I dropped it.
A little girlie picked it up,
And put it in her pocket."

Virtual Duplication

The remaining sixteen bars are all about what the one little girlie did with the letter to the other little girlie's mommy, but it will be seen from this much that Ella and her collaborator virtually duplicated the basic words of the old rhyme.

After Abe Olman, general manager of the music house, closed the deal for the song in the Savoy Ballroom in Harlem in May, it wasn't long in becoming a hit.

Then came the recordings and after that—well, Ella has about a dozen evening gowns in her dressing room now, and about that many more at home, and fully that many more in the stores, which she's going to buy for fall.

Hollywood has even come through with a $5,000 bid.

Ella spurned it, remembering that it was Chick Webb who picked her up from an amateur hour at the Harlem Opera House four years ago. Ella says it's not true that she was A. W. O. L. from Riverdale Orphanage at Hastings-on-the-Hudson that night.

"I was sixteen, in the second year of high," she said.

Chick, who was about twenty-five at the time, said he adopted this lonely orphan girl, "jist to give her protection." And now when rival band leaders make her offers, she says: "You'll have to see my legal guardian, Chick Webb."

Which is fine for Chick.

NINA BERNSTEIN
THE GAP IN ELLA FITZGERALD'S LIFE
New York Times, 1996

This very dramatic article appeared shortly after Ella Fitzgerald died. It gives a graphic account of Ella's sojourn in a segregated reform school, where she was sent for being a truant. This is a different school from the one cited by biographers Stuart Nicholson and then Geoffrey Mark Fidelman; the article's author did her own research to come up with this shocking information. It was part of Ella's secret, conscious life, which she chose never to talk about for public consumption. Perhaps she never talked about it to anyone. Certainly the information confirms this anthropologist's long-held belief, or instinct, that Ella experienced a wretched adolescence, and that part of her life could constitute a gripping book all by itself. —LG

Ella Fitzgerald sang jazz in a voice so pure and perfected that it admitted no pain—and America loved her for it. In her sound we soared over the darkest passages of our nation's history, to a place where race and class lost all dominion.

Yet the public never knew the full measure of her accomplishment, because for over 60 years she kept the cruelest chapter of her own history a secret: her confinement for more than a year in a reformatory when she was an orphaned teen-ager.

The unwritten story survives in the recollections of former employees of the New York State Training School for Girls at Hudson, N. Y., and in the records of a government investigation undertaken there in 1936, about two years after Miss Fitzgerald left. State investigators reported that black girls, then 88 of 460 residents, were segregated in the two most crowded and dilapidated of the reformatory's 17 "cottages," and were routinely beaten by male staff.

At a time of renewed calls for institutions to rescue children from failed families, this lost chapter in the life of an American icon illuminates the gap between a recurrent ideal and the harsh realities of the child welfare system.

Like Miss Fitzgerald, most of the 12- to 16-year-old girls sent to the reform school by the family courts were guilty of nothing more serious than truancy or running away. Like today's foster children, they were typically victims of poverty, abuse and family disruption; indeed, many had been discarded by private foster care charities upon reaching a troublesome puberty.

When Thomas Tunney, the institution's last superintendent, arrived in 1965 and tried to bring back former residents to talk to the girls of his own day, he learned that Miss Fitzgerald had already rebuffed invitations to return as an honored guest.

"She hated the place," Mr. Tunney said from his home in Saratoga Springs, where he retired some years after the institution closed in 1976.

"She had been held in the basement of one of the cottages once and all but tortured. She was damned if she was going to come back."

Not in the Choir

A more generous image of Miss Fitzgerald's experience there was painted by E. M. O'Rourke, 87, who taught English at the school in the 1930's and remembers Miss Fitzgerald as a model student. "I can even visualize her handwriting—she was a perfectionist," she recalled. There was a fine music program at the school, she said, and a locally celebrated institution choir.

But Ella Fitzgerald was not in the choir: it was all white.

"We didn't know what we were looking at," Mrs. O'Rourke said. "We didn't know she would be the future Ella Fitzgerald."

She did sing in public at least once while she was at the reformatory, according to Beulah Crank, who later worked as a house-mother there. Mrs. Crank, 78, said she was with her parents at the A.M.E. Zion Church in Hudson the day Miss Fitzgerald performed with a few other black girls from the school; she would have been no more than a year away from her legendary victory in a talent contest at Harlem's Apollo Theater.

"That girl sang her heart out," Mrs. Crank remembered.

Gloria McFarland, director of psychology at the reformatory from 1955 to 1963, found Miss Fitzgerald's record in the musty files. "She was a foster care kid when she came," said Dr. McFarland. "She was paroled to Chick Webb's band." Later, the institution's old juvenile records were destroyed by order of the state.

All her life, Miss Fitzgerald was intensely reluctant to talk about her past. As recently as 1994, when this reporter first stumbled on evidence that she had been at the school, Miss Fitzgerald kept her silence.

The silence left a mysterious gap in her obituaries when she died June 15. But her history can now add a cherished face to an often abstract debate about other people's children.

Abused by her stepfather after her mother was taken in at 15 by an aunt in Harlem—the equivalent of today's kinship foster home, but without the financial support. The girl who had excelled in her old Yonkers school dropped out to scrounge for money; she ran numbers at one point and worked as a lookout for a "sporting house," knocking on the door in warning if the police were around.

Her most recent biographer, Stuart Nicholson, has surmised that the authorities caught up with her and placed her in the Colored Orphan

Asylum in Riverdale. It was after running away from the orphanage, he suggests, that she found her lucky break in show business.

Out of Room

But the Riverdale orphanage—the only one open to black children—was overwhelmed as the Depression converged with the great migration of poor blacks from the rural South. With so many younger children in need of a bed, a runaway teen-ager was a perfect candidate to send on to the state reform school.

The institution at Hudson, near Albany, had opened in 1887 as the House of Refuge for Women, the first state reformatory targeting unwed mothers. In the "homelike" brick cottages, discipline meant solitary confinement on bread and water, shackles and beatings. Later, the mission changed to younger girls loosely defined as "wayward," "incorrigible" or "in need of supervision." But the solitary confinement and abuse remained endemic. The buildings now house a men's prison.

"Institutions at their best are no damn good, and I'm old enough to see the pendulum swing back," lamented Mr. Tunney, who closed the "punishment cottage" but found himself re-introducing some of the old practices in a "behavior modification unit."

Like many adolescents leaving the foster care system today, Miss Fitzgerald lived hand to mouth after she left Hudson.

"You ask me how did she eat," Charles Linton, a singer with Chick Webb's orchestra, has said of the gawky, unwashed girl who was dancing for tips on 125th Street until he persuaded the band leader to let her sing with them. "She lived with people she talked to, and she ate with them, she slept wherever she could."

Still shy of 18, she was officially in state custody. Today, we would call her homeless. Her "parole" to a band performing at the Savoy Ballroom was only formal sanction for what she found by her own extraordinary talent and luck.

If she was almost lost to us, how many like her have been?

"How many Ellas are there?" Mr. Tunney asked. "She turned out to be absolutely one of a kind. But all the other children were human beings, too. In that sense, they are all Ellas."

This excerpt from the book Amateur Night at the Apollo *is particularly notable for Ralph Cooper's recollections of Ella's debut at the theater. Ella undoubtedly didn't win twenty-five dollars. First prize was only ten dollars in 1942, when Sarah Vaughan won it, and so it couldn't have been twenty-five dollars in 1933, the year Ella is believed to have won. Neither did Chick Webb hire her on the spot, for he wasn't there that night; nor did Ella get to claim her prize of a week's performance at the theater because she was so unkempt. The first contest she won probably took place at the Harlem Opera House. Although she acquitted herself well in the amateur shows, they didn't launch her career, in part because she looked so messy that nobody wanted to hire her.*

And she surely didn't record "A Tisket, A Tasket" for several years to come. She did her first recording with Webb in 1935, and it wasn't that song. Cooper was at the Apollo as master of ceremonies the night that Ella won. —LG

Anyone who has read about hubris in old books can watch it work on the Apollo stage, where the smug and cocky routinely crash and burn, and where the meek and trembling can surprise the world with voices full of more power and emotion than they ever guessed they had in them.

It happened to Ella Fitzgerald over fifty years ago. The future First Lady of Jazz was just a teenager then, and so scared she almost blew the performance that launched her career. Nearly half a century later, a terrified kid named Luther Vandross got booed off our stage four times before he finally won over the crowd. If he hadn't been dedicated enough to come back for a fifth try, the soul star would be just as meek and unknown now as he was then.

Ella and Luther are proof of the truth: As long as there is an Amateur Night in Harlem, there will always be some brand-new nobody with the chutzpah to stand on our stage and dare to be somebody. Ella has said that she had planned to do a dance number that night (of the Amateur Contest), but when she saw a really hot dance group compete ahead of her, she changed her mind. At the last minute she decided to sing a Connee Boswell song, "The Object of My Affection."

I should have known that even Ella, whose confidence was anchored in real talent, could be blown off course by a sudden and furious gust of fear. And that's just what happened. "I'm always nervous when I sing," Ella told a newspaper reporter a few years later. "Sometimes I can't even remember the words and then I get along on riffs. Mostly I picture what I'm singing. If it's a river, then I get a picture in my mind of a river."

But Ella's visions failed her that night at the Apollo. She came out onstage all jumpy and unnerved. She told that reporter that she first tried to do a little dance step, but she was so intimidated by the audience, her feet felt like they were stuck in cement. When she started to sing, she was off-key, and her voice sounded like a hoarse croak.

I could feel the audience start to rumble. They didn't boo immediately, but I could feel the blood rising. So I stopped Ella in the opening verse and said, "Folks hold on now. This young lady's got a gift she'd like to share with us tonight. She's just having a little trouble getting it out of its wrapper. Let's give her a second chance."

That's all the help Ella Fitzgerald needed. As soon as she composed herself, she tore the place apart. She found her voice, and the audience loved her and made her that night's twenty five dollar winner with a week's appearance at the theater. But, of importance, Chick Webb hired Ella as his vocalist on the spot. At Chick's next recording session, Ella recorded "A Tisket, A Tasket" and gold and fame poured into her basket.

MARION BUSSANG

ELLA FITZGERALD—CHICK WEBB: BAND LEADER'S DEATH MADE HER RICH—SHE'S BEWILDERED
New York Post, 1939

In an interview for an unidentified New York daily newspaper (the piece was reprinted the following year in Down Beat magazine), Ella talks about her reliance on her mentor, Chick Webb, who had died of spinal tuberculosis in 1939, and the ways she misses him. The comings and goings of the personnel suggest the major responsibility thrust upon Ella when she inherited Chick's band. Hunchbacked and crippled for all of his life, Webb nevertheless had the stamina, musical ability, and intellectual capacities for controlling and uplifting his band in a milieu filled with talent and competition. All of his band members had liked Chick, and in his drum work he had been a driving accompanist and an exciting, daring soloist.—LG

When Ella Fitzgerald, the big, light-colored gal, bounces into the spotlight these days and nights, she feels there's an empty space behind her.

The boys are there, all right, playing hot or sweet or lowdown obbligati to her voice.

But there's a new man behind the drums, and that makes Ella feel uneasy, because he's sitting in the seat, smack in back of her, that was Chick Webb's place.

Chick Webb Is Gone

Chick, the small dark boy with the big hump on his little back, has been dead for four weeks. Now, for the first time in her life, Ella has to perform without his comforting presence at her back.

"I didn't always look at him when I came out," says Ella. "But I knew he was there. He'd tap out the beat and I'd listen and then I'd sing."

Ella never sang with any one but Chick.

When she was fifteen, she ran away from a colored orphan asylum in Riverdale to Harlem. A skinny little colored girl, she ran right into an amateur night at the Harlem Opera House.

Chick was out in the audience. Band leaders used to drop into the opera house, looking for talent, and when Chick heard Ella, he knew he had found some.

Sang at Yale Prom

"He sent around some money an' tol' me to get an evenin' dress," Ella says. "I'd never had a evenin' dress before. He took me up to New Haven 'cause he was playin' at some prom up there at Yale. Well, the Yale boys, they liked me a lot, so Chick kept me on.

"An' I stayed."

The courts made Chick Ella's legal guardian. He was a small, patient man. He trained her and worked with her and taught her how to put the breaks in her voice that send little shivers up and down the spines of listeners when she sings.

And when Chick died, leaving no will, Ella was declared his legal heir. Ella doesn't seem to understand yet that she's a very rich woman.

She was polite but bewildered when asked how rich she was. The band's business manager explained that the band is all Ella's, and that it nets $150,000 a year. This doesn't include the revenue from records and sheet music and arrangements, or the money that is Ella's own for writing the song that made her famous, the nursery rhyme swing tune, "A Tisket, a Tasket."

"I guess I just haven't got a head for figures," sighs Ella. "I guess I just like to sing."

Weight Her Big Worry

It hasn't occurred to her yet—and probably it won't—that she can go out and buy herself a big, shiny car or a flock of jewelry. She's proud of the diamond ring Chick gave her for Christmas one year, and the wrist watch she bought herself out of her salary. She'd always wanted a wrist watch, she confides.

She's got just one real worry in the world—her weight. Ella wishes there wasn't quite such a lot of her to waggle when the band goes in the groove.

She's had two offers from Hollywood and has turned them both down.

"I just couldn't go out there and have them take pictures of me for everybody to see with me like this, now, could I?" asks Ella, giving herself a resounding smack.

SHAKEUP HITS ELLA'S BAND; BOB STARK OUT
Down Beat, 1941

Here is another article suggesting the difficulties Ella faced in managing the Chick Webb band once he was gone. But Chick's arranger, Edgar Sampson, was still helping out.—LG

New York—Substantial changes in the Ella Fitzgerald personnel are being made. Bobby Stark, trumpeter, has already left and Irving "Mouse" Randolph, from Benny Carter's band, is in his chair.

"No more big bands for me," says Stark. "I will probably work with Kaiser Marshall's gang at the Victoria in Harlem, just to get my kicks."

Pneumonia Hits Fulford

Pianist Tommy Fulford, stricken with pneumonia, was rushed home, his place taken by "Ram" (Roger Ramirez), top-notch swing pianist who had only returned a couple of days before after several years in Europe.

Wayman Carver, saxist-arranger with the Fitzgerald band, was set to leave as soon as a replacement could be found, and chances were that trombonists Sandy Williams and Nat Story would be out before long.

Edgar Sampson Back

It is also expected that Edgar Sampson will again come into the band on fifth sax when Ella moves from the Savoy to the Famous Door shortly.

MALCOLM JOHNSON
ELLA FITZGERALD AND HER BAND AT THE NEW CLUB TROPICANA— WHO WAS WHERE
1940

Malcolm Johnson, in a New York daily newspaper on October 30, 1940, discusses the band's bookings and appeal.—LG

What may very well be Harlem's last stand on Broadway, now that the Cotton Club is no more, is the new Club Tropicana, recently opened at Broadway between Fifty-second and Fifty-third streets, in quarters previously occupied by a series of unsuccessful night clubs.

The Tropicana clings steadfastly to Harlem talent for its entertainment, but bows to the current rage for South Sea Island atmosphere in night clubs by providing a tropical setting. It is all quite attractive, much brighter and cheerier than the somber, dull red decorations of its immediate predecessor, the Hollywood Cabaret.

Ella Fitzgerald and her band, which she inherited from the late Chick Webb, are the big attractions at the Tropicana, and deservedly so. It is a good band for dancing or for listening, playing in a subdued vein as an effective background for Miss Fitzgerald's singing, which is the highlight of the show. In her work at the Tropicana you'd hardly recognize Miss Fitzgerald as the creator of the swing song "A Tisket A-Tasket." Although she can and does swing out in the hot tunes, she apparently is willing to let "A Tisket A-Tasket" remain in the dead and buried past. For that, we, for one, are grateful.

Ella Fitzgerald is a Negro girl who impresses her listeners as a sensitive, sincere and talented performer. She resorts to no tricks; she just stands up there with her hands behind her back and sings—simply and with a warmth of feeling that is strangely moving. She does a particularly fine job with Gershwin's "Summertime," which tugs at the heartstrings as she sings it. Perhaps the finest critical compliment to her work is that her night club audience listens to her with rapt attention—drinks, food, everything else forgotten.

This is true even in the last show, at 2:30 A. M., when audiences are likely to be noisier and much gayer than earlier in the evening.

Orphan Girl

Ella comes to the Tropicana after a country-wide tour with her band. She is only 22 years old, was born in Newport News, Va., but spent most of her childhood in an orphanage at Riverdale. Chick Webb, the Negro band leader, discovered her one night in an amateur contest at the Harlem Opera House. Ella had entered the contest as a dancer, but when her turn came she was so frightened that her knees gave way and, acting on impulse, she started to sing. The judges gave her the gong. Webb, who was in the audience, didn't agree with the judges, looked her up and offered her a job with his band. After four months of coaching Ella made her debut with the band at a Yale prom. She was sharing featured billing with Chick Webb. A short time before his death, Webb legally adopted Ella. When he died she took over his band.

The floor show at the Tropicana is first-rate entertainment of its kind. Much of its talent is familiar to habitués of the late lamented Cotton Club and this fact is no reflection on the Tropicana, since the Cotton Club made its reputation on presenting the finest Negro talent available.

The principals in the show include Flash and Dash, a team of fast steppers; Avon Long, "The Boy in Brown," who sings; Swan and Lee, comedians; Mae Johnson in her acceptable imitation of Mae West, and Babe Wallace, who acts as master of ceremonies. All in all, a fast-moving show typical of the best that Harlem has to offer. There are three shows nightly, at 8, midnight and 2:30 A. M. Ella Fitzgerald's orchestra alternates with Socarras and his rumba band in music for dancing.

ELLA FITZGERALD WILL QUIT AS LEADER
Music and Rhythm, 1941

Ella was getting set to front her own vocal group for a while.—LG

New York—Ella Fitzgerald will definitely quit as a bandleader in July, but until that time will appear with her band intact in theaters and on one-nighters. Moe Gale, who manages and books the singer, revealed that Miss Fitzgerald would appear exclusively with a new Philadelphia vocal-instrumental group using the name "Three Keys," comprising the Furness brothers, who sing and play piano, bass and guitar.

Gale told *Music and Rhythm* that Ella is signed to appear as soloist on an NBC program. Her orchestra will not disband in July, however, inasmuch as the musical director, Eddie Barefield, will continue with Gale's office backing him.

Barefield is a Des Moines boy noted for his clarinet playing and arranging. He first became prominent with the old Bennie Moten ork.

Miss Fitzgerald took over as leader of Chick Webb's band a few weeks after his death in June, 1939. She'll play theaters and one-nighters with the Keys, Gale said, in addition to her radio show. Barefield will undergo a Gale buildup to make his unit a strong box-office attraction.

MARK MURPHY
TISKET, TASKET—IT'S RHYTHM: ELLA FITZGERALD IS BACK FROM ROAD
New York Post, 1941

Ella is at home talking to Mark Murphy of the New York Post *about rhythm and her romantic life, but she doesn't discuss the burdens of managing her band. Note that Murphy actually means drummer Bill Beason, not Skin Beaton, in the sixth paragraph of this story.—LG*

Ella Fitzgerald was trying to explain rhythm. She moved one hand and then the other.

"It's like . . ." she said. Then she started over. She moved one hand and then the other. "It's like . . ." she said.

She halted again. She pulled her eyebrows together to denote thought and said finally:

"Most all of this is what you get the beat from."

She thereupon waved in the general direction of the band which was practicing on a rehearsal stage at the Paramount today. The beat was there, definitely. Taft Jordan, a lean sort of man, about the color of expensive luggage, was, as they say, giving with his horn.

Deadpan at the Drum

He was being backed up by Skin Beaton on the drums. Skin was very lean, looking like a dissatisfied Iroquois, and he was deadpanning his music, working hard, but showing no particular emotion besides "we don't like it here."

Teddy McRae, who does some of the arranging for the band, was coming in now and then with his saxophone, and his notes were quite warm.

"See," said Ella. "Listen. That's what the beat's from."

Ella then left her chair in the back of the room and stood in front of the band. She gave a reflective kick and began to sing. There wasn't any microphone there and you couldn't hear her. It seemed funny, Ella Fitzgerald singing but not being heard.

She sang "Muffin Man," and then some other song about a man. Then she sang "I Tisket, a Tasket," which is Ella Fitzgerald's song. That was the song that made Ella Fitzgerald.

How It Started

She was just a kid in Harlem, who had been raised in an orphanage and didn't have much of a chance in this world, when she appeared one night on a Harlem amateur program. She tried to dance, but got scared and her feet wouldn't move. Then she tried to sing—in a scared voice.

Chick Webb, it happened, was in the audience and although the rest of the audience didn't think much of the chunky girl on the stage, he liked that scared voice. He went back stage, met her, gave her a job in his band and taught her stage business. Then came "Tasket."

Chick, when he died, left Ella his band, and she's been carrying on. She said that Beason, who took Chick's place at the drums, is awfully good.

Ella, dressed in a blue tweed suit with yellow glints in it, said she's glad to be back in New York after a few months on the road when she was in love—with a guy in Count Basie's band. Being in love is good for a singing girl, Ella implied.

She's Kind of Scared

She said she was kind of scared about her Paramount engagement, would feel more comfortable in Harlem, but then, too, liked the idea of playing a midtown theatre—it made for prestige, she thought. But the audiences have been liking her and so that suits.

As soon as Ella and her show wind up the Paramount stand, they will go out in the willow-frond circuit for a couple of engagements and then come back to the Savoy Ballroom.

There will be dancing and rejoicing in Harlem Streets that night.

PART TWO

How High
the Moon

On Her Own,
Recording with
Decca, 1939 – 55

"Ella's style was complete by the time she broke up the Webb band. The little-girl voice that bounced along through her early records had grown nearly as much as it ever would, give or take a new low register, a loosening vibrato, and heavier timbres. The fact that her voice never became womanly that both her slow, cushiony ballads and her leggy up-tempo scat numbers had a preternatural smoothness, made her seem ageless."
—Whitney Balliett, 1993

Ella was essentially on her own from the day that Chick Webb died in 1939. She led the band for a couple of years, and then she worked with the Three Keys. Not until the late 1940s did she find her way into Dizzy Gillespie's band, where she met her husband, Dizzy's young bassist, Ray Brown. Her connection with Ray Brown led her to capture Norman Granz's serious attention. In the mid-1950s she moved increasingly under Granz's wing, and in December 1955 she signed with his label, Verve. If there is one consistency in Ella's life in the two decades prior to that exclusive contract, it was her recording career with Decca and producer Milt Gabler. Many of Ella's great records and some important, or at least charming, commercial hits carried her along in her Decca years.—LG

TED YATES
ELLA FITZGERALD FOUND HER "YELLOW BASKET"
1945

Ella was no longer working with the Three Keys, and, out on her own, she was playing at the Zanzibar in midtown Manhattan and

had been held over for a fifteen-week engagement. The club also featured other great African-American entertainers in the 1940s— Louis Armstrong, Duke Ellington, and Nat Cole, among others. Ella had great dreams—"Please say I want to be a star like Ethel Waters with a Broadway show," she said—and still talked about how wonderful Chick Webb had been.

She had hired Dizzy Gillespie in the early 1940s, after he had gotten into a fight with bandleader Cab Calloway. Nobody wanted to hire Dizzy, for people were afraid of him, but Ella welcomed him into the Webb band. Later, when she was at a loss for direction, Dizzy would repay the favor by hiring her for his group and taking her on the road. In Dizzy's band she would become immersed in modern music and emerge as a great scat singer. She would also meet her second husband, Ray Brown, the bassist.—LG

SHE FOUND HER YELLOW BASKET: Ella Fitzgerald skyrocketed to fame swinging her nursery rhyme: "A Tisket, A Tasket, I Lost My Yellow Basket." At 16 she went AWOL from the orphan asylum she lived in to dance in an amateur contest at the old Harlem Opera House. Numb with stage fright she lost her feet, and in desperation found she possessed a voice. Chick Webb, a great spirit that glowed in a broken body, heard her. He was with his manager, Moe Gale, up front in the audience. Chick and Mrs. Webb adopted her. When Chick died in 1939 Ella had the unique experience of inheriting his entire orchestra, and that great manager, Gale.

. . . "Three years before that I stopped Mr. Webb on the street and it was Winter," said Ella. "I asked for his autograph and his hands were freezing cold, but he signed that autograph for me."

Ella will always be the guileless little girl who can laugh and mean it. And cry, too. For she's real. With real ability, and with a kindness and humility she inherited from her many young years in the orphanage.

Ella comes from Newport News, Va. When her father died she was sent to the Riverdale orphanage in New York. After Chick and his wife adopted her she traveled with his band for two years and never sang once. That's because Chick kept saying "Don't come up like a shooting star and drop just as fast. Take your time. Build."

But when Chick thought she was ready he wanted her to record music with him. The record company rejected Ella at first. Chick refused to make records unless she was on them. Chick won.

She made her first professional appearance at Yale. Then he gave her the acid test by putting her in the Savoy Ballroom up Harlem way.

"They're real critics in Harlem. If I was accepted there, I'd go places."

She did go places—clear across the country, blazing on every college campus, in every major theatre, and right to Hollywood and pictures.

After Chick's death Ella kept his band going for three years, then gave it up, fulfilled a hungry ambition on a coast to coast radio show over the Blue Network, teamed up with the Four Keys, launching them once again with her reputation as a power among quartets. When she moved into the Cafe Zanzibar in New York the Keys were able to make their own way in cafes and theatres. Still at the Zanzibar Ella has been held over for 15 weeks.

She has composed enough words and music to make the ASCAP membership—she's the youngest in the revered songwriting organization. She picks her tunes out naturally with one finger on the piano.

"Then the piano player writes down the chords. Wish I knew how because sometimes those chords sound barberish to me—like the tunes they played in the old barber shops."

"What do I want most!! Please say I want to be a star like Ethel Waters with a Broadway show!"

But Ella can never talk about herself without remembering Chick Webb. He was sick and deformed, and like Ella, started life struggling against bitter poverty.

"He was the kind that comes once every 1,000 years. Most people always have an angle not he. Always thinking of others, and always in pain, but no one ever knew it. If he'd have taken the same time that he applied to helping people, and rested he'd have lived longer than his 29 years. And there was so much music in that man."

That's Ella Fitzgerald! A veteran of nine years of trouping at 25, but still loyal to the memory of the great little man who made her famous and happy—Chick Webb! Someday she hopes to build an everlasting memorial in Harlem to the diminutive drumming genius. Maybe after the war. We'll all help, won't we?

BETSY LUCE
SOMEDAY ELLA'LL BUY
New York Post, 1943

Betsy Luce wrote about the arts for the New York Post, among other periodicals. Here is a view of Ella in '43.—LG

Ella Fitzgerald, Harlem's gift to swing, has two kind of audiences.

The first kind is comprised of Broadwayites who 'hang' on the ropes of the Cafe Zanzibar every night while she gives out with "Take It From There" and other current favorites.

The second kind is comprised of the neighborhood kids who swarm ever her Harlem apartment when she's home in the daytime.

Both audiences love Ella.

She Likes Kids

Of the second audience Miss Fitzgerald had this to say today:

"I like kids. They come up to the apartment a lot. Sometimes I give them a quarter to go out and buy something, and sometimes they just come up and hug me.

"Sometime I'm going to buy myself a home, a real home, where I can go to rest," she said. "I think it's a good idea, putting maybe $60 or $70 a month into a house that'll be your own some day."

With soft wonder she said that now that she's in ASCAP she gets $100 a month. If she'd been in when she wrote "A Tisket, A Tasket," she'd have made much more, she was told. Some day she'd like to write enough hits to be up in the $10,000-a-year class. The last song she wrote was, "It Was Just One of Those Nights."

Marriage Annulled

She recently had her marriage to Benny Kornegay annulled. He was a defense worker, and they were married less than a year.

Now she has her cousin, Georgie Henry, keeping house with her. The two girls like to cook their own meals. Miss Fitzgerald is on a diet.

"I want to get my hips down," she said. "I want to reduce enough to wear a size 14. But, my oh my, when we go to those Army camps to entertain! All the butter and ice cream they give us!"

She plays the piano, but her main ambition now is to be junior defense worker.

Born in Virginia

Miss Fitzgerald was born Newport News, Va., 25 years ago. Her father died while she was a baby and her mother married again and moved to Yonkers.

Ella was 14 when her mother died. She was put in an orphanage in Riverdale but "left." At 15 she was discovered by the late Chick Webb, Negro band leader who developed her into a singer.

"I'm always nervous when I start to sing," she said. "Sometimes I can't even remember the words, and then I get along on 'riffs.'

"Mostly I picture what I'm singing about. If it's a river, then I get a picture in my mind of a river. I like sweet music, not just swing alone. I guess I just love music."

CARTER HARMAN
ELLA HAS A WAY WITH A SONG
New York Times, 1951

The Times *writer lovingly portrays Ella as a warm, versatile performer, noting that she was never known for singing the blues. Among the singers she emulated were the Boswell Sisters, particularly Connee Boswell.—LG*

Band men who play with Ella Fitzgerald have been heard to say they tune up to her voice, so true is it. Other singers spare few superlatives in her praise. She is publicized as the "First Lady of Song" and the consensus seems to be that she has earned the title in her seventeen years before the public.

The remarkable thing about Ella is her ability to sing any kind of a song and do it with more spirit, with more impact on her listeners and with more purely vocal personality than other performers who specialize in style. When you see her—which you can do Saturday midnight when she sings in the "Jazz at the Philharmonic" program in Carnegie Hall—she will doubtless offer a wide variety.

As she prances into the spotlight, your impression may be of a large, cheerful child. Her smile is entrancing in her cherubic face; her eyes twinkle with more than a touch of mischief; her body—no longer sylph-like, you will agree—seems light and responds eagerly to the bouncing rhythms.

Cold Feet

As a matter of record, Ella wanted to be a dancer as a child in Newport News, and she finally entered an amateur contest at the Apollo Theatre to dance. Cold feet—or wobbly knees—led her to change her mind at the last minute, and she sang instead. The late fabulous drummer, Chick Webb, heard her there and, after a few months, had her singing with his band. She was the one who kept the outfit running for a while after Webb's death, which indicates how high she stands with other musicians.

On a club date or on a theatre stage she will start by singing a rhythm tune of the day. In 1936 it might have been "A Tisket, a Tasket," the old nursery rhyme endowed with a spirited jump setting by Miss Fitzgerald herself.

Ten years later it might have been "How High the Moon?," that sentimental song which she cooled, heated-white, molded into the then-fashionable bob shape and then tempered like steel.

When the cheers die down she will abandon the shiny-surfaced voice for one of sweet, husky, controlled texture and deliver herself of a wistful ditty such as "Sunday Kind of Love." Ballads are really her favorite material, she admits, but she loves to sing anything.

In the same group she might include a new favorite of hers, "Smooth Sailing," an arresting item which as yet has no words. Burbling syllables are used instead, and the melodic line grows into arabesques of instrumental precision and agility. Ella is supposed to have said that she "should have been a tenor man." She makes up for the error by singing the kind of music a saxophonist might play, and as easily as he would play it.

From such exhibitions of "advanced" style one might infer that the singer has theories about it, but she insists that she merely "sings songs." After enough listening one believes her, too. She sings each song the way she feels it and, for her, it is right.

Sitting with her and her friends recently, watching her distastefully eat a box of ice cream because it soothed her sore throat, one got the impression she had the same attitude toward other performers. When someone said that one style sounded "like" another, Miss Fitzgerald overcame her shyness long enough to object: "People are always talking about somebody sounding like somebody else," she complained. On the other hand, the unanswerable retort of a singer who is accused of getting too "advanced" is: "Ella's doing it!"

A musician's spirit seems to be almost more important to her than his ability; she once complained mildly about a man who had accompanied her in an orchestra, not because he played badly, which he did not, but because she didn't think he joined in the fun.

Ella also likes the blues, but she doesn't sing the "suggestive" ones. She tried it once, and was told that it did not suit her. Her voice and interpretations are somehow too pure for smutty lyrics.

Like any sensitive performer, she immediately feels what kind of an audience she has before her. When she sees that her listeners are pleased she smiles her winsome smile and gives them what they like.

One time she sang ballads "all night" for a receptive crowd. On other occasions she indulges in her delightful talent for mimicry. She can growl a chorus that sounds for all the world like Louis Armstrong, or twitter and chirp in devastating imitation of Rose Murphy, the "chee-chee girl."

However she chooses to sing, in whatever vein or idiom, few people who have heard Ella Fitzgerald ever fail to recognize her.

STANLEY DANCE
FOUR TO KEEP
Jazz Journal, 1954

Stanley Dance, one of the greatest authorities on the swing era, wrote this perceptive piece about Ella's early Gershwin album produced by Milt Gabler. Dance recognized the special support and chemistry between Ella and her piano accompanist Ellis Larkins. Critics would always refer to this album as one of Ella's best and most important achievements.

Like Leonard Feather, Dance emigrated to the United States and wrote for magazines. Dance then distinguished himself as an authority with such books as The World of Earl Hines, The World of Duke Ellington, *and* The World of Swing.—LG

Four records lead the field by a long way this month. First and foremost is Ella Fitzgerald singing Gershwin songs on Brunswick LA 8648.

This seems to us to be well-nigh perfect and to possess something of the timelessness of great art. The Gershwin numbers, music and lyrics, will really only have sounded dated to those who were contemporary with their creation. Ellis Larkins, at the piano, reveals how strong the Garner influence was at the period of this session, but his work is always intelligent and constructive. Ella's voice and artistry are so personal, so inimitable, as to be quite unique in our time. Fortunately, this is one of the instances where they are not squandered in poor settings on poorer material.

It is probable that Ella's "Somebody Bad Stole de Wedding Bell" (Brunswick 05271) will make far more quick money. (Incidentally, the backing, "Melancholy Me," is a lovely performance). But in the long run it is records like this LP by which Ella will be remembered, and which will either have to be retained in the catalogue or be periodically re-issued.

What we have here is real, mature talent seriously and conscientiously employed. Ella and Ellis, to be familiar, work like a perfect team, in sympathy with one another, in sympathy with the material. They are confident artists who have no need to demonstrate their brilliance in any deliberate flights of virtuosity or exercises in complexity. They treat the songs with respect and affection, but they cannot help swinging them. Note how effortlessly they set such numbers as "Maybe" and "Soon" rocking.

The notes on the sleeve tend to sentimentalize the great story of Ella's discovery and career with Chick Webb. The truth was more impressive. For instance, when Chick found Ella he was earning around thirty-five dollars a week, out of which he paid for the band's arrangements! According to the sleeve, Ella toured two years with the band without singing in public. That doesn't ring true at all, for those were hard times. Chick had made it the hard way, was the gamest little fighter jazz ever saw, and just wasn't the feather-bedding kind.

Three requests to Brunswick: (1) that Ella now be recorded in a selection of Ellington songs; (2) that her version of Duke's "The Greatest There Is" be not withheld too long; (3) that the LP of Harold Arlem numbers played by Ellis Larkins be given us soon.

BILL COSS

ELLA

Metronome, 1953

Coss, too, praises Ella's early Gershwin recordings for Decca, and he discusses her lack of confidence—a quality that he believes is a key to her character. It may have been the reason that she tried to sing her heart out every time she went on stage: just to be sure

people knew she was trying hard. Perhaps that is how, from the
beginning, she outdid everyone else.—LG

ella!
    everybody thinks she's the greatest
    except maybe miss fitzgerald, herself

When we talk about quality in jazz singing, we always mention Ella. There's no need to say Fitzgerald, everyone knows about whom you're speaking. Everyone shares, at least in part, the admiration that you have for *The First Lady of Song*. Read the polls, ask other singers, quiz music critics, buttonhole the nearest jazz lover. Ella is always the first or second choice.

In the midst of all this acclaim, much more than any other jazz singer has had, she is a sometimes majestic, sometimes ingenuous, woman who has a certain hesitancy off-stage, revealed by a certain turn of words or posturing of body. I say hesitancy because there is no other word to describe the personal reservations that she makes. Everyone praises Ella, but what does she think about herself?

In the last two months, I have made some attempt to subtly discover just that. In a recent interview the questions were introduced particularly for that reason. And, during this time, I heard Ella at La Vie en Rose, Birdland, the Chicago Theatre and the Paramount. My devotion remains unassailed: only marred by the fact that such great and consistent talent is too often thwarted by Decca. For Ella wants to sing ballads, project moods, and, most importantly, record with small groups.

This is the age of huge backings for singers, partly to cut through the noise that surrounds the average juke box, partly to cover up the inadequacies of the singer. Ella doesn't need protection for either reason and she finds that the big accompaniment hurts the feeling of intimacy that she wants to achieve.

She got her chance to sing ballads at La Vie and the welcome change made her hungry for more. She sang with a small group at Birdland and the freedom was particularly thrilling for her. At all four places she received ovations that must have buoyed even so modest an ego as she has.

Through the years, Ella has remained almost an enigma to me. The shy, inordinately modest woman, who sings "How High the Moon" on the nation's biggest stages is not much different from the young girl who wrote and sang "A-Tisket A-Tasket" with the Chick Webb band. In fact, the years between her use of the word "rebop" ("for no reason at all") at the end of a scatting chorus on "Taint What You Do," and her more accepted use of the word bop today, seem only to have made her more shy—less sure of herself.

For Ella, who has always sung simply, those early days of bop were something of a nightmare as she describes it now. "I felt that I was being left behind, and I was," she says. And in an effort to catch up she started scatting to the modern idiom—"All I did was sing 'Moon.' It seemed like the only song I ever sang."

I was told once, by a prominent arranger, that he had complimented Ella after a recording session only to be met with what he described as "wide-eyed disbelief, as if she was certain that she had made one of the worst records of her career. Actually, it was one of the best." It was this kind of lack of confidence that turned her into a singer in the first place, because she had entered the Harlem Opera House to enter the amateur contest as a dancer, then got too scared to dance and sang instead. But it is strange to see it remaining in a woman who is patently thrilled about her acceptance in Europe on the recent JATP tours. Perhaps, not so strange, if you heard her explanation—"I suppose it's because they don't see us very often."

I dwell on this subject because it's a real and an important part of Ella, without knowledge of which you can hardly know the whole woman. It is the inconsistent part of her life, considering the charity which she brings to her judgments, the catholicity of her taste for others' music and the particular delicacy of the taste she brings to her own work. She says, for example, that she likes "all kinds of music, as long as it's played well. Like hillbilly music, it tells a story, and that's good." And this master story-singer should know, for no one can get as much out of a lyric as Ella. Yet she wouldn't have this much charity for her own rendition of a folk song which would be infinitely better than the average rachitic tune from the hills.

I think that there are one or two exceptions to her self-abnegation. She's happy that there's a picture of herself on the wall of a Norway night spot: proud that she was asked to autograph it. And, I believe that she is satisfied with the Gershwin album that she did for Decca. She says that it was the only chance that she has ever had to record with arrangements that really matched her ideas.

But most of the excitement that she feels is about others. About Europe. About working with Woody Herman on the last tour ("Art Mardigan is a wonderful drummer.") About Basie's band—"what can you say?" And about bands in general—"we need bands to make people appreciate music again." She exclaimed about several musicians whom she had met in Europe although she had forgotten most of the names—a vibist and pianist in Paris, a small group in Switzerland and a girl vocalist in Italy. About music in Europe she said that "there are certainly modernists everywhere, not just in the northern countries."

But I still wonder and am sad about so much timidity amidst so much grandeur, and, perhaps you do too, whether you are being made cognizant of it for the first time or reminded of it for the seventh. I sit enraptured, listening to a voice that is at once bright and hauntingly beautiful, hearing and watching a grace that transcends a frequently awkward gesture. I sit and hear good tunes, fair tunes and bad tunes, all given stature and meaning because of her. But most of all, more than any song, I hear Ella.

NAT HENTOFF

ELLA TELLS OF TROUBLE IN MIND CONCERNING DISCS, TELEVISION
Down Beat, 1955

In this piece, Hentoff, an extremely sensitive writer, makes it plain that little is known of Ella's private thoughts. He attempts to get her to speak candidly on a variety of subjects, including the types of songs she is given to sing and the distribution and airing of her recordings by disk jockeys. She never came right out and said that she hadn't gotten a regular television show to do because of racial prejudice, but she named a number of her colleagues who had also been denied that opportunity.

This article appeared as Ella was on the cusp of having her recording career taken over completely by Norman Granz for Verve, and so the regular radio or television shows that she wanted—and which were out of her reach because of racial prejudice—became an academic issue. She didn't need a regular show. She would travel another road and become a concert artist and recording star.

Hentoff is a well-known, highly respected jazz historian and critic. He contributed regularly to Esquire *and* Down Beat *and has written liner notes and books. He has also distinguished himself as an important civil libertarian in his books and his articles for the* Village Voice.—*LG*

New York—"We had a request to sing," Ella began over the applause— and suddenly she stopped. "You know," she grinned, "we really didn't have a request. This is just our next number." Ella had displayed again the candor that has been hers for 20 years in the music big leagues.

Yet, despite this open-hearted honesty, very little is known about what Ella really thinks on subjects closest to her career and emotions. For, except with intimate friends, Ella is one of the shyest people in the entertainment business.

Backstage one night at Basin Street, however, Ella relaxed and spoke openly of several things that long have troubled her.

Potential Scope

Ella, though she underrates herself, is conscious of the warm esteem in which she's held, and often revered, over much of the world. But she is also conscious of the potential scope of her vocal skill and warmth, a potential that never has been realized as fully as it deserves—for reasons that have nothing to do with her undeniable talent.

Take records, for example, Ella has in her repertoire an arrangement of "Teach Me Tonight," one of the current pop best-sellers, that is musically a delight and is as commercial as any direct expression of emotion (with close attention to the melody line) can be.

Yet she has not had a chance to record the number for Decca, nor does she often get a chance to record any really "hot" pop material for the label.

"And," Ella adds, "it's been so long since I've gotten a show tune to do, except for the album. Or a chance to do a tune like 'The Man That Got Away.' Frank Sinatra came into Basin Street often while he was at the Copa, and he asked for that song every time. And he also asked, 'How come, Ella, you don't have a number like *that* to record?'"

"Don't Know Myself"

"I don't know why myself," Ella told him. "Yet I never do get a chance at the songs that have a chance. They give me something by somebody that no one else has, and then they wonder why the record doesn't sell.

"I'm so heart-broken over it. Maybe it's me, but there are so many pretty songs I *could* sing on record. I need a record out. I know that, but I don't know what they're doing at the record company. There must be something I can make that people who buy records would like to hear.

"The album (*Ella*, Decca 12" LPDL 8068) was something I was pleased with. It got such wonderful write-ups, and I remember when I was on the coast it seemed like everybody was playing it. But the disc jockeys claimed that the company didn't give them the record. In fact, we had to go out and buy the record and give it to those disc jockeys that didn't have it."

What's Main Interest?

"Now I don't like to say anything against anybody, but maybe it's because that record company is mainly interested in pictures now that they don't give as much attention to the records. But I sure would like to record with someone who would give me something to record."

Then there's the matter of Ella Fitzgerald and television. "Like every singer," Ella said, "my ambition for a long time has been to have a TV show of my own, but," she shook her head, "I don't like to think too far ahead. What I mean is I don't know anybody who has one. Do you understand what I'm trying to say?

"Sammy Davis, Jr., for example. He didn't get his show, and no one certainly could get tired of looking at him for 15 minutes. Do you remember how great he was on the *Colgate Comedy Hour?* And there's Lena Horne, Jimminy Crickets! If Lena doesn't have a show of her own! We have so many wonderful artists who deserve a TV show. But I don't know . . . the way things are. . . ."

"Someday Maybe"

"I hope someday maybe," Ella continued, "somewhere I can get a TV show. Even if it were just a New York program. So I could stay home a little. It's not that I don't like the road, but traveling all the time, year in and year out, isn't as easy on a woman as it is on a man. And you've heard how guys complain about the road.

"I can dance, you know, if I get a show. I don't say I can read lines," she smiled again, "but for the kind of show I want to do, that wouldn't be so necessary, I'd like a program that was like inviting the audience into my home. The feeling that Peter Lind Hayes and Mary Healy had on their show. It would be informal.

"One evening, for example, we could do a song two ways, fast and slow, and see which turns out better. I could have guests drop in—people like Sarah or maybe a dancer. The routines wouldn't always have to be rehearsed, and if there were mistakes on the program, we'd just do the song or dance over again."

Commercial Twist

"If the show turned out to be a commercial one," Ella animatedly went on, "instead of reading the same commercial every night, we could make up new words and change it every night. And as for talent, if the show wasn't on too late, we could even have somebody drop in with some talented kids from time to time.

"I'd even write music for the program," said ASCAP member Fitzgerald (whose credits include "A-Tisket, A-Tasket," "You Showed Me the Way" and "Rough Riding"). "Lately I've lost all my ambition for songwriting. Every once in a while, I do write a new song down and put it away some place, but when I go to find it, I don't know where it is. But if I had a TV show of my own, I'd be real eager to write some music for it.

"Oh, I have gobs and gobs of ideas, but . . . well, you dream things like that, and that's what these are, you know—my day dreams."

NAT HENTOFF
ELLA FITZGERALD: THE CRITERION OF INNOCENCE FOR POPULAR SINGERS

Liner notes for a Decca label compilation (MCA2–4047), The Best of Ella . . .

Decca reissued two 33-rpm LPs of songs Ella recorded in the 1940s and 1950s, with jacket material contributed by several writers, among them Nat Hentoff and Dom Cerulli, an associate editor of Down Beat. *In his section of the notes, Nat Hentoff makes observations about Ella's relationship to popular music and jazz, while Dom Cerulli concentrates on Ella's voice, which he likens to a tenor saxophone. (For other writers, she called to mind the alto.)*

In general, liner notes for Ella's albums in the 1950s and 1960s, when she recorded for Decca and Verve, were not very interesting—at least, that's the impression made on this anthologist after

*a perusal of liner notes in one collector's library. Writers praised
and promoted her and rehashed sketchy, old misinformation about
her life, when they talked about her life at all. These refreshing
pieces by Hentoff and Cerulli offer some focus.—LG*

"Hey nonny no!
Men are fools that wish to die!
Is't not fine to dance and sing
When the bells of death do ring?
Is't not fine to swim in wine,
And turn upon the toe
And sing hey nonny no,
When the winds blow and the seas flow?
Hey nonny no!"
—An Anonymous Elizabethan

There are fewer and fewer certainties in our civilization of quicksand; but among the predictabilities that remain (aside from mortality and deficit spending) is that when a singer of popular songs is asked his or her favorite vocalist, the IBM answer is: "Ella Fitzgerald."

Such suzerains of the field as Bing Crosby and Frank Sinatra have been proclaiming Miss Fitzgerald's position as a criterion of pop singing for many years, long before that opinion was the fashion. In the past few years, however, everyone has joined in the chorus of hosannas to Ella, and I suspect that there have been some new singers confronted with their first interview who have given Ella's name mainly because they dimly realized that choosing her was a bridge to musical respectability, sometimes a stronger bridge than their own voices.

In any case, the accolades for Ella in this context are exactly deserved. By my own nonconformist criteria, in fact, Ella is more consistently entertaining as a pop singer than in jazz, a field in which she also sweeps most polls, official and conversational. I do not mean to minimize her supple skill as one of the rare "jazz" singers who do fit naturally into an instrumental jazz setting, but I have suspected for many years that Ella became a jazz singer less through fierce personal conviction than through the gradual force of circumstances. As it happened, she did and does possess an instrumentalized approach to singing, a jazzman's concept of phrasing, and a wholly flowing beat. But in general, the most inflammable and irreparably convincing jazz—instrumental or vocal—has been the self-expression of souls that somewhere within them have had more of the tiger than the lamb. I mean Louis Armstrong, Billie Holiday, Miles Davis, John Lewis, Ivie Anderson, and many other jazz players and singers.

It is not that Ella does not sing jazz; but she is happier, I feel, in the less naturalistic pop world where she can sing popular songs and standards in a jazz-influenced style and never meet anything more forbidding than the Wizard of Oz. The conditions of the two worlds—jazz and pop—are different, although there have been viable enough singers, like Ella, to wander in both. Essentially, however, the pop singer does not have to expose her own feelings as nakedly and urgently as the jazz singer; nor, in fact, does she have to draw on the depth of awareness of her own experiences that a jazz singer requires. She can be an innocent at home because, except for the work of a few writers of standards, pop music concerns paper moons more than it realistically examines empty beds. And even in those more urbane standards that are used as often in the jazz as in the pop world, the pop singer doesn't have to reveal the inside of herself as much as she has to be reasonably musical and reasonably faithful to the intentions of the writers.

Ella is a gentle, ingenuous woman. She is still startled that movie stars are among her fans; still nervous at each concert as if she can't quite believe yet that she has an established position in show business; still trusting beyond most others' capacities to imagine trust; and above and underneath all, a romantic. She loves to sing ballads, and her normally intense admiration for Frank Sinatra was even more fired when the first question he asked her at rehearsals for her guest appearance on one of his TV shows was: "Which ballads do you want to sing?" Most often on television, she has been typed as a "rhythm" singer, but it's the ballads she feels most lingeringly. And she is more likely to believe in a ballad that speaks in the idiom of Edgar Guest than she is to comprehend Billy Strayhorn's "Lush Life," although she has sung the latter.

Left to herself, I think you would find that Ella would pick many more of the pop hits of the day to record than she would material better suited to jazz. Ella has never denied wanting a "hit," but unlike other singers who have deliberately "condescended" to sing "hit" material, Ella likes most pop ballads—if they're gentle and innocent enough. It's partly because she is so honestly a resident of the pop world that she can sing most pop songs so much better than her contemporaries. And she not only has the necessary belief in the material to project to her audience, but she also has such superior musicianship. She is an innocent with the musical capacity of a sweet wizard.

Ella, by being herself, has become the best of all pop singers; and by being so accurate a musician in the process, she has set a standard for skill in the field that has given even the most insensitive apprentices a firm idea of what excellence actually is. Meanwhile, her personality has remained about as unspoiled as in the time of "A-Tisket A-Tasket," and it is another Elizabethan poet, Nashe, who for me conveys the characteristic unaffected quality of Ella in this salute:

"Spring, the Sweet Spring, is the year's pleasant king;
Then blooms each thing, then maids dance in a ring,
Cold doth not sting, the pretty birds do sing,
Cuckoo, jug-jug, pu-we, to-witta-woo!"

DOM CERULLI
ELLA ... THE JAZZ HORN
Liner notes, The Best of Decca

Ella knows her way around her voice as very few singers today.

But there are times when she seems to be unaware there are things a human voice just doesn't do.

She does them.

Lately, Ella has included a scat up-tempo tune in her night club and concert repertoire. Most generally it's "Air Mail Special," although at times she sings "How High The Moon" or "Flyin' Home."

She gets into a rhythmic groove and fires a breath-taking barrage of scat words, syllables, snatches of other tunes, interpolations to the audience, asides to her rhythm section; and then brings the piece to a dazzling conclusion by swooping on an open tone up some three octaves to the very top of her range.

It's an electrifying experience to see and hear.

And it must be an exhilarating experience to do.

Ella apparently does it without thinking. She, like any competent jazz musician, works easily within the bounds of her range, saving that climactic extra for the out chorus.

Ella has always had a little of the tenor sax in her voice. Other singers have had touches of other instruments to color their way of singing; Jo Stafford and Sarah Vaughan, to me, have always phrased with a trombone-like clarity, saving a bit of vibrato for the end of a line or phrase for that polish which fully rounds it out; Anita O'Day has a bit of muted trumpet in her voice, and in the way she builds a solo with apparent disregard for bar lines and straight 4/4; and Dinah Washington certainly has the brassiness and brashness of an open-horn trumpet in her forthright singing.

But Ella's voice, as a vocal instrument, has always had the fluidity of a tenor, even when singing words. She somehow manages to slide around words and syllables, no matter how constricting, with the ease of a tenor in the capable hands, say, of Lester Young or Stan Getz.

There is this firm articulation and carry of tone in her sound which comes through like a tenor.

On up tunes, particularly the scat songs, she improvises in a steady flow, much as a tenor would. She jumps octaves and adds little breathy after-thoughts to phrases, much as a tenor.

And she builds vocal riffs exactly the way a tenor would.

It seems, too, in the syllables she uses for improvising, she chooses the ones most easily adaptable to the flow of a tenor sax.

And her vocal timbre is akin to the range of that horn. She has the depth (sometimes, to the delight of everyone listening, she can and does toss in an appropriate honk) of the instrument.

She adopts many of the phrasing devices of the tenor. There are many times when she will take a word like in and sing it "i-hin"; or and will emerge "a-ha-ha-ha-hand"; and she will have improvised within the word or a vowel, in the chord, and with the mannerisms of a tenor.

Perhaps it this facility of voice coupled with a consciousness of the aspirate device in phrasing, and climaxed with an amazing ability to create supple, intricate cadenzas that sustain this image of Ella as a tenor.

The early instrumental uses of her voice which started with her Decca recordings of "Lady Be Good" and "Flyin' Home" in the mid-40s have carried her into her ballad work and today's instrumental uses of her voice.

One thing for sure: as a singer, Ella is also a great instrumentalist.

BOB BACH
THE FIRST LADY OF SONG
Metronome, 1947

Bach calls Ella's absence from the airwaves an example of the "malodorous color line in radio today." Nat Cole had had his own show, and in the 1950s, Mahalia Jackson would have one on CBS for a while, but Ella never did. The joys and headaches of a regular broadcast would never be hers.

Nor did she appear often in the movies. For all her hard work and celebrated image, she never had a decent acting role. In her best movie role in Pete Kelly's Blues—a Jack Webb film about the jazz life in Kansas City when it was run by gangsters (even before Count Basie led his first band there in the mid-1930s)—she played a great African-American singer. But she stayed within the professional confines of her neighborhood club. The great white jazz singer Peggy Lee didn't fare very well in that film, either being depicted as a platinum blonde, alcoholic gun moll or an aspiring singer whose life fell apart in the fast lane. Such was jazz's image. In truth, for those less famous than Ella and Peggy, the jazz life afforded one of the hardest existences for any artist.—LG

Everybody who is anybody in the music business agrees that Ella is the greatest but still she isn't on the air: Bob Bach gives the subject an airing.—*Metronome*

How many ways can you say it:

> *the greatest*
> The Greatest
> THE GREATEST

Ella Fitzgerald has been called The Greatest and The First Lady of Song and almost every other superlative for so long now that it begins to become one of those accepted bromides like an apple a day keeps the doctor away, etc.

All right, so don't take my word for it. Take the words of all the top singers in the business. They listen carefully, super-critically, and they ought to know. Here's what they have to say about Ella Fitzgerald:

Bing Crosby—Man, woman or child, Ella's the greatest!

Mildred Bailey—Ella is one of my favorite singers, one whose interpretations I especially admire.

Perry Como—She has been one of my all-time favorites for many years and still is—she's terrific!

Mel Torme—Ella's fabulous . . . one of the greatest singers alive.

Dinah Shore—(*Metronome* Sept. '46) Of course there's Ella . . . I love her!

Peggy Lee—(*Metronome* Feb. '47 Blindfold Test) Two of my favorite singers on one record . . . Louis and Ella!

Dick Haymes—(*Metronome* June '47) Among the girls there are Margaret Whiting and Ella Fitzgerald, who never use any of the overrated schmaltz.

Add to this list other Fitzgerald raves from—in *Metronome* alone—Vaughn Monroe, Art Lund, Judy Garland, Beryl Davis and others. Margaret Whiting is an enthusiastic Ella booster and girls like Bea Wain, Monica Lewis, and Liza Morrow, go all-out in their praise of The Greatest.

Ella kills everybody—musicians, other singers, fans, hard-boiled recording men—but somehow or other she has been unable to get on the radio with a program of her own or a regular spot on a big show. Ella Fitzgerald, the greatest pop singer of them all by years of almost unanimous acclaim, cannot be heard on the great American wave lengths, while such obvious vocal foul balls as Milena Miller, Dorothy Lamour, Dorothy Shay etc. etc. are to be heard all over this great free air. Need we draw any neon arrows to lead you to the large and disgraceful spectre of Jim Crowism behind American radio? It's so and I throw this charge at every advertising agency and network, along with the back of my hand. If you want one small example of the malodorous color line in radio today I will simply cite the answer I was given by one advertising bigwig when I suggested Ella for an opening on a big network show: "She wouldn't look so good for pictures." Television isn't that close, bud.

Well, maybe by this time Ella is used to the hard facts of life. She had to win three amateur night contests in order to get her first stage job. Her mother died just two weeks after The Street Singer's manager had signed a contract to put the 14-year-old girl on the air. The contract was null and void because Ella was a minor. She was left pretty much alone at this early age and had to scuffle hard to keep going.

The Greatest among today's pop singers might never have been a singer at all if it hadn't been for stage fright. When she walked onto the stage of the old Harlem Opera House in 1935 Ella was going to dance! But she got scared and sang instead—the song was "Judy." The theatre went wild (this writer was lucky enough to be there that night) and Ella won the contest and with it a week's engagement at the theatre. Some people spoke to bandleader Willie Bryant and advised him to sign up the talented kid. He wouldn't. Neither would Willie's rival bandleader at The Savoy, Chick Webb. (Decca's notes in the recent Fitzgerald album are wrong in saying that Chick was in the theatre the night of the amateur contest and signed her on the spot.)

Bardu Ali, who fronted Chick Webb's band, was the guy who discovered The First Lady of Song and insisted upon her being hired for Chick's band. The little drummer refused to listen to her and Bardu had to smuggle Ella into the bandleader's dressing room, lock the door and practically hold Webb in his chair while she sang. Chick was sold but still not convinced that a girl singer with a swing band was a good idea. "We'll take her with us to Yale tomorrow night," said Chick, "and if she goes over with the college kids she stays." "Boola Boola" and "Hold 'Em Yale!" The prom crowd was sent by the plump little singer, even though she only did three numbers with the band—"Judy," "Believe It Beloved" and "The Object Of My Affection." Ella stayed.

At the Savoy Ballroom Ella Fitzgerald began attracting attention with Chick Webb's great band. He made her do mostly rhythm numbers and said he would gradually let her break into the ballad field after she had absorbed enough experience. When Maxine Sullivan became the rage of the country with "Loch Lomond," Ella asked Chick why she too couldn't become as famous with a special number. Chick, a wise little guy, comforted her by saying. "Don't ever want to go up to the top fast . . . build your reputation slowly and you'll stay on top longer."

Chick Webb was right. Outside of a sensational novelty "A-Tisket A-Tasket" (which still plagues her when the requests start flying), Ella Fitzgerald has built her reputation slowly and with impeccable musicianship. As a matter of fact, she's more of a musician than nine-tenths of the horn blowers and rhythm men in the business (friends, like Ellington's Ray Nance, often kid her by asking for her union card). She's come up the hard way, intelligently, the way the late Chick Webb told her to. In *Metronome's* pages over the years Ella's popularity with those who really know music has described a peculiar line of up and down:

'39 .... *1st*
'40 .... *1st*
'41 .... *4th*
'42 .... *7th*
'43 .... *11th*
'44 .... *13th*
'45 .... *8th*
'46 .... *5th*
'47 .... *4th*

The Ella Fitzgerald cycle seems to be on the way back to the top. A recent record of "Lady Be Good," which is one of the good things that has happened to The Queen, represents her awareness of the Gillespie school of jazz (which will be still further exploited through "How High The Moon") and her intelligent musical progress. "Lady Be Good" may become another and more representative "A-Tisket A-Tasket" for Ella Fitzgerald. Believe me—and all the country's smart singers—it couldn't happen to a more gifted person.

P.S. The Greatest pop singer of them all still ain't on the radio.

LEONARD FEATHER

ELLA GIVES CARMEN, PEGGY, HACKETT 5 IN THE BLINDFOLD TEST

Down Beat, 1955

This test is reprinted to show how enthusiastic Ella was about other singers and how tactfully she could criticize or dodge criticizing another singer outright. The piece contrasts in an interesting way with the pieces heaping praise on Ella. While not her only Blindfold Test, it reflects the spirit in which she took all of them.

Feather originated his Blindfold Test for Metronome *magazine, and when it ceased publication, he moved his creation to* Down Beat. *Carmen McRae had just begun winning polls and public acclaim, after about fifteen years of struggle. Helen Merrill was emerging as an important jazz singer. Peggy Lee was very well known, having distinguished herself with Benny Goodman's band and gone on to become a star. Pianist and singer Jeri Southern was brought to New York to sing at Birdland, had hit recordings, and eventually went to write music for films in Hollywood. Barbara Carroll became well known in the bebop era and later on in her career played often as a pianist in the Hotel Carlyle's Bemelman's Bar.*

Ella didn't so readily recognize the instrumentalists, but she knew very well that alto saxophonist Frank Morgan worshipped Bird and that Bobby Hackett was a brilliant trumpet player. Her legendary ears revealed themselves in her answers.—LG

Ella Fitzgerald has been on the receiving end for so much critical comment about her own work—all of it 100 percent favorable—that it constituted a logical reversal to put her in the critic's chair herself.

Since Ella, as can be deduced from her singing, has long maintained an active interest in the instrumental aspects of music, the records selected for her Blindfold Test included a couple of instrumentals in addition to some interesting recent vocal releases. Ella was given no information whatever, either before or during the test, about the records played for her.

The Records

1. Frank Morgan. "Chooch" (Gene Norman). Frank Morgan, alto sax; Wild Bill Davis, organ; Conte Candoli, trumpet.

I don't know who that is. Funniest thing is, the organ sounds like some things that Oscar does. It doesn't have to be; probably isn't. The song sounds like "'S Wonderful." Is that the title they gave it? I like the beat.

I don't know who the alto player is, though. In fact, I don't know who the trumpet player is. Yardbird really started something with that style. With the exception of a couple of fellows like Sonny Stitt and a couple of other fellows, you always think of Parker; unless they do exceptionally well, it doesn't mean anything.

I liked the beat, and I liked the organ, and the rhythm section. I'd give it three stars.

2. Barbara Carroll. "By Myself" (Victor). Joe Shulman, bass; Ralph Pollack, drums; Barbara Carroll, vocal and piano.

Seems to me like it's somebody who is a piano player, who's singing to herself. Sounds a little like Barbara Carroll. I remember catching her in a club one time. It sounds to me like a person with her style of playing; I could be wrong.

There's a nice beat to it, and I liked the rhythm section very much. The song is cute. It's got a cute meaning—you know, I go by myself alone—it's got a little story. I'd give it about four stars.

3. Carmen McRae. "Tip-Toe Gently" (Bethlehem).

Five stars, Carmen McRae. That's my girl. She sings with so much beat, so much feeling. She just kills me. I like everything about the record.

I have the record. When you played it, right away I knew. There is nothing more to be said. Just five!

4. Helen Merrill. "You'd Be So Nice To Come Home To" (EmArcy). Clark Terry, trumpet; Quincy Jones, arr.; Oscar Pettiford, bass; Jimmy Jones, piano.

I liked the beat. It sounds like something that Dizzy had something to do with. It sounds like Dizzy on trumpet, and if I'm not mistaken, that might be that girl Betty St. Claire. It sounds a little like her. She sings in tune. I think she sounds nice.

There are a couple of words, like when she says paradise, you can't understand too well. It's a nice moving record, though; I like the arrangement . . . I like the solos. For a while I though it was Dizzy playing on piano. You know sometimes he plays on the records. Some of the chords sounded like him. I like everything about it with the exception of little things in the diction. I'd give it four stars.

5. Paul Quinichette. "You're Crying" (EmArcy). Quincy Jones, arr. and comp.

Pretty tune. Sounds like a song you'd take and put words to. I don't know who it is though. We've been traveling around the country, and I've lost all contact with music. I like the solo; I like the record. I thought it was very nicely arranged. It sounds a little like Stan Getz, but I've been goofing so much, through not keeping up with music lately, that I couldn't say for sure. I'd give it four stars.

6. Peggy Lee. "Ooh, That Kiss" (Decca).

Five stars!!! I heard this record before in Detroit, and when I heard it, I tried to buy it right away. I think it's the cutest thing; the beat, the arrangement, and the way that Peggy sings it. Of course, Peggy is something to me like Jeri Southern. Just certain songs they sing, they get that sexy feeling in their singing. This seems like it was just written for her. No complaints at all.

7. Helen Carr. "I'm Glad There Is You" (Bethlehem). Don Fagerquist, trumpet.

Boy, that trumpet solo coming in like that surprised me; really surprised me! I don't know who the singer is, 'cause I'm not down with all the singers now. She sounds like Lady Day. She's got a cute voice.

The song is such a pretty song. This reminds me of when I made a record of "Lover Come Back to Me," and the fellows said they didn't like it because it was too pretty a tune to be swung like that.

This type of song is something you don't play fast because you lose the feeling. I liked the first part of it. I thought it was very intimate and warm. I didn't particularly like the swinging part of it. But who am I to say? I have no hits! I'd give it three stars.

8. Bobby Hackett. "Lazy River" (Capitol).

I'd give that five stars. That's a pretty record. I think it's a beautiful instrumental. It's a nice tempo; its nice and soft. He's not playing too much; he's just playing a nice pretty solo from the heart with soul, with feeling shall we say. I don't know who it is though.

I think I'm going to have to buy a whole lot of records. I can't catch up with the music. There are so many singers and musicians coming up now, I don't know who's who. But I like the record very much for an instrumental.

Afterthoughts by Ella

My favorites that you haven't played that I would give five stars? Well, there's Frank Sinatra, and there's Nat. You haven't played any Lady Day. I haven't heard any Lady Day records lately. They say she's got a wonderful album out now.

There are so many new people nowadays that it's hard to know where to start. There are so many girls, especially, coming up. I think there are more girl singers coming up than male.

PART THREE

Everything I've Got

Norman Granz and the Songbooks, 1955–65

"On standards, show tunes and ballads, she is wonderfully warm, with exquisite phrasing, a perfect ear and that dollop of melancholy that gives body to her easy, sometimes jaunty, often honeyed delivery. The Fitzgerald persona communicates as pure and humble, and most of her peers rate her as their favorite singer."

—Linda Dahl, "Stormy Weather," 1984

Sometimes Ella Fitzgerald's relationship with Norman Granz would become stormy. Ella would eventually tell of episodes when she and Granz didn't speak to each other for weeks at a time. The bond between them was extremely strong, however, and their commercial success was spectacular. As she grew older, Ella would say, she learned that, by not taking everything to heart, she could keep their relations running along smoothly.

First Granz had replaced Moe Gale as her manager formally in 1953 and straightened out Ella's debt to the I.R.S. Previously no one had made sure that her taxes had been paid, and her income was considerable. *Time* magazine reported she was grossing fifty thousand dollars a year from Norman Granz's tours, Jazz at the Philharmonic, apart from her other public performances and her recordings. According to the man who is today her most authoritative biographer, Stuart Nicholson, Granz paid her debt to the I.R.S. out of his own pocket. Then Granz bargained her contract away from record producer Milt Gabler at Decca and tucked her firmly under his own wing at his label, Verve.

In 1956 her first songbook album—Norman's idea for the direction her career should take and a fulfillment of Ella's own yearnings for beautifully expressive songs to sing—came out. This and subsequent songbook albums of great American composers and lyricists would dazzle audiences and sell in the millions. In her songbook period she became a superstar.

Exactly at which point she became a legend is hard to say, but, by the 1960s, when the Beatles personified the new pop superstar image, Ella was, like Louis Armstrong, impossible to topple from her throne. When Ella and Louis sang and recorded together, their recordings became major hits.

Granz fell in love with jazz when he was a college student in Los Angeles. Legend has it that he learned a great deal about jazz from Nat King Cole. Granz constantly asked Cole questions about jazz when they met regularly at Sunday jam sessions in a leading club in town. On July 2, 1944, Granz launched his career as an entrepreneur with his first Jazz at the Philharmonic concert. It was a great success, and Granz went on to establish a Jazz at the Philharmonic concert tour and to found record companies. He nurtured many careers with his enterprises, focusing especially on Canadian-born jazz concert pianist Oscar Peterson and Ella Fitzgerald. For his artistic, business, and civil rights achievements, Norman Granz is one of the most important and interesting figures in jazz history.—LG

R.J.D. (DIC DOYLE)
ELLA SINGS THE DUKE AND IT'S A TREASURE
Globe and Mail (Toronto), 1958

Here is one of the flattering reviews of Ella's Ellington songbook album. Some other reviewers had reservations, but later they saw the error of their ways and revised their opinions. This piece reflected the reverence that would ultimately be accorded this album. A second album review by John E. Hasse is included here to provide a perspective from a distance of more than thirty-five years.—LG

Having enriched the world of records with her Cole Porter and Rodgers and Hart Song Books, it was only a matter of time until Ella Fitzgerald got around to Edward Kennedy Ellington. She does so on the widely heralded *Ella Fitzgerald Sings the Duke Ellington Song Book* (Verve MGV 4009–2), a two-volume set of four discs on which the Duke, with small combos and big band, provides the accompaniment.

Of course, it's a treasure house for those who savor the memory of the remarkable things Mr. Ellington has done in the course of bringing sophistication to jazz. And it's a surprise too that so much of his music—written in many cases for the peculiar and particular talents of various Ellington soloists—translates into made-to-order material for Miss Fitzgerald.

Despite its length, the Song Book does not attempt to tell the story of Ellington the composer. His first song, "Soda Fountain Rag," written 40 years ago when the teen-aged Duke was playing a Washington spot called the Poodle Dog Cafe, is not included, nor is any item from Ellington's first show, *The Chocolate Kiddies*. Also omitted are works from some of his more ambitious suites of recent years—like "Such Sweet Thunder" and "A Drum Is a Woman."

Instead, the Song Book concentrates on the thirties and forties, when it seemed that Ellington could do no wrong.

Most of the best of the Ellington standards are included—"Mood Indigo," "In a Mellotone," "Do Nothing Till You Hear From Me," "Sophisticated Lady," "I Let a Song Go Out of My Heart," "I Got It Bad and That Ain't Good," and "I'm Just a Lucky So and So," to name a few. Occasionally the listener would swear that the Duke had Ella in mind when he composed. Certainly there's grounds for the conclusion in a moody crooning of "Don't Get Around Much Anymore," a free-swinging ball with "It Don't Mean a Thing" and the vocal love affair with "I Ain't Got Nothing But the Blues."

Ellington includes, in the style of his latter-day suites, a four-part "Portrait of Ella Fitzgerald" with appropriate Ellington remarks. The grand finale to it all is "The E and D Blues," as joyful a bit as you'll find on all four disks.

As always, Ellington is well served by his instrumental soloists. They include Stuff Smith, Barney Kessel, Oscar Peterson, Ben Webster and the admirable Johnny Hodges.

But the Song Book is Miss Fitzgerald's property. In *The Book of Jazz,* Leonard Feather speaks of "Ella, the voice of light, swinging in insouciant and bell-clear tones an endless parade of trivial songs dominating and conquering the material in a gaily rhythmic challenge."

Here, of course, Ella has a good deal to work with which isn't trivial but still the Feather comment on her career applies. Perhaps the fault lies with producer Norman Granz but the weakness of the Duke Ellington Songbook is that it is too much of a good thing. Ellington has written some great music; beside it, his lesser works seem even less than they are. This is particularly true in many of the instrumental bits in which Ella scats and bops her way around the lack of lyrics. If Granz had had the courage to edit his four-record book into a two-record package, the results might have been sensational. As it stands, they are merely very good.

ESSENTIAL ELLINGTON, 1956–1965
From Beyond Category: The Life and Genius of Duke Ellington, 1993

Nearly all of Ellington's work was instrumental. Of interpretations of his songs, however, one of the most notable albums came in 1957 with *Ella Fitzgerald Sings the Duke Ellington Songbook* (Verve), the first and best of their collaborations. While Fitzgerald is perhaps too sunny to be the definitive interpreter of Ellington songs, she brings much to this album, including her lovely and warm voice, splendid rhythmic sense, and improvisatory gifts as a superb natural melodist. She recorded half the album with the Ellington orchestra (sounding somewhat unrehearsed), the other half backed by a small group including Ben Webster playing strikingly. The thirty-eight pieces on this three-CD set include the expected Ellington songs, new pieces such as the "E and D Blues" and the sixteen-minute instrumental "Portrait of Ella Fitzgerald," and unexpected mutations such as a recomposed "Caravan" and Fitzgerald scatting a new melodic line in the instrumental "Rockin' in Rhythm."

LEONARD FEATHER
ELLA
In From Satchmo to Miles, 1972

British-born Leonard Feather—a pianist, songwriter, and critic— emigrated to the United States, where he became immersed in the jazz world in the 1940s. He learned firsthand about the lives of the jazz musicians from observing them up close.—LG

Ella Fitzgerald's story is strikingly different from Billie Holiday's, even though both were initially handicapped by being poor and black. The difference was a temperamental one: Ella would no more have become identified with "Strange Fruit" than Billie would have with "A-Tisket, A-Tasket." Although Billie was deeply involved in the world of popular music, such songs were not endemic to her style and personality. Ella, on the other hand, can fashion from the most trivial material a performance that appeals to mass audiences—without losing her jazz fans. Billie sometimes accepted songs of little artistic value: Ella often embraced them.

At the beginning of 1936 it was my intense pleasure to travel uptown on any evening I pleased (and I pleased on many evenings) to hear Chick Webb's music at the Savoy Ballroom. In an article for the *Melody Maker* whose prose style can be excused only in the light of its author's age, I tried to capture the experience.

Amid that dark world of Lindy Hoppers, of laughter and light ale [the Savoy serves no hard liquor], of low lights and swing music, of fellowship and fights, the arrangements of Chick Webb and his Chicks stood out like the Aurora Borealis in a sullen sky. . . . There is here something more than the pure, unalloyed swing that has been admired in the work of the early Armstrong, in Oliver and other sepia jazz pioneers. There is the sophistication . . . the artistry and painstaking rehearsal, the brilliant orchestration combined with the loop-holes for grand improvisation, combining to make the perfect swing orchestra of 1936.

Accompanying the story was a photograph I had taken of arranger Edgar Sampson and a slim, pretty Ella Fitzgerald with comments that concluded as follows:

"Please, Mr. Webb, may I sing this number?"
The audacity of seventeen-year-old, witching-eyed Ella Fitzgerald in clambering onto the Savoy bandstand, making this request, and collaring the mike, led to her immediate leap in the Webb aggregation as featured artist on records and from the ranks of unknown amateurs to permanent membership broadcasts.
Ella is a rarity: the only vocalist whose interruptions of a Sampson arrangement can be tolerated, even welcomed with open ears.

Ella Fitzgerald's life will never be made into a movie. The worlds of alcoholism, addiction, and degradation—stepping stones to Hollywood's wide screen—are alien to her. Even the story that she was raised in an orphanage is untrue.

She was born Ella Fitzgerald in Newport News, Virginia, on April 25, 1918. She never knew her real father or her native town: her mother and stepfather moved to Yonkers when she was a child, and she spent much time shuttling back and forth between her mother and an aunt.

As a young girl Ella loved to dance and sing. During lunch hours at junior high school, she would sneak to the theater with a couple of school friends to catch Dolly Dawn with George Hall's orchestra; at night she listened to the Boswell Sisters on the radio—Connee Boswell soon became her favorite.

"Everybody in Yonkers thought I was a good dancer," Ella says. "I really wanted to be a dancer, not a singer. One day two girlfriends and I made a bet—a dare. We all wanted to get on the stage, and we drew straws to see which of us would go on the amateur hour. I drew the short straw, and that's how I got started winning all these shows."

Ella's first appearance, at Harlem's Apollo, won her a prize. "Benny Carter saw the show and told John Hammond about me; they took me up to Fletcher Henderson's house, but I guess they weren't too impressed when I sang for Fletcher, because he said, 'Don't call me, I'll call you!'"

The round of amateur hours continued, and word of her reached the CBS offices. She won an audition to appear with Arthur Tracy, the "Street Singer," and a contract was drawn up in which she was promised a "build-up like Connee Boswell." The bubble burst suddenly when Ella's mother died, leaving Ella orphaned and a minor, with nobody to accept legal responsibilities for her. Hoping to find work, she was forced to resume the weary amateur hour routine. She lost a contest for the first—and last—time when she tried to sing "Lost in a Fog" and ran off the stage to an accompaniment of boos. ("The pianist didn't know the chord changes and I mean I *really* got lost!") But her long-delayed professional debut came soon afterward—a week's work at the Harlem Opera House, for $50.

"Tiny Bradshaw's band was on that show," Ella remembers. "They put me on right at the end, when everybody had on their coats and was getting ready to leave. Tiny said, 'Ladies and gentlemen, here is the young girl that's been winning all the contests,' and they all came back and took their coats off and sat down again."

The orchestra that followed Bradshaw's was that of Chick Webb, a frail, humpbacked drummer from Baltimore who, although barely literate, had risen to form one of the greatest bands of the day. Chick resolutely refused to enlarge his vocal department, which comprised a male ballad singer and a trumpeter whose vocal style resembled Louis Armstrong's.

"He didn't want no girl singer," Ella recalls, "so they hid me in his dressing room and forced him to listen to me . . . I only knew three songs: 'Judy,' 'The Object of My Affection' and 'Believe It, Beloved.' I knew them all from Connee Boswell and I sang all three of them. Chick still wasn't convinced, but he said, 'OK, we'll take her on the one-nighter to Yale tomorrow.' Tiny Bradshaw and the chorus girls had all kicked in to buy me a gown. The kids at Yale seemed to like me, so Chick said he'd give me a week's tryout with the band at the Savoy Ballroom."

"The first time she came to my office," said Moe Gale, who was Webb's manager, "she looked incredible—her hair disheveled, her clothes just terrible. I said to Chick, 'My God, what can you do with this girl?' Chick answered, 'Mr. Gale, you'd be surprised what a beauty parlor and some makeup and nice clothes can do.'" And Edgar Sampson remembers: "We all kidded her. It would be 'Hey, Sis, where'd you get those clothes?' We all called her Sis. And 'Sis, what's with that hairdo?' But Ella always took it in good spirits."

Ella was still slim during her first months with the band, despite her fondness for Southern cooking. While the Lindy Hoppers at the Savoy grew familiar with Fitzgerald in person, her voice was slowly becoming known to radio listeners everywhere as the band broadcast late-night remotes. Eventually her fame forced Chick to include her in a record date for Decca.

"I'll never forget it," said Ella. "The record was 'Love and Kisses.' After we made it the band was in Philadelphia one night when they wouldn't let me in at some beer garden where I wanted to hear it on the piccolo [jukebox]. So I had some fellow who was over twenty-one go in and put a nickel in while I stood outside and listened to my own voice coming out.

"Things went so good that by the fall of 1936 Benny Goodman had me make some records with the band for Victor. But Chick was under contract to Decca and they made them call the records back in." (There were three tunes, all collectors' items today.)

By 1937 she had become famous enough to win her first *Down Beat* poll, which she shared with Bing Crosby. Jimmie Lunceford, whose band she revered, offered her a job at $75 a week; he later retracted the bid out of respect for Webb, but Chick raised her salary to $50 and then to $125.

The Fifty-second Street era was now in full swing. Jazz clubs were blossoming, and the phrase "swing music" was on everybody's lips. The demand was for anybody who could "swing, brother, swing." Stuff Smith tried it on the fiddle, Artie Shaw had a string section in his band for a while, and Maxine Sullivan, swinging folksongs at the Onyx Club, was the new national rage as the "Loch Lomond" Lady.

If you could swing a folksong, why not extend the concept? One day the band was at a rehearsal in Boston when Van Alexander, who was doing some of the vocal arrangements, heard Ella fooling around with an old children's rhyme. He suggested they add some lyrics and a middle part. The result was Ella's smash hit for Decca, "A-Tisket, A-Tasket." "If they'd been giving out gold records in those days I imagine we'd have gotten one," says Ella.

The Webb band and Ella were flying high with their hit records when Chick's health began to deteriorate rapidly; he had tuberculosis of the spine and only his superhuman stamina enabled him even to sit behind his drums. After playing on a riverboat outside Washington, he was rushed to Johns Hopkins for an operation. Chick's will to live carried him through a whole week, then the pain-racked little giant looked around at his friends and relatives, asked his mother to lift him up, said, "I'm sorry—I gotta go!" and died.

At Chick's funeral Ella's voice achieved a poignant beauty it could never surpass. "There were thousands of people," said Moe Gale. "It was the biggest funeral I had ever seen—and I know there wasn't a dry eye when Ella sang."

Gale decided that the band should continue, with Chick's name but with Ella fronting and with one of the saxophonists as musical director. There were more tours and records, and Ella won her third straight *Down Beat* victory.

When the band hit Los Angeles, some of its members were invited to earn an extra $6 by playing an occasional jam session run informally at a nightclub by a tall, intense young man named Norman Granz. "Sure, he used my musicians, but he didn't want me—he just didn't dig me," says Ella. ("I never used Nat Cole either," says Granz.)

The bandleading period, although successful, was not a very happy time for Ella. She had contracted a bad marriage that was ultimately annulled. The draft had decimated the band. Her career as a bandleader was soon over. Gale teamed her with a vocal-instrumental group, the Four Keys, and they had one big hit record, "All I Need Is You," before the Keys themselves were drafted. Ella then joined forces with a series of road shows.

The bop revolution never fazed Ella; she had Dizzy Gillespie in her band for a while in 1941, and her ear grasped the harmonic intricacies of the new style well enough to enable her to incorporate it into a series of wordless performances known as scat, or bop singing. "Flyin' Home" in 1946, "Lady Be Good" in 1947, and a series of follow-ups established her reputation among the same cognoscenti who combed the record shops for the latest Diz and Bird recordings.

A young bassist from Pittsburgh, Ray Brown, was an early bop musician who, after a long apprenticeship with Gillespie, began to play dates with Norman Granz. By now Granz had moved out of nightclubs and into concert halls. Ella's interest in this new kind of music began to focus on Brown. When she visited him in 1948 at a Jazz at the Philharmonic concert, admiring fans spotted Ella in the audience and asked her to sing. Granz grudgingly consented and Ella won Granz over; he offered her an immediate contract. That same year she married Ray Brown.

As soon as she boarded the Granzwagon, Ella's prestige rose even further. She remained with Granz who, even after his move to Switzerland in 1959, continued to manage her. She made a number of albums for Granz's Verve label. He teamed her with Louis Armstrong on one album, gave her a flock of Cole Porter songs for another, followed it up with Rodgers and Hart, and kept her constantly on the best-seller charts. Ella's business alliance with Granz proved more durable than her marriage to Brown, which ended in divorce in 1952.

Ella Fitzgerald has never fully recognized the extent of her fame or talent; she is constantly amazed at her reputation. She is not publicity-conscious at all, is reluctant to give press interviews, and hates cameramen as well—especially the type whose flashbulb explodes during the more tender moments of a love song. "That's the one thing that can drive her crazy at concerts," Granz once said, "that and nervousness. I have yet to see her do a show when she wasn't nervous. We can be at an afternoon concert playing to a small house in Mannheim, Germany, in the fifth week of a tour, doing the same show she's done every day, and she'll come backstage afterward and say, 'Do you think I did all right? I was so scared out there!'"

The views of Ella's managers and fans alike concerning what songs are best for her conflicted violently for many years. A frustrated ballad singer, she once burst into tears when Chick Webb ("He didn't think I was ready to sing ballads") assigned to the band's male vocalist a tune that had been specially arranged for Ella.

"She was temperamental about what she sang," says Tim Gale, Moe's brother, whose booking agency handled Ella for many years. "However, she would sing *anything* if her advisers insisted. One of her records was a thing called 'Happiness.' She cut it under protest; I brought the dub backstage to her at the Paramount, and she said, 'It's a shame. A corny performance of a corny song.' It turned out to be one of her biggest sellers.

"She once played a club in Omaha when Frankie Laine's 'Mule Train' was a tremendous hit. One of the biggest spenders in Omaha came in constantly and demanded that she sing it. She kept ducking it until finally the club boss begged her to please the money guy. Ella said to herself, 'I'll sing it in such a way that he'll never ask for it again,' and proceeded to do a burlesque so tremendous that she kept it in the act and scored riotously with it everywhere—even at Bop City."

Granz's first move on assuming the managerial reins was to steer Ella away from the jazz rooms and into the class clubs. Skeptical at first, Ella gradually took to the new plush environments when she found that audiences at the Fairmont in San Francisco or the Copa in New York were as susceptible to "Air Mail Special" and "Tenderly" as the hip crowd at Birdland.

The quantity of Ella's performances has caused more disagreements than the quality. "I'll ask her to do two ballads in a row, to set a mood," says Granz, "but some kid in the back will yell 'How High the Moon' and off she'll go. Or I'll say I want her to do eight tunes and she'll say, 'Don't you think that's too many? Let's make it six.' And she'll go out there and do the six and then if the audience wants fifty she'll stay for forty-four more. It's part of her whole approach to life. She just loves to sing."

"Every tour I ever made with her convinced me that singing is her whole life," says guitarist Barney Kessel. "I remember once in Genoa, Italy, we sat down to eat and the restaurant was empty except for Lester Young and his wife and Ella and me. So while we waited to give our breakfast order I pulled out my guitar and she and Lester started making up fabulous things on the blues.

"Another time, when we were touring Switzerland, instead of gossiping with the rest of the troupe on the bus, she and I would get together and she'd take some tune like 'Blue Lou' and sing it every way in the world. She'd do it like Mahalia Jackson and like Sarah and finally make up new lyrics for it. She would try to exhaust every possibility, as if she were trying to develop improvisation to a new point by ad-libbing lyrically, too, the way Calypso singers do."

"Ella does that even on shows," recalls another musician who toured with her for years. "If there's a heckler she'll interpolate a swinging warning to him in the middle of a number, or the mike'll go wrong and she'll tell the engineer about it in words and music.

"But she's terribly sensitive socially. Whenever she hears a crowd mumbling she feels that they are discussing her—and always unfavorably. I think she lays so much stress on being accepted in music because this is the one area of life into which she feels she can fit successfully. Her marriages failed; she doesn't have an awful lot of the normal activities most women have, such as home life, so she wraps herself up entirely in music. She wants desperately to be accepted."

This analysis may be accurate, but Ella often gives the impression that she is a happy extrovert. One of the gang to her fellow workers, she is a whiz at tonk or blackjack when the cards are pulled out on bus trips. She also has the naively enthusiastic qualities of one of her own fans. ("Do you know who caught the show the other night?" she said to me one day in 1960. "Judy Holliday—and she came backstage afterward to see me! And she went on and on about how she liked me! Imagine that—Judy Holliday!") Once when a restaurant owner for whom she had just tape-recorded an interview picked up the check for her dinner, she was both astonished and grateful—as if this gesture were without precedent.

Today Ella is firmly established within the jazz world as a great artist. She has kept pace with the times by sometimes adapting current tunes to her style, although her attempts to gain a foothold in the pop record market by recording with unsympathetic rock arrangements have proved less than successful, both musically and commercially.

She continues to travel frequently. In the summer of 1971, however, one of her European tours was cut short when, shortly after she had recuperated from a cataract operation on her left eye, her right eye hemorrhaged. While she recovered at home in Beverly Hills, she studied Portuguese "so when I do those Brazilian songs I'll know what I'm singing about."

The arguments concerning her stature as a jazz singer have long since subsided. With the shrinking emphasis on categorization, the central fact has stood out in sharper perspective than ever: Ella Fitzgerald's is one of the most flexible, beautiful, and widely appreciated voices of this century.

Perhaps the best assessment of it was made by Mrs. David Frisina, wife of the Los Angeles Philharmonic concertmaster, after a historic concert at the Hollywood Bowl in 1957: "Ella Fitzgerald," she said, "could sing the Van Nuys telephone directory with a broken jaw and make it sound good. And that," she added, "is a particularly dull telephone directory."

JOHN TYNAN

IT TOOK A HIT ALBUM TO MAKE MISS F. A CLASS NITERY ATTRACTION

Down Beat, 1956

Here, Ella reveals her career in full swing, as she works hard for the Jazz at the Philharmonic tours and begins reaping the benefits of her songbooks. She still has dreams of having her own television show, and she talks about doing a Duke Ellington songbook.—LG

"Every year I wait for the tour. It's pretty rough going sometimes, but I think that my being with Jazz at the Philharmonic helps win me fans."

That's about it. ". . . Pretty rough going sometimes, but . . . helps win me fans." After 10 years with Norman Granz's annual concert tour—and 22 years in show business—Ella Fitzgerald fairly sums up her raison d'etre. Seemingly indefatigable, with a current engagement schedule that permits her little time off till mid-January, when she can relax in her new Los Angeles home, Ella feels that so long as she's singing and reaching a wider appreciative audience, her life is full and swinging.

On her last date at the upper-crust Mocambo (the third there in 1 1/2 years) owner Charlie Morrison says she drew better than Roberta Sherwood's act that immediately preceded her. The significant fact here is that Miss Sherwood opened on the Sunset Strip following an almost unprecedented publicity campaign conducted by Walter Winchell. Conversely, Miss Fitzgerald bowed into the "Mo" with a minimum of advance fanfare and played to turn-away business every night.

Ella contends the main reason for this triumph is that for the first time in her career she's got a best-selling album package working for her, Verve Records' *Cole Porter Songbook*. In support of this reasoning is the fact that during her last stint at the club early this year business was clearly disappointing. More often than not, she sang to a room half full, a clientele more of noisy bon vivants than admirers. Then, this summer, her album of Cole Porter tunes was released by Norman Granz, the artist's first LP since leaving Decca. Since then it's been near panic wherever she appears.

Resting between shows in the Mocambo's fire-engine red dressing room, Ella talked good humoredly to visiting fans Jerry Lewis and Monty Clift. Clift was apologizing for calling requests too loudly during her show. Ella laughed and said it was good to know he was digging her. Lewis yawned and grumbled about a 6 a.m. call to his movie studio. La Fitzgerald grinned as she recalled her own early calls during the filming of *Pete Kelly's Blues*. When the visitors had left, Ella relaxed a bit.

"What was that you were asking me? Oh, yes, the harmonica." She gave a mock wince and chuckled. "More people have been asking me about that darn harmonica. Well, here's the true story.

"Oscar and 'Herky' (that's what we call Ellis) bought one in Europe to tease Norman. They'd play it hillbilly style to rile him. I used to play in school and one day I got hold of theirs and started blowing. Then, for a gag I played it at a concert one night. In Europe, I mean. Norman thought it was a pretty good bit, said he'd have me play on our tour back home. And that was that."

Asked how she felt about playing it onstage, Ella smiled and commented, "It was something a little different. A bit of fun, you know. Like a challenge in a way. But then, I'd like to learn vibes, too. . . . That'd be a ball."

Returning to the subject of recording, Ella spoke of her just-completed *Rodgers and Hart Songbook*. "It's so pretty," she said. "I did it mostly with strings, and I've always wanted to sing with lots of strings. Then, I think the average layman knows the songs better, so it should sell more than Cole Porter. Another thing is that we didn't have to rush it like we did the first album, so I think the whole feeling is more relaxed."

Of the Rodgers and Hart songs, she especially mentioned "Spring Is Here" ("I like that") and "Bewitched" ("I got real sexy on that one") as evoking particularly warm feeling.

There was good news that evening concerning television, an entertainment medium thus far denied this superb entertainer. It had just been announced by NBC that Nat Cole was to have his own network teleshow, albeit a scant 15 minutes and only on what the network executives call a "trial basis." But Ella was deeply happy for Nat.

"I'm so proud for him," she smiled wistfully. "Nobody deserves it more than he does. All I can say is that I hope I'm the first woman . . ." Her voice trailed off and she looked away.

As conversation reverted to in-person performances, the topic of audiences naturally predominated. "In 10 years of making concert tours I think the audiences have matured quite a lot," she observed. "Particularly the JATP audiences. This year I believe we had the nicest houses so far, and a great deal of credit must go to Norman. You know, he even wrote a little instruction on the JATP program this year on how they should behave. And it worked. Oh, you'll always get a few loudmouths. Guess it can't be helped. I think the Modern Jazz Quartet, too, helped make them quiet this year. When they play, people just have to listen."

With characteristic modesty, Ella omitted to mention the part she has played in improving audience habits over the last 10 years. She didn't tell, for example, of the time about three years ago during a JATP concert at Los Angeles's Shrine when a typical "screamer" kept interrupting her rendition of a beautiful ballad. Without altering tempo or melody, Ella extemporized four bars on the bridge, directed to the noisemaker, that went: "Some people like to hear a ballad/Won't you please give them a chance . . ." As she returned to the original lyrics, the auditorium was hushed and remained thus throughout the rest of her set.

Just before they left on the latest JATP tour, Ella suggested to Norman

Granz, her personal manager, that she do an album of Ellington tunes. With Stuff Smith on violin, Ben Webster on tenor, and a rhythm section comprising Barney Kessel, Paul Smith, Joe Mondragon, and Alvin Stoller backing her, she recorded such fine samples of Ellingtonia as "Satin Doll," "Azure" (with new set of lyrics), "Rocks in My Bed," "Squeeze Me," and "Don't Get Around Much Anymore."

Supporting her for the Mocambo engagement, Ella chose four of the coast's most accomplished musicians. On guitar was Kessel; on bass, Max Bennett; piano, Jimmy Rowles; drums, Larry Bunker. "You know, we hardly had any time to rehearse. But these boys catch on so quickly."

As she spoke, Ella answered a quiet knock on the dressing room door. Barney entered, guitar under his arm. Ella had been in a talking mood. "Well," she apologized, as Barney sat down, "got to work out the next set now. We're on in ten minutes."

IRVING KOLODIN

RODGERS AND HART, ELLA AND ELLINGTON

Saturday Review, 1957

Some critics thought that the popular songs of Richard Rodgers and Lorenz Hart were the best vehicles for Ella. Irving Kolodin was an influential music critic for the Saturday Review *covering jazz, classical music, and opera.—LG*

At the current rate of record production, that old division into "popular" and "classical" music is about as useful as a prewar map of Europe. There are a dozen different areas, from progressive jazz to calypso and back again, in which there can be happy hunting with no thought of the Broadway show with that name. What's better still, each is being energetically serviced without neglect of others. At the moment, those devoted to Rodgers and Hart, Ella Fitzgerald, and Duke Ellington will find their interests especially well served.

More than thirty of the notable collaborations of Richard Rodgers and Larry Hart have been brought together on a pair of LPs (Verve MGV 4001-2, $9.96) with the silky voice of Ella Fitzgerald as the thread on which they are strung. For a lady who made her first fame in terms of a nursery rhyme ("A-Tisket A-Tasket") Fitzgerald has come a long way to deal on even terms with the verbal niceties of "It Never Entered My

Mind," "Little Girl Blue," "I Wish I Were in Love Again," and "I Could Write a Book," not to mention "Dancing on the Ceiling," "A Ship Without a Sail," and "To Keep My Love Alive," the last of these a jaunty bit about mayhem from "Connecticut Yankee" of 1927.

What Ella Fitzgerald can now do with a melodic line is a treatise on self-improvement, in which thought and taste (plus a considerable amount of intuition) have given the one time baby band-singer rank with the bygone Mildred Bailey. If there is higher praise in this area, somebody else will have to think of it. Though Ellis Larkins is not identified among the members of Buddy Bregman's band which provides the most appropriate backgrounds, it seems likely that it is he who does the pianistic hem-stitching on such tunes as "Spring Is Here."

In addition to those mentioned, the roll-call includes "Bewitched," "Blue Moon," "Blue Room," "Everything I've Got," "Give It Back to the Indians," "Have You Met Miss Jones?", "Here in My Arms," "I Didn't Know What Time It Was," "Isn't It Romantic?" "I've Got Five Dollars," "Johnny One Note," "Lover," "Manhattan," "Mountain Greenery," "My Funny Valentine," "My Heart Stood Still," "My Romance," "Ten Cents a Dance," "The Lady Is a Tramp," "Small Hotel," "This Can't Be Love," "Thou Swell," "Wait Till You See Her," "Where or When," "With a Song in My Heart," and "You Took Advantage of Me." It's all very well to recognize the present status of Rodgers as a past master, but let's remember these were the creations that made his reputation when Gershwin, Kern, Youmans, and Porter were the day-to-day competition.

A related view of a similar matter is offered on Bethlehem BCP 6005 in which Duke Ellington suggests how "My Funny Valentine" might have sounded if he had written it. This is one of a series of performances projecting the solo talents of his current bandsmen (here Jimmy Hamilton, clarinet; Quentin Jackson, trombone; and Ray Nance, trumpet). In Gershwin's "Summertime" it is "Cat" Anderson's trumpet, in Raksin's "Laura" the tenor sax of Paul Gonsalves, in the other Duke's (Vernon) "I Can't Get Started," Nance on violin and vocal, in Herbert's "Indian Summer" the fluid alto sax of Russell Procope, and in Peter de Rose's "Deep Purple," Hamilton again.

Add to these such older Ellington compositions as "Cotton Tail," "Day Dream," "Everything But You," "Frustration," and a "Blues," and you have a rich cross section of the timbres and the humors which have made Ellington's name unique in the lore of music. Another phase of his long career is recalled on RCA Victor LPM 1364, in which sixteen sides from the brilliant 1940–1942 period are brought together on a single LP. "Take the

'A' Train" is the first, "What Am I Here For?" the last, with such memorable matters as "Perdido," "Rumpus in Richmond," "Sepia Panorama," "I Got It Bad and That Ain't Good," "The Flaming Sword," "A Portrait of Bert Williams," and "Cotton Tail," this time in its original version with Ben Webster. Any doubt that it is Duke who made his musicians rather than vice versa is dispelled by the consistent quality of sound, the high standard of accomplishment at both ends of a fifteen-year period, though Harry Carney on baritone sax, Johnny Hodges, and Nance, are the only holdovers.

Ellington's periodic efforts to break out of the confinement of the four-minute piece has now produced "A Drum Is a Woman," in succession to such efforts of the past as "Black, Brown, and Beige," the "Liberia" and "Harlem" suites, together with sundry unrealized stage pieces (a new one is in prospect for Broadway production next fall). "I am not a drum, I am a woman," in Ellington's voice, is the beginning of Carribee Joe's romance with the instrument he finds in a West Indian jungle. On a thin thread of story, involving the woman-drum, now named "Mme. Zajj," are projected mood pieces related to New Orleans, Congo Square, New York, 52nd Street, etc., also a spoken narrative, filling two LP sides.

Most of the musical ideas have the vivid Ellington quality—the calypsonian "What Else Can You Do With a Drum," the low down "Hey, Buddy Bolden," the swinging "Ballet of the Flying Saucers," etc., but Ellington doesn't solve the organizational problem much better than in "Black, Brown, and Beige." The individual sections have varying degrees of interest without adding to much of a totality . . . and the spoken text on the "drum is a woman" theme is either pretentious or childish. It's understandable, and admirable, for Ellington to think of himself in terms of something other than "miniatures," but, so far, it's the "miniatures" that have the concentration of a real expression.

Johnny Guarnieri pinpoints this fact in a disc titled "The Duke Again!" in which he reverts to such striking Ellington "strains" as "Scattin' at the Kit Kat," "Birmingham Breakdown," "Rockin' in Rhythm," "Mississippi Moan," and "It Don't Mean a Thing If It Ain't Got That Swing" for pianistic purposes (Coral CRL 57086, $2.98). A rhythm section with drummer Don Lamond, bassists Wendell Marshall and Arnold Fishkind, and guitarists George Barnes and Mundell Lowe provides Guarnieri with a tonal backdrop for his well-fingered impressions. Needless to say, the more "commercial" Ellington of "Sophisticated Lady," "Mood Indigo," "Solitude," "In a Sentimental Mood," and "I Let a Song Go Out of My Heart" is not forgotten.

THE AUDIENCE LOVED ELLA'S EVENING
Boston Traveler, 1959

This review is typical of those Ella garnered in mid-career. Bob Freedman, a jazz musician and composer, wrote record reviews for the Jazz Review, *a well-respected periodical of the time.—LG*

Ella Fitzgerald walked onto the stage of Symphony Hall last Friday night and delivered 14 songs to a near-capacity audience before taking an intermission.

Despite the size of the audience and some unforgivably disconcerting mis-manipulation of a single spotlight, Miss Fitzgerald drew two of the most satisfying things a singer can ask for—complete silence while singing, and literally overwhelming applause at the end of each selection.

Herb Ellis Star of First Number

Her opening number was "Like Young," on which the four-man rhythm section came closer to swinging as a unit than they were able to do during the remainder of the concert. Of this group, Herb Ellis was the obvious star, both musically and visually.

Sitting confidently upstage of the rest of the quartet, he was the perfect accompanying guitarist. His performance was marred only by the relatively insensitive playing of the other musicians.

If you were at the concert you recognized at least 95 per cent of the songs that Ella sang. This is because the format of the show was standards—Standard songs sung in such a way as to reach virtually anyone who took the time to listen.

Miss Fitzgerald's voice has achieved a trueness that must appeal, whether the listener might be a so-called jazz fan or not. I doubt that the majority of the people who applauded Ella as sincerely as she sang to them would have appreciated a fine performance by the Modern Jazz Quartet.

Yet no real jazz musician or enthusiast could have been bored or left unstimulated by her singing Friday night.

"But Not For Me," taken at ballad tempo, was applauded after the first few bars. "Angel Eyes," also a ballad, was done by Ella more meaningful than I've ever heard it done.

"Eight-To-The-Bar," an authentic sounding piece from the Boogie-Woogie era, may have shown some of the younger members of the audience that Fats Domino is perpetuating a tradition, not imitating one.

Much has been written and said of Ella Fitzgerald's "horn-like" quality and approach to singing. The actual basis for this terminology is her ability to sing all intervals without having to slide from one pitch to the other. She has what is called in musical circles a tremendous ear, plus a control over her voice that enables her to sing according to the demands of that ear.

The one bothersome characteristic of the audience was its lack of sense of humor. Many times during the evening, the crowd missed the humorous impact of special-material lines. Ella may have been making reference to this when, in the course of a long blues number, she sang, "People wonder what I'm singin' about!"

Ella a Master at Finger-Snapping

Whatever else Ella Fitzgerald is, she is a master finger-snapper. Many times during the evening the thumb and first two fingers of her left hand kept a beat going that the band was unable to match.

I noticed a fan in the eighth row attempting to emulate her technique. Would that the numerous finger-snapping jazz lovers might absorb a fraction of Ella's natural rhythmic "feel." Dream on. . .

At the scheduled end of the concert, the applause for Miss Fitzgerald was long, loud and lovely. About half a dozen people went for the exists. The rest stayed in place, demanding more of Ella Fitzgerald.

When the noise had subsided somewhat, she said, "I'm not going to leave that applause."

"A-Tisket, A-Tasket" came off like a firecracker, featuring a kiddie bit by Miss Fitzgerald that made you want to get that basket back to her at any cost.

Opinion: A fine show!

RHYTHM SECTION
Wichita, Kansas, Beacon, 1958

This piece was syndicated and probably first appeared in the San
Francisco Chronicle, *for which Gleason regularly wrote from
1950 until his death from a heart attack on June 3, 1975. As
usual, Gleason within a few paragraphs reveals the power and
impact of a performer and, in particular, the issues and opportunities facing Ella. As she became very famous with her songbooks she was accused of going pop and Hollywood and of
abandoning jazz. Writers, many of them astute critics, who
would later call her indisputably a jazz singer, began categorizing
her as a pop singer. Ella explained that she was simply building
on her achievements.*

*Ralph Gleason wrote articles and liner notes about jazz and jazz
artists; for his pithy and pertinent work, the jazz world revered
him. In honor of his memory, there's an annual music book competition, the Ralph J. Gleason Awards, sponsored by Broadcast
Music Inc., New York University, and a magazine he helped found,
Rolling Stone. Some of his pieces for the* Chronicle *and for magazines and his album liner notes have been collected in a Da Capo
paperback,* Celebrating the Duke and Louis, Bessie, Billie, Bird,
Carmen, Miles, Dizzy and Other Heroes.—*LG*

Ella Fitzgerald, Queen of the Jazz singers, has been scoring heavily in
recent months at top hotels and supper clubs. Sometimes her jazz audience
sees this as indicating she is leaving jazz and going "commercial."
    Backstage at one of her recent appearances, Miss Fitzgerald answered
this charge directly and forcefully.
    "I'm not going Hollywood," she told me. "I'm trying to sell records
and give the people something they can hum; some familiar melody.
    "You know what I'm trying to do? I'm trying to be myself. I'm not a
glamour girl and I'm not a dancer. I'm just me. I could do all the acting
with a song, all the stuff with the hands and those gimmicks if someone
showed me and I learned it. But it's not me.
    "You want to hear a funny story? I did it once in Chicago. I was
singing 'Witchcraft'—I do the verse, and when Sinatra heard it he didn't

know what song it was! So I was doing it one night and I acted it all out with the gestures and my gown down off one shoulder.

"And when I finished, some guy in the audience said, real loud, 'That's fine. Now let's hear Ella Fitzgerald do it!' I was so embarrassed!

"But what I want to do is to sing a song on stage like you asked me to sing a song to you here now. Just the two of us. I want to get that personal feeling. I like to sing sweet songs. You can still be jazzy and sing sweet songs. I still do my jazz numbers, I get my bop singing into 'Alexander's Ragtime Band' and I finish with 'How High the Moon.' I'm not changing.

"Why have I started to feature the ballad medley sitting on a stool on the stage? My manager, Norman Granz, wanted me to use the stool for the ballads but I was scared. Oh, I didn't want to do it at all. But when I did it, the people seemed to like it and so I've kept it as part of my act.

"I'm just trying to be myself out there and get over some of that self-consciousness I have. I try to give the audience a little bit of everything. I sing current popular tunes and even some rock 'n' roll. And I do a little Dixieland.

"The people seem to like it, and I know it's been good for me. I'm feeling so good these days, so ambitious. There's so many things I would like to do and now I'm starting to do them. I'm studying French. Wouldn't it be a kick to sing a song in French? Not one that's been done a lot, but one that hasn't been done before.

"It's a good feeling for me to do something new. Like the Broadway tunes and the songbooks I've done. Some people thought maybe I shouldn't do them, or couldn't do them, so it was a challenge. I did them and they were successful."

In a day when the music business is top heavy with vocalists and small groups, Miss Fitzgerald is a one-girl crusade for big bands. "You know I'm a firm believer in the big bands. We have to get them out again and bring back dancing. I love big bands. When I was out on the concert tour this fall, we had several dates around New York and Count Basie was at Birdland and I rushed into New York every night to catch the last set. One night we had some trouble with the car and I missed the band and it ruined my whole night!

"I love the big bands and I love sweet songs. I'm making an album of sweet songs next. All pretty ones. We made lists of sweet songs and picked out the best ones. We had maybe 50 to begin with and then cut it down.

"I'm not a complicated person and I can't do a complicated show. I'm not like that. I'm just me. And I like to talk to the audience and sing requests for them. I'm at home that way."

MISS ELLA
Show magazine, 1961

Although this magazine was primarily a fashion magazine filled with pictures of pretty models, it also published some interesting articles on the arts. Douglas Watt was a well-known New York–based jazz critic who ordinarily wrote for the Daily News. *Here he assesses the songbook series.—LG*

A single record, recently released on the Verve label, presents us with Ella Fitzgerald in free-form vocal interpretations of two old chestnuts "Mr. Paganini" and "You're Driving Me Crazy." They are also part of a collection to be issued this month on an LP called *Ella in Hollywood*, and they present Miss Fitzgerald in the dazzling, riff-singing style that was her stock in trade until, some five years ago, she gave us the first of her *Song Books*.

That first *Song Book* was an investigation of Cole Porter's vivacious and often haunting combinations of words and music. With it, Miss Fitzgerald immediately won the affections of that somewhat aloof and stoutly principled group, the show-tune buffs; composed of fanciers of the popular song in its more artful manifestations, usually to be found in Broadway show scores, this group was squarer, perhaps, than her old fans, but at the same time more sophisticated. At any rate, its interest in the Porter collection was considerable enough to inspire five more *Song Books*, devoted variously to the output of Rodgers and Hart, Duke Ellington, Irving Berlin, George Gershwin, and Harold Arlen, in that order—most of them two-record sets, like the Porter. During this period, Miss Fitzgerald's nightclub salary leaped, and she made occasional guest appearances on television.

The last of the *Song Books*, the Arlen one, came out late last winter. There are, at this writing, no plans for any more. Left waiting in the wings are Jerome Kern, Vincent Youmans, Arthur Schwartz, and a few other hopefuls. The select body of new fans she acquired with her *Song Books* may well be disappointed, for the series, in addition to providing a fresh insight into the art of modern song writing, sharpened Miss Fitzgerald's own art.

The *Song Books* vary a good deal in both content and appeal. The least of them, to my way of thinking, is the one concerned with Irving Berlin's product. The master of simplicity is here revealed as perhaps too simple to be taken in such a large dose. Then, too, a particular facet of Berlin's writings—his long preoccupation with two subjects, the weather and dancing—is likely to induce monotony in the course of any survey of his works. The blandest of the *Song Books*, it supports the soloist with competent but scarcely notable orchestral arrangements by Paul Weston. But Miss Fitzgerald can make almost any song come to life, and when the innocent world of Berlin achieves the insipid, as it frequently does, she takes off on some fanciful vocal flight to avoid tedium.

It is probably in the Rodgers-and-Hart set, featuring skillful instrumental arrangements by Buddy Bregman, who served in the same capacity for the Porter *Song Book*, that the singer faces her greatest challenge. For more than any of the other collections, the Rodgers-and-Hart one emphasizes the character song. (The Gershwin set, voluminous though it is, does not include anything out of *Porgy and Bess*.) "Bewitched," for example, is the confession of a middle-aged sophisticate, first stimulated against her better judgment and then wryly disillusioned. "Ten Cents a Dance" is a taxi dancer's catalogue of debasement. "To Keep My Love Alive," an added number in the 1943 revival of *A Connecticut Yankee*, the team's last collaboration (the Rodgers-and-Hammerstein *Oklahoma!* had already begun its career), consists of the arch admissions of a medieval murderess. "Give It Back to the Indians" is a New Yorker's ironic listing of the city's follies. I am of two minds about Miss Fitzgerald's treatment of this material. Being the kind of singer she is, interested primarily in musical values, she makes no attempt at all at characterization. On the other hand, her clear and always musical expression of the pungent lyrics is often enough to make them carry conviction, as, for instance, in "Ten Cents a Dance."

The Gershwin cavalcade, running to ten sides, is probably much too long, except for the most indefatigable show buffs. (True, the records can be purchased singly, and the programming, which follows no chronological order, invites the buyer to shop around.) After all, not every song Gershwin and his lyricists, of whom his brother Ira was the principal one, wrote is indelible, and there are several that I could do without, though a few of them, very early products, undoubtedly have historical interest for the musicologists in the crowd. But oh, the velvety beauty of "Embraceable You" and so many others in which the singer and the conductor-arranger, Nelson Riddle, found a perfect meeting ground!

The recent Arlen *Song Book* finds Miss Fitzgerald in extremely compatible surroundings. For Arlen's work not only has great rhythmic and harmonic interest; it also is the product of a man who has long been associated with Negro performers and who achieved a distinctive style through a kind of wedding of the cantor's keening art and the Negro's blues-and-spiritual art. The *Song Book* goes no further (except for "The Man That Got Away," an old Arlen tune that Ira Gershwin equipped with a lyric for the 1954 movie *A Star Is Born*) than the 1948 film *Casbah* in covering Arlen's career, but it offers a good, representative collection of his hits, from his early association with Ted Koehler to his later one with Johnny Mercer, and the Billy May arrangements are peppy and incisive.

The recent album called *Get Happy* contains two items left over from the *Song Books*—Gershwin's "Somebody Loves Me" and Berlin's "Blue Skies." For the rest, we have "Cheerful Little Earful," "St. Louis Blues," "You Make Me Feel So Young," "Moonlight Becomes You," and such nondescript items as "Like Young," "Cool Breeze," "Gypsy in My Soul," "Goody Goody," and "Beat Me Daddy Eight to the Bar." It is a grab-bag representation of Miss Fitzgerald's art, as is the forthcoming "Ella in Hollywood." But whether or not there are to be more *Song Books*, the five collections stand as one of the more significant contributions to recorded popular music of the last decade or more.

SHE WHO IS ELLA
Time magazine, 1964

In early 1964 Time *published a perceptive article about Thelonious Monk, and at the end of the year, the magazine continued its excellent jazz coverage with a witty piece effectively describing Ella's scat singing style. The piece was unsigned, in the spirit of group journalism dominant in news magazines in those days, and one wonders about the identity of the well-informed jazz lover (or lovers) who wrote this story.—LG*

"Ella," says her manager offhandedly, "Drake Brown is in the audience tonight."

"Who?"

"Drake Brown. You mean you've never seen his picture in the papers?"

Ella Fitzgerald tenses fearfully when she hears this. The most popular jazz singer in the world for 27 years and only now reaching the peak of her career, she remains a celebrity fan non-pareil. So out on the stage she goes and sings her heart out to impress Drake Brown. It is unimportant that Drake Brown does not exist. In jazz the end justifies the means.

Last week, in a new and stunning blonde wig, she was at her greatest in the pink and purple Flamingo Room at Las Vegas, appearing before a mass of abnormally hushed conventioneers, all of whom were in the palm of her hand. Ella is 46 now. Countless other singers have entered and left the scene during the span of Ella's career. A British magazine recently conducted a poll to determine the second best female singer; it was understood that the first was Ella. As a true jazz musician, she has never sung a song twice the same way. She still makes her old classics like "How High the Moon" sound fresh and new, and in recent years she has reached out to include anthologies of Cole Porter, Jerome Kern, Rodgers and Hart, Irving Berlin, and George Gershwin.

Her incredible improvising runs are effortless. She can take off from a melody, go over it, around it, through it, under it, moving at twice the speed of nine-to-five Man, tossing in casual doodles in the abstract expressionism of sound. When other singers' jugulars would be bulging, Ella isn't even panting. She seems to breathe through her ears. Her range goes from lower owl to upper sparrow. Her voice sounds all of 20 years old. Her manner, for all her speed, is soothing. Just when you think she might be turning into Bonnie Baker, however, she kicks the lid off and begins to scat: "Scoodee-oo-da-do-dee-uba-ty-ty-ta-roo."

She is the chair professor of the art of scat singing, wherein a singer abandons comprehensible lyrics in the middle of a song, and she can scoodee-oo-da for 800 bars without running out of fresh gibberish. For added sparks, she tosses in little shards of the classics, such as, say, a bit of the "William Tell Overture." Then suddenly she turns to a robust fragment of "Did You Ever See a Dream Walking," only to return quickly to the riverbed of perickety-bip-delip-deluda-bry-bry-kanoo.

But play as she will with the originals, she respects their integrity, if they have any. Her imitators shred songs; she explodes and reassembles them. Much of her genius in performance may arise from her ability to write songs as well as sing them. She made her name, after all, when she wrote "A-Tisket A-Tasket" in 1938, turning a nursery rhyme into the No. 1 tune in the nation.

Ringo Way

Born in Newport News, Va., orphaned and raised by an aunt in Yonkers, Ella Fitzgerald in her early days was a skinny girl, but over the years her stature grew in both senses. She is supersensitive about her weight, and understandably cried through the night once when—after she had performed with another heavy singer—a critic wrote: "Last night the stage contained 600 lbs. of pure talent." The talent moves as well as sings. One of Ella Fitzgerald's secrets is that she really wishes she were a dancer. When she feels good onstage, she becomes as physical as she is vocal, cutting steps left and right to underscore her song.

Ella is a hypo-millionairess now, can afford a Don Loper wardrobe, and endlessly redecorates her house in Beverly Hills. She is also kind, thoughtful, and painfully unsure of herself. She spends her free evenings sewing or watching television or writing new songs. She has just written one in homage to Ringo Starr, the Beatle:

Don't knock the rhythm of the kids today;
Remember they're playing the Ringo way.

Once married for four years to Bass Player Ray Brown, Ella has a son, Ray Jr., who plays football and basketball for Hollywood High School and is a drummer in a combo as well. She herself was educated only through the ninth grade; unthinking people hurt her deeply by imitating her weak grammar or by ascribing to her an accent she does not have. The mere mention of a high school dropout will start her lecturing: "You never know, one of these kids may have something but not the money or means to finish."

She is pleasantly informal, but she does have her formal side. "It used to bother me when people I didn't know came up and called me Ella," she says. "It seemed to me they should say 'Miss Fitzgerald,' but somehow they never do." Perhaps this is because there are several million Fitzgeralds but only one Ella.

LEE JESKE
ASK NORMAN
Jazziz magazine, 1996

Norman Granz, a virtual Houdini for Ella's career and for that of the great pianist Oscar Peterson, rarely gave interviews about his management techniques. One of them appeared in Jazziz *magazine, the cover of which featured a svelte and stunning-looking Ella dressed in a red suit and matching pillbox hat, leaning against a fashionable car, and carrying a leopard coat—one of the most glamorous pictures ever taken of Ella. Granz took over the reins of Ella's career completely in 1955, and even when he moved to Switzerland, he ruled from his aerie there via his Los Angeles office.*

Lee Jeske, a New York–based critic, has been writing about jazz for many years. He has served as a jazz critic for the New York Post *and contributed to* Rolling Stone, Cash Box, *and the* New York Times.*—LG*

If anyone had a question about Ella Fitzgerald, they were referred to Norman Granz. And while other divas groped around for fashionable material, Granz helped Ella to uncover an enduring canon of music, one that forever changed our view of American composers. More than anyone else, Granz helped establish Ella a seat of royalty she'd forever keep—First Lady of Song.

It was just one of those things. Ella Fitzgerald began working with Norman Granz in 1946, when they were both in their twenties, and their relationship lasted until Ella's death, an even 50 years. Granz was her personal manager (beginning in 1949) and became her record producer (beginning in 1956, when he wrested her contract away from Decca), but he was much more: he was her advisor and protector, steering her career brilliantly, keeping the world away from her door (as she wished), and helping make her (and himself) enormously wealthy in the process.

If Fitzgerald was the great American singer, Granz was the great American impresario/entrepreneur, and with the help of the great American songwriters, the two left a series of recorded monuments for his labels, Verve and Pablo Records. There were the incredible songbooks of the '50s, of course—which swooped Ella out of the clutches of novelty songs and strained attempts at pop hits—but so much more: the amazing live recordings (Berlin, naturally, but also the great Montreux performances of the '70s), the splendid collaborations with Louis Armstrong and Joe Pass, the intoxicating Antonio Carlos Jobim recordings and the landmark meetings with the bands of Ellington and Basie.

While Granz was mostly a hands-off producer, devoted to his "Jazz at the Philharmonic" ethic (recording session-as-jam session), with Ella he was intimately involved in every nuance of every recording. (There are handfuls of lesser Fitzgerald recordings made after she left Decca but look closely and you'll notice that they were recorded in the '60s, when Granz left record producing to indulge his passion for art collecting.)

"Ask Norman" was the response you'd get when you had an Ella inquiry but, like Ella herself, Granz rarely submitted to interviews. This exchange was conducted in 1990, upon the release of *All That Jazz*, Ella's last studio session and the last recording produced by Granz.

Lee Jeske: How did you come up with the idea for the songbook series?

Norman Granz: Well, Ella had been under contract to only one record company for about 20 years—that was Decca. And the jazz things were okay, where she scatted, but then they started giving her a lot of tunes that were really not terribly good, but which they thought were commercial.

I had proposed the Cole Porter songbook to Decca, but they rejected it on the grounds that Ella wasn't the kind of singer who did that material. Well, I could understand it from their point of view, because they had one thing in mind and that was finding hit singles. I was interested in how I could enhance Ella's position, to make her a singer with more than just a cult following amongst jazz fans.

Then I had the chance to get her contract. So I proposed to Ella that the first project we do would not be a jazz project, but rather a songbook of the works of Cole Porter; I envisaged her doing a lot of composers. The trick was to change the backing enough so that, here and there, there would still be signs of jazz. So we never had just the big orchestra with Nelson Riddle's arrangements, we would also have maybe a trio with Ben Webster. In a sense, it created a whole new public for Ella, and I think that her regular jazz-oriented following liked it as well.

LJ: How did you go about choosing the songs?

NG: The routine I used with Ella was—in fact, the rest of the time I recorded Ella I used pretty much that routine—I would get together a hundred songs that I thought would suit Ella lyrically and would lend themselves to all kinds of backings. I would sit down with Ella, and I'd say, "Okay, here are the hundred songs that I think would work, now let's go through each one." In many cases Ella would know the song, or she could hear the melody in her head. Of course, she had to really dig the song. Then I had to go over the verses with her to see whether she felt comfortable with them—most singers ignored them. And on record dates, you also had the time factor: I didn't care how long a song took, it took what it needed. So that gave us a kind of variety—the song might be eight minutes, if it was worth it, or it might be two minutes, just one chorus. And it might be just a piano player or it might be a 50-piece orchestra.

Of course, I always recorded live, we never recorded and then had Ella track. In that way, you had to have very flexible arrangements, where you could say, "Let's pick up the tempo here" or "Let's drop this" or whatever, during the session—which most companies, of course, wouldn't countenance because it was too expensive. But that was the way we did it. Well, Ella would finally narrow it down to maybe 50 songs, and then I would have a piano player do the 50 songs so she could hear them, just a chorus each. Finally, *finally*, we would whittle it down to, say, 35 songs. And if the album finally came out with 30, we had some alternates.

The first one, the Cole Porter, was an enormous success. I think not only because of Ella, obviously, but because a lot of Cole Porter fans had never had the chance to hear the songs done in that fashion; there were some songs that people didn't even know Porter had written.

LJ: Is it true that you played The Cole Porter Songbook for Cole Porter?

NG: Yeah, sure. I had recorded Fred Astaire, and through Fred I met people like Cole Porter. It was quite simple for me, after I finished the album—before I began the production of the sleeve and all the rest—I called up Cole and said, "Look, I'm coming to New York, I'm going to bring the acetates of your songbook." He said, "Great." So I flew there, Cole let them know he was not to be disturbed, and for two hours, he played them over and over again. I was very curious to see what he was going to say, and he was honest enough that if he didn't like something, he'd tell you. I wouldn't have changed it, I must say, because I felt that what we did we thought was right. Cole was very pleased with it.

The one that was the most fruitful, from my point of view, was the Gershwin. Because I was a very good friend of Ira Gershwin, and Ira helped—we'd sit down and go over the numbers I proposed for Ella, and he'd say, "Wait, there's a song we had in a show that we never used, let me dig it up for you." And he even wrote some additional lyrics for me on some old standards.

LJ: Is that why that was five LPs?

NG: I think that Gershwin's songs lent themselves more easily to jazz than some of the others. But I had a special feeling for Gershwin, and the fact that I had the chance to work closely with Ira meant that I really had a chance to stretch out and do 60 songs. If I were working for a major label they would have thrown me out—you can sell many more if you just do 12 for an LP. But that was the luxury of owning my own company and doing what I thought would help my artist.

I never was concerned with sales. I mean, I was fortunate enough to subsidize my recording activities with my concerts. So I didn't really care if five LPs sold or not. I knew ultimately it would retrieve its cost. You do an opera, it might take you 20 years to get your money back. And I was quite content, with the songbooks, to wait as long as it took.

LJ: You really were taking advantage of the LP. . . .

NG: Most record companies looked upon the LP as merely a collection of 78 tracks. So if you look at the early LPs of any good singer, you'll find they were really collections of three-minute takes on maybe 12 songs. The LP was simply another vehicle, so instead of having six 78s, you'd have one LP.

I felt different about it, I felt you should enjoy the LP, and if I wanted to do one number that ran 20 minutes I could do it, if it was warranted. So the LP to me was an enormous advantage to really stretch out on certain things. And for a singer like Ella—who could keep going on different choruses, because she could change keys, she could scat—we could really reinterpret the songs in a way the 78s would never allow.

LJ: It's ironic—while singers like Sarah Vaughan and Dinah Washington were recording songs aimed at crossover appeal during that time Ella was recording great American songs, which, in their way, achieved the crossover success the others were aiming at.

NG: I don't blame the A&R men or the producers, because the singers you just named—Sarah and, certainly, Dinah—could call their own shots. I think the trick was to have them do great material, even if it didn't sell at the time; I mean, material that suited them. But I think that sometimes they were the victims of trying to make it for that particular period.

Say, for example, you like painting, and you want to be a collector—and you know the insane prices that art can get. If you were to come to me and say, "I'm going to buy a Cezanne"—because you think it's a good investment—I would first ask you, "Do you like the picture?" And if you said you don't like it, I'd tell you, don't buy it. On the other hand, if you like the picture—it doesn't have to be Cezanne, it could be anybody—and you buy it because you like it, inevitably it's going to turn out to be the most valuable thing you could have done. Because the worst that could happen is, if you ever wanted to sell it, you've enjoyed it for years.

LJ: In your long experience with Ella Fitzgerald, what is it about this woman that makes her appeal so wide-ranging?

NG: It's simple, it's what makes the difference in almost any kind of music. The first thing that people are aware of—it's almost involuntary—is time. You'll tap your foot almost unconsciously. She had the quality of time, which is the simplest thing that people become aware of. That's a big plus. I mean, a great singer like Billie Holiday had a different kind of time. Ella's is more acceptable and more easily felt. Not understood, but felt.

The other thing is, Ella respects melody. So that instead of showing off, which she can do harmonically, which is the third part of all music, Ella stressed the melody, so you knew what she was doing. And she swung. Well, if you have those elements, that takes in an awful lot of people. You don't have to stretch out and show how harmonically hip you are and reinterpret a song so that, for many people, they don't even know what you're doing. Now that's not to say that she's deliberately trying to be more commercial, it's just something that she does innately.

FRANCIS DAVIS

ELLA

In Outcats: Jazz Composers, Instrumentalists, and Singers, 1990

Francis Davis, a Philadelphia native, has written articles and reviews for newspapers and magazines, including the Philadelphia Inquirer *and the* Atlantic Monthly. *His essays have been collected into the books—*Outcats *and* In the Moment. *He published a new collection,* Bebop and Nothingness, *with Schirmer Books in 1996, and he is at work on a biography of John Coltrane. In recent years he has had several fellowships, including a Guggenheim, a Pew*

Fellowship in the Arts, and a Morroe Berger–Benny Carter Fellowship.—LG

Ella Fitzgerald's girlish, unshadowed reading of "The Man That Got Away" was recorded in 1961 for her just-reissued two-record *Harold Arlen Songbook* (Verve 817-526-1). Unlike Judy Garland or Billie Holiday, Fitzgerald is a presentational singer who imposes no subjective weight on her material and unlocks no secret, ambivalent yearnings in herself or her audiences. She is no wild Duse, and no diva, either. Songs rarely become mere props for her virtuosity, as they often do for Sarah Vaughan's. Even at her best, Fitzgerald offers no pleasures deeper than those of hearing a good song superbly sung. But her genius is that she usually manages to make this seem like enough.

Even more than her free-flying scat, what we marvel at in Fitzgerald is her ability to disappear in words and melody without leaving a trace. The most beguiling demonstration of this remains the durable songbook series she recorded for Verve beginning in the late fifties, and the Arlen set is the pick of the bunch, possibly because Arlen was a fine jazz singer himself early in his career and had the good fortune to collaborate with lyricists (like Ted Koehler, Yip Harburg, Johnny Mercer, and Ira Gershwin) who could hook his melodies to everyday figures of speech that jibe wonderfully with Fitzgerald's matter-of-fact delivery. There's a delightfully vulgar bounce to Arlen's songs—an urban snarl beneath their veneer of wit and sophistication—that helps them resist the sacred-text treatment favored by American Popular Song epigones (the sort of people who insist on the upper case). Arlen's melodies are ideal for Fitzgerald, who exploits their full improvisatory potential merely by holding fast on their hairpin turns. The brassiness of Billy May's horn charts underlines both Arlen's enduring vitality and Fitzgerald's innate swing; even his string arrangements have a sparkle that suits the material. May and Fitzgerald excel at staging full-blown Arlen production numbers, like "The Man That Got Away," "Stormy Weather," "Over the Rainbow," and "Blues in the Night." But the most engaging Arlen songs (and the most fruitful Fitzgerald and May interpretations) are those that sound tossed-off: "Let's Fall in Love," "As Long as I Live," or, best of all, the previously unissued "Sing, My Heart," which finds Fitzgerald riffing on vowels like a saxophonist executing a precipitous scalar run. The solos of Ben Webster and Stuff Smith make *The Duke Ellington Songbook, Volume Two* (Verve VE2-2540) a superior jazz showcase, but the songs are better here (though he was a great composer, Ellington was no match for Arlen as a songwriter—nobody was).

Moreover, on the *Arlen Songbook*, the brief interludes by the alto saxophonist Benny Carter, the tenor saxophonist Plas Johnson, and the trumpeter Don Fagerquist, though infrequent, are worth waiting for. And though Fitzgerald's five-record Gershwin box (Verve 2615-063) may be the more definitive composer's retrospective, the overripe colors of Nelson Riddle's arrangements sound faded next to May's deft, workmanlike sketches for the Arlen tunes.

Fitzgerald's songbooks were such masterpieces of their kind that encores were inevitable. I wish I could hail *Nice Work If You Can Get It* (Pablo D2312-140), her newest collection of Gershwin, as a latter-day triumph. Failing that, I wish I could pin all its shortcomings on the slumming lapses of her accomplice, the pianist André Previn. (Was doing "Let's Call the Whole Thing Off" in three/four time his bright idea?) But Fitzgerald is the real culprit. Not only is her voice not what it used to be (that much is forgivable), her adherence to melody isn't what *it* used to be, either; and her uvular gymnastics risk self-parody (on "A Fog-gog-gog-ey Day," in particular). Previn's rococo touches hardly encourage the singer to toe the line. Still, he and the world-class bassist Niels-Henning Orsted Pederson are frequently right on the money. *Nice Work If You Can Get It* brims with felicities, including a brisk, efficient "Who Cares?" and an understated reading of "How Long Has This Been Going On?" on which Fitzgerald expertly registers a playgirl's awed first brush with true love as Previn splashes ambiguous dissonances behind her. But even on these tracks, the overfamiliar material works against the singer, who has, after all, recorded impeccable versions of these songs in the past.

At her best, Fitzgerald inhabits a song with her total being, yet leaves it much as she found it—a feat more difficult and gratifying than it sounds, like a novelist holding the proverbial mirror up to life without leaving his messy fingerprints all over the glass. In her selfless interpretations, the works of the great American songwriters become a colloquial poetry that speaks both to us and for us. Which is not to say that standards are superior to rock tunes, only that like Garland, Holiday, or Sinatra, rock singers and songwriters have been trained to go for the kill. When they succeed, it can trigger revelation, but when they fail, you want to echo Gatsby's dismissal of Daisy's feelings for Tom: it was only personal.

ELLA FITZGERALD—LONELY AT THE TOP
New York Post, 1965

Leonard Feather, one of the most important and influential jazz critics of the century, had Ella's confidence. For his interview she greeted Leonard poolside at her Beverly Hills home. Here she speaks candidly of her legendary insecurity. She also touches upon the isolation and loneliness that a musician can feel when he or she lives primarily on the road. For Ella, the predicament was worse than for others, because, as the musicians in her groups noticed, she did her job—her concert—and then went back to the hotel with her staff, usually consisting of her cousin Georgiana, who worked and traveled with Ella for so many years. Ella almost never hung out with musicians or other singers.

Carmen McRae and Sarah Vaughan were buddies and spent many nights and days together, relaxing, joking, laughing, and raising hell. Sarah was famed for staying up three days and nights at a time to socialize and partake of all the refreshments of the world, and Carmen could run her a close second when she felt like it. But Ella didn't smoke or drink; she had no bad habits at all, except for her great appetite and overindulgence in food. Feather's column gives the reader a rare peek at the way Ella's lifestyle tended to strand her as a superstar on stage with an ocean of strangers at her feet.—LG

A small mountain peak is a lonely place. There is only room for one at the top.

Ella Fitzgerald was singing with Chick Webb's band in Harlem when she won her first popularity poll in 1937. Last week she sat in a handsomely appointed, lawned and pooled home on Beverly Hills, just a couple of months past that notable success symptom, a collapse from overwork, that had sent her home from Europe a bundle of nerves.

"You can get into a bad situation," she said. "The audiences are wonderful and you don't want to turn down the jobs, so you suddenly come to realize that you're working too hard to enjoy yourself."

Like most of her contemporaries who were raised under the impression that singing was a profession rather than a fast-buck kick, she views the present scene with several sets of dim tinted glasses. Through one pair, she sees the inroads of the teen beat.

"I won't put it all down. I don't care what people say about the Beatles; they've proven they do know some kind of music, and I'd love to make an album of their songs. But too many of these beat combos want to start right out making a few dollars a night instead of spending their time studying—like the group Raymond plays in." Ray Brown Jr., 16, from whose father Miss Fitzgerald was discovered 13 years ago, now attends Beverly Hills High and plays weekend gigs as drummer with what Ella calls a "Ringo Beat" combo.

Ella's wafer-thin skin protection against criticism is a second source of insecurity. When Frank Sinatra impugned her phrasing and breathing in a recent magazine article, she says, "I was so upset I could hardly sing for a week." She had looked forward to the European tour as a desperately needed morale booster: "I was beginning to be afraid, I felt maybe I just didn't have it, and I had no hit record. It took a lot of people to convince me that there are more important things."

Through another pair of dark glasses, Ella sees herself, as a consequence of an inexorable show business process, torn from her natural milieu.

"With so many clubs gone, there's no night jobs left in this country except where most people can't afford to come to see me—a couple of big hotels and the casinos in Las Vegas.

"Sure, we're all in business to make money, but sometimes you can find you're way up on top and all by yourself. It can get pretty lonely up there and you miss all the kicks.

"It would be so nice to be able to play a small jazz spot and feel at home. Like a home cooked meal—you don't pay as much for it as you do in a fine restaurant, but you're gonna dig it twice as much. It's bad to lose contact with the very people that made it possible for you to be where you are. Instead of enjoying the singing and the entertaining, you find it becomes just a thing of how much can I get out of it?

"I think my manager, Norman Granz, has realized now that in order to sing and enjoy yourself, once in a while you have to get back in that old bag."

One means to this end will be a series of albums that marks a departure from her standardized "Song Books" of works by Tin Pan Alley kingpins. Recently she taped an LP of some of her own favorite tunes, with jazz-oriented background written by Marty Paich. Next week she joins

forces with the Duke Ellington band for their first joint album
years.

In the final analysis, she feels, the seasoned pros must win ou.
at the ones that had real experience, in night clubs, like Andy Williams, u.
as band singers like your Peggy Lees, Vic Damones, Carmen McRaes, Kay
Starrs. Not all of them are selling millions of records, but they have secu-
rity and respect, along with a certain maturity that you're bound to recognize."

CONTROVERSY COMES WITH THE TERRITORY

*Rarely did Ella ever show up in an article that addressed anything
but her performances. Below I've reprinted a couple of completely
uncharacteristic peeks behind the scenes.*

*The first striking news clip requires some introduction. One
October evening in 1955 she was arrested backstage in Houston,
Texas, where the police, disgruntled because Norman Granz
insisted upon racial integration in his audiences, burst in on the
musicians and found trumpeter Dizzy Gillespie and tenor saxophonist Illinois Jacquet shooting dice. Ella was eating a piece of
pie. Granz posted bail for everyone; the musicians got back to the
theater for the second show, and they left town at the crack of
dawn the next day. The charges ended up being dismissed by a
judge who recognized the reason for the policemen's zeal.*

*In 1957 Ella, Georgiana Henry, pianist John Lewis, and Norman
Granz won an out-of-court settlement of $7,500 from Pan
American World Airways. They had been trying to fly from
Honolulu to Australia, on the last leg of a trip taking them to a
performance. But they were bumped, and they charged that preju-
dice was the reason. They asked for $270,000 in damages.*

*And the Associated Press reported on May 3, 1958, that Ella's lug-
gage was searched—perhaps ransacked would be a better word—
by customs agents in England looking for drugs. Her vitamin pills
were sent to a laboratory for testing. The linings of her coats were
examined. Norman Granz's toothpaste tube was split open.*

Touring with Jazz at the Philharmonic, Ella wasn't accustomed to such treatment. She certainly never used drugs.

Once, in concert with Louis Armstrong and the Lionel Hampton band, Ella was attacked on stage by a madman who shared her last name and decided he was her husband.

Then there were items about Ella's love life, a subject that rarely surfaced in the press. In 1947 Ella was seen wearing an engagement ring, and she wouldn't say who had given it to her, except to admit that he was an American and not a musician. It had to be Ray Brown, whom she married soon afterward.

A 1957 story on the United Press wire out of Monte Carlo said she had married a Norwegian, whom she may actually have married briefly. He turned out to be a fortune hunter, and he may have had another fiancée. Granz quashed the story and may have arranged for the marriage annulment, or he may simply have helped to break up an unsuitable engagement. In essence, the story was so confused in the United Press version and in every rumor relating to it that the truth never did come out in a definitive way.

Later on, the press also discovered and revealed that Ella was living in Denmark to spend time with a young lover who worked for an airline. Eventually they went their own ways, and Ella moved back to Los Angeles.

Perhaps never has so little been said about such a famous star's romantic life.—LG

Houston Dice Cops Give Ella & Boys a Bad Shake

Houston, Tex., Oct. 8 (U.P.).—A vice squad broke up a dice game in the dressing room of singer Ella Fitzgerald but waited until the first performance was over before taking her to the station.

Vice officers at a one-night stand of "Jazz at the Philharmonic" walked into the singer's dressing room just as saxophonist Illinois Jacquet rolled his point.

But the officers, led by Vice Squad Sgt. W. A. Scotton, beat Jacquet to the pot and scooped up $185 and the dice.

Others Seized

Miss Fitzgerald, Jacquet, trumpet player Dizzy Gillespie, singer Georgianna Henry and producer Norman Granz were arrested.

At the station, Miss Fitzgerald, dressed in a décolleté gown of blue taffeta and a mink stole, dabbed at her eyes with a wispy handkerchief.

"I have nothing to say," she said as she was booked for shooting dice. "What is there to say? I was only having a piece of pie and a cup of coffee."

Not Actually Shooting

Sgt. Scotton agreed that Miss Fitzgerald was not actually shooting dice when they entered.

Granz posted $10 bond for each on the misdemeanor charge and police drove them all back to the Music Hall in time for the second show.

The troupe left Houston at 8 A. M. It was presumed the bond would be forfeited.

Man Attacks Jazz Singer

Atlantic City, N. J. (UPI)—A Negro jazz fan went berserk Saturday night, leaped on the stage of the Warner Theater and punched singer Ella Fitzgerald in the jaw while she was singing a song.

"You've got another man," the assailant screamed as he swung a roundhouse which caught the blues singer on the right side of her jaw. Miss Fitzgerald reeled back under the blow while musicians and a policeman rushed from the wings and grabbed the man.

The attack occurred before some 2,000 persons attending a jazz show featuring Miss Fitzgerald, Louis Satchmo Armstrong, and the Lionel Hampton band.

The man later was identified as William Edward Fitzgerald, 29, of Atlantic City, no relation to the singer. Police said he had a record of a narcotics arrest in 1950. Fitzgerald said he had been treated at the Veteran's Hospital at Lyon's N. J. for a mental disorder.

Police physician Oscar Harris examined Fitzgerald and said he was a "mental case." He ordered him to the Ancora State Hospital for further examination.

Miss Fitzgerald said she would delay lodging charges pending the outcome of the examination and a conference with her attorneys.

LADY DAY AND LADY TIME
In Jazz Singing, 1990

The iconoclastic, highly opinionated jazz critic, Will Friedwald, often surprises readers with his novel views of musicians and singers. He doesn't disappoint in this excerpt from his book, in which he draws an analogy between Ella and Leo Watson, a little-known, zany, very creative scat singer who had a brief heyday in the 1930s and 1940s. It's possible, as Friedwald suggests, that Ella heard Watson's recordings but doubtful that she ever imbibed his influence for her own style. In New York he sang primarily on 52nd Street, or Swing Street, in the tiny clubs there. By that time Ella's career was already well established. Nevertheless, it's intriguing to think of Ella studying Watson's fresh work—and a shame that it's not impossible to ask her if she knew or admired him.

Friedwald applies himself to analyzing and evaluating her recordings at various stages of Ella's career. It's interesting to compare his ideas about her songbooks with those of other critics. He closes with a paean to Ella's artistry, exulting, "If this isn't drama, I don't know what is."—LG

Any connections between musicology and biography decrease from vague to nonexistent in Ella Fitzgerald, whose far-out scat lines have no parallel in her controlled and well-managed career. On the face of it, she has more in common with the life and art of her most immediate inspiration in this area, Leo Watson, the only scat singer of note between Armstrong and Fitzgerald. Personal descriptions of Watson range from Leonard Feather's "a mad genius" to just plain "flaky." The stories of his adventures outzany those of any other figure in jazz, even certified cuckoos like the maniacal Jack Purvis and the perverse Joe Venuti. Nonetheless, in the long run, we'll remember Watson more for his singing than for his insanity.

People first heard of Watson, born in Kansas City in 1898, when his vocal-instrumental group, the Spirits of Rhythm, became so popular that they established not only themselves but the Onyx Club and all of 52nd Street in the early thirties. Otis Ferguson, who wrote the only important article on the group besides Feather, describes the Spirits getting started as "kids helling around with ukuleles," although John Chilton reports that they didn't come together until Watson had passed thirty. After the Spirits disintegrated, a number of major pop stars tried to help Watson on his solo career. Artie Shaw used a wordless Watson chorus on Cole Porter's "I've a Strange New Rhythm in My Heart" (1937, Brunswick), perhaps the first time anyone ever got away with scatting on a new plug tune in place of the usual vocal refrain. Gene Krupa hired him as a regular vocalist (concurrent with Jan Savitt's Bon Bon) for eight months, until Watson picked a fight with a Pullman porter and put his fist through a train window. The Andrews Sisters made their only significant contribution to music by persuading their contract company, Decca, to award Watson his first solo recording session. Slim Gaillard took him into his kooky combo as drummer, vocalist, and resident meshuggener in the funniest series of jazz programs ever broadcast. But these periods of productivity only amounted to intervals in a life of (unprovable) rumors of marathon drum solos that could be silenced only by the police, arrests for possession of illegal substances, spells outside music where he worked as a waiter and in a munitions plant, percussion accompaniment to race riots, naked sprints through hotel lobbies, and other causes for commitment. When Watson died in Los Angeles in 1950, the killer was officially pneumonia, but I suspect that he was just too crazy to live.

Only a superficial hearing would offer evidence that his seemingly nonsensical scat choruses betray a turbulent state of mind. Ultimately, the only time Watson was under control was when he was singing. His vocals, especially the scat choruses, reveal a marvelous sense of construction, symmetry, and interior logic. Even tranquillity, as Dan Morgenstern suggests, citing his solo on "Way Down Yonder in New Orleans" (with Red McKenzie and the Spirits of Rhythm [1934, Decca]) as one of the earliest examples of the relaxed feeling Lester Young later brought to jazz, as does his markedly ungospel antiphonous second-to-last chorus of "I'll Be Ready When the Great Day Comes" (1933, Brunswick).

Watson made the first significant extension of the scatter's vocabulary since Armstrong and Crosby. Though voices had been imitating instruments since Cliff Edwards's time, Watson developed ways for singers to learn from horns without having to mimic them. Some of his admirers, like Jon Hendricks and writer Carlton Brown, mention his trombonelike approach, but Watson used long, smeary glissandi long before he actually learned to play the trombone (Feather says he picked it up—literally—for a date with the unzany John Kirby Sextet in 1937). On his great 1939 "It's the Tune That Counts" (Decca), Watson comes armed with short, percussive phrases that refer to his experiences as a drummer and with the guitar family. Watson also standardized another Armstrong technique that the trumpeter had never fully developed in his singing, the quote. In improvising, Watson's mind frequently lighted on fragments from older tunes, generally nursery rhymes and folk airs (this being before the body of American popular songs grew large enough to support its own circulating library of references), and he'd combine these extracts, sometimes with, sometimes without the accompanying lyric, with his variations on the original theme as well as completely improvised material, creating what George Simon called "singing in shorthand" and Leonard Feather dubbed a "vocal stream of consciousness." Watson's work was so complete that around 1939, when he met Eddie Jefferson, then a young dancer who told Watson of his desire to do something new in jazz singing, Watson told him that everything possible had already been done with scatting[1]—this before the mature Fitzgerald, Anita O'Day, Mel Torme, Betty Carter, and everyone else.

Watson had only a few opportunities to freeze his innovative sounds for posterity before he went to that big wangadoodle in the sky, but his ideas caught on quickly. His short burst of notoriety, combined with the longer stays in the spotlight of the considerably better-known Cab Calloway and Louis Armstrong, guaranteed that scat singing would be one of the more steadily demanded novelties of the swing era. The trumpeter-leader and occasional singer Bunny Berigan, who shared Watson's structural genius as well as his propensity for screwing up, functioned an extremely Watsonian vocal on the quasi-nonsensical "Mama, I Wanna Make Rhythm" (1937, Victor), loaded with slurred phrases and hard g and k sounds.

In fact, to judge Fitzgerald on her Chick Webb–era sides alone, including the pre-1939 titles under her own name (she had just turned twenty-one at the time of Webb's death, having spent the last four years on the road with that great band), we might dismiss her scatting as simply the best to come along in the path of Watson and her ballads merely as the finest of Connee Boswell's heiresses. Throughout the years, Fitzgerald repeatedly scats along trails blazed by Watson, especially in her instrumental noises (the air-bass solos) and her method of quoting (especially the nursery rhymes). In her first modern masterpiece, Fitzgerald squeezes in the same "crazy over horses" lick that Watson played on "I Got Rhythm" (1933, Brunswick) and sang on "Junk Man" (1934, Decca).

Though Fitzgerald never completely escaped Watson, he still amounts to only one of her influences. She told Murray Kempton once that she "remembers everything, absorbs everything and uses everything," and continued, "I steal everything I ever heard." The singers she's studied go way beyond Watson and Boswell, as you can tell from her impressions. At a 1949 club date and other references that she drops as she recalled for George Hoefer a year later, while her bassist soloed on "Basin Street Blues," she hummed the lyrics behind him in a Louis Armstrong fashion. Her drummer, Lee Young, encouraged her to take it out front and the imitation became part of her act. When recording "Basin Street" in 1952, she worked in a whole chorus à la Armstrong. She used the bit as part of an introduction to "St. Louis Blues," and when sharing a bill with Satchmo at the Hollywood Bowl in 1956, did "I Can't Give You Anything But Love" like him for one chorus and like Rose Murphy for another (an imitation that went back to 1950). It remained a staple of her act for years: Fitzgerald, inimitable herself, creating impressions of female singers as uncannily accurate as Sammy Davis, Jr.'s imitations of male vocalists. One 1964 specialty number, "Bill Bailey," gave her the chance to do Sophie Tucker, Della Reese, Pearl Bailey, and Dinah Washington. With Mel Torme's arranger, Marty Paich, she borrowed the vamp Torme and Paich used to introduce "Lulu's Back in Town" for her own "If I Were a Bell" on *Ella Swings Lightly* (1958, Verve).[2] This album offers Fitzgerald's tributes to Bon Bon Tunnell in "720 in the Books" and to Roy Eldridge in "Little Jazz."

Fitzgerald's earliest scat lines stay closer to home rhythmically, especially the 1-2-3 beat of "The Organ Grinder's Swing" (1936, Decca), than do Watson's high-flying phrases. In 1945, Fitzgerald recorded "Flying Home," and listeners forgot that anyone else had ever scatted. The first of hundreds of versions of "Flying Home" reveals as many differences from Watson's method as it does similarities, virtually all of which she would expand on later. She takes the piece at a more relaxed long-form approach, possibly learned from Holiday, which contrasts with Watson's compressed and manic outbursts, giving her greater opportunity to build up tension and then disperse it. She also incorporates well-known jazz solos and arrangements into her vocal improvisations, like the Illinois Jacquet "honk" climax of "Flying Home" and the shape of the Count Basie–Bill Davis chart of "April in Paris" into her own version of the piece (the latter from a 1957 Newport set issued by Verve). "Flying" also offers a link to Connee Boswell through a quote from her "Martha." This incorporation is more satisfying than the vocalise movement of Eddie Jefferson and King Pleasure.

Nonetheless, over the long haul, Fitzgerald was only revving up her engines in "Flying Home," and only really took off following her involvement with the bop movement a few years later. "These bop musicians have stimulated me more than I can say," Fitzgerald related at the time in *Ebony* magazine. "I've been inspired by them and I want the world to know it. Bop musicians have more to say than any other musicians playing today." Not only by absorbing modern jazz, but by publicly allying herself with the new music, she became its most identifiable figure at the height of the bop controversy. Only a handful of swing-era stars—Woody Herman, Coleman Hawkins, and Benny Goodman—and only one star singer—Fitzgerald—came out in support of bop, although a few others capitalized on its notoriety. Fitzgerald learned bop at the hands of its originators: during a tour with Gillespie himself. "I used to get thrilled listening to them when he would do his bebop," she later told Al Fraser. "That's the way I learned to what you call bop. It was quite a new experience and he used to always tell me, 'Come up and do it with the fellas. . . .' That to me was my education in learning how to really bop." In 1947, Fitzgerald married Ray Brown, the new music's leading bassist.

In the early forties Anita O'Day had experimented with increasingly shorter notes that anticipated bop's rhythmic style, but Fitzgerald dove headfirst into bop's harmonic maelstrom. Just to keep up with the chord patterns of swing improvisation took more musicianship than almost any singer had in the band era, and in the late forties only five or six perhaps fully understood the advanced bop changes. Fitzgerald, as Martin Williams has pointed out, took it even farther; her ability to make musical sense out of the spaciest intervals and harmonic patterns imaginable established her as one of the most important minds in modern jazz. Of the dozens of vocalists to try their tonsils at scatting, only Fitzgerald could keep an audience entertained with nothing else but this. Only Fitzgerald would never repeat herself, never grow monotonous. She's always had the showmanship never to try this for more than one or two numbers a set, to mix in scat features with familiar standards and current tunes at varying speeds and extraslow ballads—but she doesn't need it.

Perhaps because her improvising is the most accomplished in vocal music, she's never had to consider the context in which it appears as carefully as O'Day or Mel Torme, whose balance of preset form and improvisation resembles that of John Lewis and the Modern Jazz Quartet. In contrast, Fitzgerald uses the bone-simplest of patterns. Her classic set piece of "How High the Moon" (1947, Decca, and endless concert versions) utilizes a few relatively simple pegs: Each performance uses the same tempo, opens with a reading of the lyric, and then goes into some special material designed to introduce the improvisation ("We're singin' it, 'cause you asked for it . . ."). The scat itself inevitably includes loads of quotes (à la Leo Watson) both irrelevant—"Rockin' in Rhythm" and "Rhapsody in Blue" on her Decca *Flying Home*; and "Poinciana," "Deep Purple," "Love in Bloom," "The Peanut Vendor," Charlie Ventura's "Whaddya Say We Go?," "Did You Ever See a Dream Walking?," "A-Tisket, A-Tasket," "Heat Wave," and "On the Trail," "L'il Liza Jane," "Got to Be This or That," "Idaho," "Smoke [Sweat] Gets in Your Eyes," and others on a 1960 Berlin concert performance (Verve)—and relevant— as on her third or fourth wordless chorus of each run-through of "Moon" when she goes into the melody of Charlie Parker's "Moon" variation and bop anthem, "Ornithology." But though she follows these rules, Fitzgerald completely improvises the content of her vocal. Like John Ford getting to work on yet another western or Chuck Jones directing his twelfth "Roadrunner" cartoon, Fitzgerald uses formulas creatively, not only to precondition her audiences as to what they can expect, but to deliver the goods.

Two mid-fifties scat features, "Later" (1954, Decca) and "Ella Hums the Blues" (1955), make clear that Fitzgerald knows the musical elements of the blues, but her one full-scale attempt at conquering the Smith girls repertoire, *These Are the Blues* (1963, Verve), reveals that she lacks the gruff, hoarse passion that even the smoothest real blues singers (such as Joe Williams) have. This doesn't make her a lesser artist, any more than Bach was a lesser artist for writing about fugal variations in D minor or Vivaldi was for writing about the four seasons. Her deeper understanding of the medium's implications may be only as cursory as Joe Williams's scatting, but she does wonders with the purely musical aspects of the form on the above-mentioned improvisations and also when the blues spirit touches a pop song, especially "I've Got a Right to Sing the Blues" and others in *The Harold Arlen Songbook* (1960–61, Verve).

Her lack of blues passion affects her work with other kinds of music, leading some of her detractors to claim that fate chose badly when it selected Ella Fitzgerald to be the one singer to record definitive collections of the essential American songs, her *Songbooks*. It must have seemed especially ironic to theater buffs that the first singer to make extra long albums of the Broadway repertoire should be one who had absolutely nothing to do with the theater, either specifically or philosophically. As we've seen, Fitzgerald's career began and stayed, for a time, with rhythmic novelties. By 1950 the gap between singer and material was widening; she was getting better and what she sang was getting worse. She reacted by pressuring Decca to allow her to record an auspicious LP of Gershwin songs (only eight of them, as LPs were only ten inches back then) with solo piano accompaniment by the brilliant Ellis Larkins. Even at the pinnacle of her involvement with bop she insisted, "Despite the different kinds of songs I sing, I still consider myself a ballad singer. I suppose I'll always be that way."

That *Ella Sings Gershwin* signifies the high-water mark of her Decca period shouldn't be interpreted as meaning that the rest of her Decca sides are crass rubbish, though MCA (which, unfortunately, currently owns the Decca catalog) would have you think so by issuing only the worst of these selections on anthologies they perversely title her "greatest hits." When we think of Fitzgerald on Decca, the worst titles tend to automatically come to mind ("Molasses, Molasses," "A Guy Is a Guy") as do the Kapp-italist extremes, the duets with Louis Armstrong and Louis Jordan (but, strangely enough, not Crosby), and the insufferable vocal groups, like the unbearably square Ink Spots, who dig their toes into the ground through seven tracks while poor Ella tries in vain to force them into the groove. In fairness, she made just as many excellent records for Kapp and his successors: *Ella*, a hauntingly beautiful 1952 reunion with Larkins; *Lullabies of Birdland*, which collects all of her scat specialties; and *Listen and Relax*, an entertaining jumble of good songs and fair songs made acceptable by Fitzgerald's singing and Gordon Jenkins's tasteful arrangements. Several cuts here forecast the future musical comedy-oriented pieces, such as two *South Pacific* songs from 1949, issued first on a single and then on *Listen*. Could she have recorded "I'm Gonna Wash That Man Right Outa My Hair" for any other reason than to show off her rhythmic dexterity? Taking the central part of the refrain at a reasonably fast clip, she effortlessly dives into the bridge at double time. Like a rubber ball bouncing up and down in an empty room, put it into a smaller space and it'll go faster because the floor and ceiling are closer together. When Ella hits that stream of short lines in the release, she starts moving twice as fast, and the effect exhilarates.

As good as some of her Deccas are, her really great years are the Verve years, 1956 to 1966.[3] Legend has it that Norman Granz didn't want her to sing with his Jazz at the Philharmonic troupe at first, and only invited Fitzgerald on stage for one number as a favor to her husband and his bassist, Ray Brown. Subsequently, her relationship with Granz lasted much longer than either of her marriages. Granz had already been making records, but Fitzgerald was too important a star (selling 22 million Decca discs by 1954 and making the cover of *Life* the following year) for Granz to record until he inaugurated his major pop music label, Verve Records. Fitzgerald began making singles for the new label in January 1956. In

March the new label announced that her first album for them would be a live set called *A Night at the Fairmont*. Though it was never released, her premier album for Verve—*The Cole Porter Songbook*—became one of the biggest-selling jazz records of all time. It made major powers out of both Verve (and Granz) and its arranger, Buddy Bregman, and if there had ever been an empty seat at a Fitzgerald club date or concert, such an animal now no longer existed.

The runaway success of *The Cole Porter Songbook* testifies more to the strength of the idea—Fitzgerald in an extended, thirty-two-song program of tunes by a single composer—than the quality of the record itself. For all the hoopla surrounding arranger Bregman in thirty-year-old liner notes, his work today comes off as routine and unimaginative, and this monotony also pervades the second Bregman-Fitzgerald outing, *The Rodgers and Hart Songbook*, also 1956, also Verve, also two records (thirty songs), and also difficult to endure without a break. The set begins to come alive when the conductor steps down and lets Fitzgerald tackle "Bewitched" with only her trio, but the singer makes too much of an effort to prolong the unorchestrated moment by doing every single verse and refrain of Larry Hart's introspective soliloquy. She meant it to be moody and ballsy ("I got real sexy on that one," she said in a contemporaneous interview), but it winds up as rambling, a seven-minute track that argues for the restoration of the 78-era three-minute limit, and also for leaving extra choruses where they belong—on the musical comedy stage. Her 1958 songbook, *Irving Berlin*, fares better under the baton of the surer-footed Paul Weston.

The songbook series includes two inarguable masterpieces, each devoted to the works of composers who straddled the boundaries of jazz and popular music: George Gershwin, Tin Pan Alley's most celebrated songwriter, who introduced the idea of working genuine jazz and black music ideas into classical music, which in turn became a building block of the jazz repertoire; and Duke Ellington, who wrote music for a jazz orchestra and soloists that, with very little finagling, belongs just as much to singers and to the theater. Fitzgerald's art relates to both men as she never crossed between pop and jazz but always kept one foot in both, making her, in retrospect, the definitive jazz singer, since before the bottom dropped out of pop in the late fifties even jazz-oriented vocalists could appeal to popular audiences.

Ellington organizes his material for Fitzgerald in three ways. On pieces that already have a vocal part or a vocal refrain, he merely recasts Ella in the role of one of his own singers, rather like Jimmy Hamilton taking over a part originally written for Barney Bigard. On "Rockin' in Rhythm," though, Ellington overlays Fitzgerald's scatting right on top of his standard arrangement as Charlie Barnet had done ten years previously with scatting dancer Bunny Briggs (also recorded by Norman Granz). Third, for some works Ellington created entirely new shapes for Fitzgerald. The new "Caravan," for instance, refers to neither of the number's two previous well-known incarnations: as vehicle for its originator, valve-trombonist Juan Tizol; and as a best-selling piece of romantic exotica for Billy Eckstine. Bandleader and singer would reteam occasionally in the sixties, for a TV special, another Verve album, and a tour to promote a potential hit single, "Imagine My Frustration," but *The Duke Ellington Songbook* remains their definitive collaboration.

By virtue of the composer's presence, *The Ellington Songbook* had to be authentic, its departures from established molds of its material done by one in a position to make them legitimate. For *The George Gershwin Songbook*, Fitzgerald and Granz strove not for authenticity but topicality, recruiting the single greatest orchestrator in all of grown-up pop music, Nelson Riddle, and Fitzgerald and Riddle jettisoned the music's original purposes to make the songs work in a contemporary context. One of the most cloying tunes Gershwin ever wrote, "Aren't You Kind of Glad We Did?" (apparently George also thought it cloying as it went unperformed in his lifetime), had previously been best known as a duet between Dick Haymes and Judy Garland. The piece's overdone coyness inspires Garland to overact more than usual, though perhaps it's only the contrast with the restrained and subtle Haymes that makes her histrionics here unbearable. The normally cool Gene Kelly flies off the handle in "By Strauss," a comic relief number in the film *An American in Paris*, which sarcastically attacks Broadway music in mock support of nineteenth-century Viennese waltzes. Fitzgerald strips each of its camp and gushiness. Riddle scores the Strauss-mock homage with just the slightest touch of Teutonic oom-pah (it would be a different song without it), and while Fitzgerald doesn't rely on the "jazz waltz" idiom ("Bluesette," "Valse Hot," "Waltzing the Blue," et al.), she makes the piece swing in an understated 3/4 time. On "Kind of Glad," she latches on to the music's gentle pulse and flows along on top of it gracefully, and gives the lyrics the same respect (or degree of respect) she affords to "Someone to Watch Over Me" or "The Man I Love" or any of the other great works in the Gershwin book.

Among other gifts, Riddle shared with Ellington a talent for making albums work as albums, which Ellington explored in classics like *His Mother Called Him Bill* and *The Far East Suite* and Riddle took to the limit in his work with Frank Sinatra. A songbook album has now a natural flow of its own; the juxtaposition of ballads with comic turns and pieces written as background for dancers gradually turns the record into a musical comedy itself. The five-record *George and Ira Gershwin Songbook* amounts to an opera, fifty-three songs[4] that cover the widest range of human situations. The early ten-inch *Ella Sings Gershwin* stands to this monument as a Picasso sketch does to his epic "Guernica."

If the Gershwin and Ellington packages are the most essential collections of Fitzgerald's work, each has a close runner-up. Her next greatest songbook, taped over 1960 and 1961, addresses Harold Arlen, whose jazz-shaped songs reflect an even greater understanding of black music than Gershwin, under the baton of Billy May, an arranger as bodacious as Riddle is subtle. Fitzgerald sounds just as good with orchestras of Count Basie and Bill Doggett as she did with Duke's. *Ella & Basie, On the Sunny Side of the Street* (1963) and *Rhythm Is My Business* (1962) demonstrate the most propulsive, impetuous, and catchy rhythmic motion (meaning swing) ever heard. On the hit instrumental "Shiny Stockings," arranger Quincy Jones reprised one Ellington method by slipping the standard Frank Foster chart behind Ella's singing of her own new lyrics. For Japanese television several years later, Fitzgerald devised a new small-group version in which she hums parts of the Foster arrangement in harmony with Roy Eldridge's muted trumpet in between her vocal choruses, working in two other Basie standards, "Every Day I Have the Blues" in Tommy Flanagan's piano introduction and "April in Paris" through Ella's hollering, "One more once!"

Fitzgerald made loads of wonderful records for Verve besides the attention-gathering songbooks and live albums, more than could possibly be reissued and then kept in the catalog even though she's one of Polygram's best-selling artists no less than Verve. Her two themeless sets with Riddle, *Ella Swings Gently with Nelson* (1961) and *Ella Swings Brightly with Nelson* (1962), are actually more consistently excellent sets than her last two songbooks with the swingin' Riddle, *Jerome Kern* (1963) and *Johnny Mercer* (1964). They gather many of the remaining great songs of the thirties and forties as do her heavily stringed ballad outings with the worthy Frank DeVol, including *Ella Fitzgerald Sings Sweet Songs for Swingers* and *Hello Love*. DeVol's Columbia albums with Tony Bennett tend to be overdone, while his work for Doris Day (and earlier for Peggy Lee at Capitol) leans toward the nondescript. However, since he knows he can't titillate and excite as consistently as Riddle, he compensates by adding two master tenor obbligatists to the mixture: Stan Getz on four tracks of *Like Someone in Love* (1957) and Zoot Sims on most of *Hello, Dolly!* (1964).

With the great modern jazz arranger Marty Paich, Fitzgerald made *Ella Swings Lightly* (1957), a jewel of a selection of big-band numbers which proved that even though she had moved up to the biggies like Gershwin and Rodgers, she could still do a great job with swing trivialities; and *Whisper Not* (1966), where top-echelon accompaniment excuses tunes like "Matchmaker" and "Wives and Lovers." Lastly, she left behind arrangements, horns, reeds, and strings altogether for two charming rhythm-section-only dates, the up-tempo *Clap Hands, Here Comes Charlie* (with pianist Lou Levy [1961]) and the lovely ballad-oriented *Let No Man Write My Epitaph* (with Paul Smith [1960]). And that's not even mentioning Fitzgerald's great live sets.

The reader will excuse me, I hope, for going on at such length about the ten years Fitzgerald recorded exclusively for Verve, but they contain so much of her best work that her earlier period seems like a mere prelude and her post-Verve years an after thought. Since 1966, Fitzgerald has made quite a few mistakes, like a religious album, *Brighten the Corner* (1967, Capitol); a group of sacred Christmas songs, *Christmas* (1967, Capitol), which is not in the same league as her secular seasonal album, *Ella Wishes You a Swinging Christmas* (1957, Verve) with Frank DeVol; and a long-awaited collaboration with Benny Carter wasted on piddling medleys. Mistakes are to be expected, but too much of her recent work seems redundant: live albums that add little to her earlier in-person recordings and a third Gershwin outing with Andre Previn, who isn't fit to polish Ellis Larkins's pedals. Compared to these, her few attempts to try something new seem ineffectual. On *Take Love Easy* (1973, Pablo), *Again* (1976, Pablo), and *Speak Love* (Pablo), she delves at length into the lyricism of voice and solo guitar, an idea she used on the verses only of "Nice Work If You Can Get It" and "They All Laughed" on *The Gershwin Songbook*, and on passages of the long "Spring Can Really Hang You Up the Most" on *Clap Hands, Here Comes Charlie*. Her double-length excursion into bossa nova, *Ella Abraca Jobim*, comes along too many years after the fact.

No one expected Fitzgerald to weather the decades all that successfully. A seventy-year-old Frank Sinatra, a Billie Holiday with a toe or two already in the grave, or a senile Mabel Mercer can get up there and still interpret a lyric meaningfully, but Fitzgerald's interpretations have always been of melodies and harmonies. No other singer depends so much on pure chops as she does. And for anyone but Ella, her recent voice would be enough. To add, or to subtract, from this, her improviser's wit and imagination may be fading as well. Those long scat lines lack the logical cohesion she once had. Again, it's too much to expect Fitzgerald to do at seventy what she could do twenty-five years ago.

As this is being written, Fitzgerald hasn't recorded—the longest period in her whole career—and one suspects that she has momentarily retreated to the wings to think carefully about her past and future. As Chick Webb's band singer, Fitzgerald perfected her pitch to the point where it was the envy of even such precise pitch-mongers as Jo Stafford. With the coming of bop she mastered modern harmony and rhythm, learning how to swing and improvise better than any other vocalist. On the 1950 Gershwin ten-incher, she conquered the slower tempi, adding new delicateness and grace to her realm of possibilities. With the 1959 Gershwin box, Fitzgerald reaches her limit. Now she can occasionally rough up her notes for effect, helping her to interject varying levels of mood (which isn't the same as emotion) into her work—mild irony, humor, and pathos.

Of her eight songbooks, she devoted only one to a lyricist, and this was that most down-to-earth of wordsmiths, Johnny Mercer. And this because, to Fitzgerald, the lyric is only something to swing on—as Claudius said in Hamlet, "Words without thoughts never to heaven go."

There are enough sultry saloon singers and balladeers in this world; we don't need to cry all the time. We need singers like Fitzgerald to remind us that our great songwriters wrote music as well as words. Ella's success with "Memories of You" (on *Hello, Dolly!* [1964, Verve]) owes nothing to "waking skies at sunrise" but to the diatonic obstacle course that leads her away from and ultimately toward the resolving five-note figure that concludes the melodic payoff. Our pulses race when Fitzgerald starts to scat. Will she follow the melody? For how long? Will a fragment of another tune momentarily pop into her head? Will she slow down the tempo, double it, or suspend the beat altogether? Will she do her crowd-pleasing "bass solo"? Will she trade fours with her accompanists, and will they be able to keep up with her endless inventiveness?

If this isn't drama, I don't know what is.

It's an enthralling experience, one, you could say, matched only by the thrill of hearing Billie Holiday interpret a ballad. They may travel completely different ways to the same destination, but the women whom Lester Young christened Lady Day and Lady Time can reach you and thrill you. That each influenced no end of other singers seems unimportant compared to the way each, when at full throttle, can still move an audience. The results make *Much Ado About Nothing* a speech that runs like iron through your blood.

1. This information from Jefferson's friend Ira Steingroot.

2. Paich used the same figure to set the stage for Art Pepper's entrance on "Anthropology" on *Art Pepper + 11*.

3. Almost every album mentioned hereinafter comes from Verve, so in the parentheses following each record title you'll find only the year; you can assume the label is Verve.

4. Completists will also want "Somebody Loves Me" and "Cheerful Little Earful," two Fitzgerald-Gershwin-Riddle tracks (the latter only by Ira) that appear only on her *Get Happy* album, as well as a 45-rpm of Riddle doing Gershwin's instrumental preludes, included only in the original box set and on a recent Japanese reissue.

LESLIE GOURSE
THE TIME OF ELLA FITZGERALD
In Louis' Children, 1984

In retrospect, writing this chapter in 1982 had some amusing moments for me. First, I could not persuade either Ella Fitzgerald or Norman Granz to let me interview them. Ella was abrupt, and Granz was vociferously opposed to my doing the chapter. He had never heard of me before I approached him. Then the great pianist, Tommy Flanagan, an exceptionally sweet man who had spent about a dozen years as Ella's distinguished accompanist, disappointed me. He was no longer in touch with Ella, and, although he admired her, he preferred not to talk about her for publication at that time. Tommy was a busy group leader and one of the greatest piano stylists in history.

Despite all the roadblocks that left me with what seemed at first to be a barren wasteland, I wrote the chapter on Ella. When the book came out, Norman Granz telephoned me and said, in essence, that he was happy with my chapter and that I could call him for any-

thing I ever wanted in the future, anything at all. Truly thrilled, I tried to call him a few times after that, but I never heard from him again. (At first, Ella's transitional group was called the Three Keys, and it may or may not have changed to become the Four Keys with new personnel before it disbanded.)—LG

Ella Fitzgerald has combined it all in one package, a peerless sense of rhythm that allows her to move like quicksilver over the notes, with perfect intonation, her voice full of ease and musical inventiveness—altogether a joyful noise. She can sound like a bell or a trumpet or a lioness at will. "No one in the world can beat Ella as a riff singer," said Ethel Waters long ago, at a time when Ethel was primarily acting instead of singing. And Ella Fitzgerald propels all of her assets with an intensely rhythmic undercurrent, sometimes only a subtle ripple, other times an awesome wave—an inexorable natural force with which she engulfs and sweeps away the audience.

She won the Apollo contest in 1934 at about age sixteen, which makes her the most senior of the two living female jazz icons, herself and Sarah Vaughan. Ella Fitzgerald's passport gives her birth date as April 25, 1918. Legend has it that Ella, a shy young woman, thought she would dance in the Apollo contest. But something changed her mind onstage; perhaps her knees turned to jelly. She still shakes with fright during performances after nearly fifty years as a performer. At the Apollo she decided to sing a tune called "Judy," several sources said, though someone else said it was "The Object of My Affection." Others noodle about the possibility of yet another tune. In any case, the audience demanded encores.

An entertainer named Bardu Ali, fronting the band for tiny, hunchbacked drummer Chick Webb at the Apollo that night, was so astounded at the girl's voice that he introduced her to Webb. He and his wife took her under their wings and into the Webb band, becoming her guardians. Her mother had died when she was fourteen, or younger, according to the most repeated version of her childhood. Very little has been written about this stage of her life.

"I thought my singing was pretty much hollering," she said, "but Webb didn't." In 1935 she made her first records with the Webb band— "Are You Here to Stay?" and "Love and Kisses"; and then three years later, "A-Tisket, A-Tasket," adapted, it was said, by Ella from an old nursery rhyme. It became a national hit and launched her as a star. She was depicted at the time in Earl Wilson's newspaper column as a fun-loving girl who liked to play cute games with pennies backstage.

Subsequently she won *Down Beat* magazine's award as Best Female Singer for eighteen consecutive years, and eleven Grammy awards, the highest awards of the National Academy of Recording Arts and Sciences, more than any other female jazz singer. She made more than 250 albums and sold over 50 million, according to one source; 100 million said another. Chick Webb died at age twenty-nine of spinal tuberculosis in 1939, after a career in which he often played in excruciating pain. Ella took over his band for three years, until the Army dismantled it. After that she went out with the Four Keys. Jay McShann recalled appearing in a show with Ella in those days. Asked to introduce her group, he got mixed up somehow and said, "Ella Keys and the Four Fitzgeralds." He also recalled the funny look she gave him. The Army eventually reduced the Keys to a skeleton. And Ella went solo.

In this period, too, she was married for the first time to Benny Kornegay, a shipyard worker. But a newspaper account of the young couple suggested that Ella's mind was more on music than ménage. While she was away on the road, Benny played her records at home, Sidney Fields wrote in his column, "Only Human," then went out to listen to more of his wife's singing on a jukebox.

"When I clown, he don't mind," Ella Fitzgerald was quoted as saying at the end of 1942. "And I'm always clowning. He understands when people like to do something it's better not to try and stop them. But I have to learn to cook. We just started our apartment and I want to get into the kitchen. We've been eating in restaurants, and he's getting tired of it. What more do I want? Please say I want to be a star like Ethel Waters with a Broadway show. I doubt it, though. Maybe I got an inferiority complex. Maybe I'm saying I doubt it because I'm hoping it will be just the opposite."

It was. It was all music, no dialogue. The girl who had come from Newport News, Virginia, to grow up in Nyack, New York, under the care of a relative, ended that marriage after two years and tried a second time with bassist Ray Brown, Sr., in 1948, when she was thirty years old. They met when they traveled with Dizzy Gillespie's band in the 1940s. "That's when she started scatting," Brown recalls. In 1950 the Browns had a son, Ray, Jr.—who became a drummer—and were divorced in 1952. She told Fields, who wrote for the *Mirror*, in 1957: "I guess I pick them wrong. But I want to get married again. I'm still looking. Everybody wants companionship." However, she never married again.

Her career as a solo recording artist for Victor, and then from 1935 to 1955 for Decca, had gone along well enough. She filled the years with albums of solid tunes with orchestras, strings and all, backing her clear, nimble voice with its brilliant, rhythmic drive. In the 1940s she had a big hit with "How High the Moon," just to toss off the name of one of her many hits. She made a few films, including *St. Louis Blues* and *Pete Kelly's Blues*, in which she sang "Hard-Hearted Hannah." In 1950 she earned $3,250 a week during an engagement at New York's Paramount Theater.

In 1955 Ella took a new manager, this time Norman Granz's. He was producing "Jazz at the Philharmonic" tours, in which Ella had already been involved, and records on the Verve label.

Granz started her on a career of recording albums of songbooks of the most famous American composers—Cole Porter, and more Cole Porter; Jerome Kern; Johnny Mercer; Rodgers and Hart; Harold Arlen; Irving Berlin; Duke Ellington; W. C. Handy; a grab bag of "Misty," "Angel Eyes," "September Song," "Let No Man Write My Epitaph" and others; a reissue of "A-Tisket, A-Tasket," "A Sunday Kind of Love," and other Fitzgerald hits; Ella with Benny Goodman in 1936, and Ella in Hollywood. In Granz she found exquisite career organization. And her career soared above almost everyone else's, prompting so many musicians to say she has been the best that ever lived.

With Granz's management she played the world—all the great music houses in the United States, with the best jazz musicians. She toured Latin America, Europe and Asia. She was the first jazz singer to appear at the Flamingo in Las Vegas and in the Venetian Room of the Fairmont Hotel in San Francisco. With Louis Armstrong, she made classic jazz recordings—another boost to her stardom.

At the height of the rock craze in the 1960s, Ella Fitzgerald thought she would like to do "Goin' Out of My Head," "Sunny," and an album of Beatles songs like "Yesterday" and "Michelle." To satisfy a fan, she learned "Ode to Billie Joe" and performed it with written notes—an effective touch by a woman whose career centered almost totally on old standards. But her greatest appeal for everyone always lay in the classics, such as "Mack the Knife" and "How High the Moon." There was never anything zany about her work to put her into the running for a piece of the rock-audience pie. Her career has been remarkably consistent—scat tunes, ballads and up-tempo numbers, with one of the most unmistakable, best-loved sounds in jazz. After so many years, she still sounded fresh, bringing people to their feet, clapping and calling for more, when she sang "Teach Me Tonight" straightforwardly, with an almost Broadway-musical bounce, at Carnegie Hall in 1982. She did a varied repertoire: "Deep Purple," "Let's Do It," "God Bless the Child," "Lullaby of Birdland,"

"'Round Midnight," "Honeysuckle Rose," which she really swung with a trombone and tenor sax, showing, as usual, that she could do it all. And "Take the 'A' Train," which she scatted and from which she darted off on a chord to "Heat Wave." At one time, so successful was she with "A-Tisket, A-Tasket," she adapted another childhood classic, "Old MacDonald Had a Farm." It has remained in her repertoire for decades, beloved of this eminent scatter and her public for the *ee-i-os*, the chick-chicks, quack-quacks, oink-oinks and moo-moos, as she keeps going up a half-tone: "Old MacDonald had a farm, what a swinging farm . . . How you going to keep them down on the farm? . . ." And she did that, too.

Norman Granz has had the ideal person to manage to superstardom. "She has no bad habits, doesn't smoke, doesn't drink, though she enjoys her food," said Jimmy Rowles, a former accompanist. "She takes good care of herself. Gets enough rest. Except when she gets bothered for interviews. People bother her. So she leaps into limos and disappears. She has things on her mind to do. And as a legend, her life doesn't belong to her. So it's hard for her to escape when she's going through a hotel lobby filled with autograph seekers. But sincerity is the first word that pops into my head when I think of what she's like. You can hear it when she sings. She likes to sing the tunes. The only time she scats is when the song requires it. Otherwise she likes to sing straight."

It's legend in the music business that Norman Granz has done all the talking for Ella Fitzgerald to her public when she's offstage. She lives very privately and self-protectively in a large house in Beverly Hills. Intrusions by the press fluster her to pique. In 1965 Leonard Feather wrote in the *New York Post*: "Ella's wafer-thin skin against criticism is a second source of insecurity. When Frank Sinatra impugned her phrasing and breathing in a recent magazine article, she says, 'I was so upset I could hardly sing for a week.' She had looked forward to [a European tour she was undertaking at the time] as a desperately needed morale-booster: 'I was beginning to be afraid. I felt maybe I just didn't have it, and I had no hit record. It took a lot of people to convince me there are more important things.'"

Feather reported in the same column that Ella Fitzgerald felt lonely at the top, so removed from the milieu in which she had grown to stardom. Her reunions with musicians from the old days took place at recording sessions and in concerts. She kept working hard—on the road a great deal of the year, with little leisure time most of her life.

When her accompanist-pianist Tommy Flanagan had a heart attack and decided to withdraw from the arduous life on the road after more than fifteen years of musical association with Fitzgerald, he and the singer had little further contact. Norman Granz continued to do the talking, while Ella continued to sing "just this side of the angels," as a headline described her work.

But in 1974 when he was still her accompanist, Tommy Flanagan, a slender man with a fringe of white hair, told writer Ernest Dunbar about her way of working:

"Sometimes Ella comes up with a tune that she's heard somewhere, or I may send her a song that I feel is especially for her. Then we get together to find the key she's comfortable in. She tells me how she feels this piece should be done—serious or playful and humorous—the kind of mood it communicates to her. I then work up an orchestration that embodies her ideas and my own and we try it together. But an arrangement for Ella is only a framework within which to move. She will still do all kinds of things within that framework. Often, she'll add a new twist for improvisation, even when we're actually onstage performing. She may lag behind the beat a bit or move ahead of it, but she always knows exactly what she is doing. What would be musically risky for some singers, she pulls off easily. She rarely sings a song exactly the same way she did it last. But we've all played together for so long that no matter what she does, we are all right there together."

Sy Oliver, who has done arrangements for Ella, implies she is a musician's dream come true to work with. "Poor little Ella," the joke goes, can't play piano, as Sarah Vaughan and Carmen McRae can. All Ella can do is sing everything right on the first take. She can play "scat" with Jon Hendricks off the cuff at parties—one of the highlights of any party I've ever heard about.

But she was and is rarely reported in any social whirl; instead, one reporter wrote, although she got along with musicians well, she lived privately. She numbered among her friends some women whom she knew for years. With close friends, she opens up and talks about music and cooking—two of her passions. She raised a niece, who was a fan of the Motown stars, as well as her own son, Ray Jr., now a rock musician, in her Beverly Hills home. "Despite her celebrity, she's notoriously shy. She's uncomfortable with strangers after all these years," notes George Wein, producer of the Kool Jazz Festivals. "A lot of black kids are shy, dealing in a white world. She was a gawky kid. When people pay her compliments, they mean something to her."

And she has fond memories of the magnificent musicians she has worked with. Dunbar wrote of her sorrow at Duke Ellington's funeral at St. John's Cathedral in New York City, where she sang a dirgelike version of Ellington's "In My Solitude" and the spiritual "Just a Closer Walk with Thee." People cried when they heard her. Later she told Dunbar:

"I didn't know what I was singing. I have the feeling I was singing the wrong words, but all I knew was that from where I was standing, I could look right across at his body, and I was sort of frozen. You knew his death had to come sometime, I guess, but I'd known him ever since I was a girl. He used to tell me a lot of things that made a lot of sense. Once I had a big problem with a love affair when he and I were working in the same theater and I turned to him for advice. He told me, 'Ella; it's like a toothache. If it hurts bad enough, you get rid of it. You miss it for a while, but you feel better afterwards.' Some musicians put other performers down, but Duke never had anything bad to say about anyone. I don't think people realized even yet how great the man was."

George Wein recalled, "When Louis Armstrong died, everyone came looking to perform. Ella flew in from Chicago, sat in a pew dressed as a mourner in front of me, and flew back out right away. She wasn't looking for publicity. She's that kind of person."

She has sung all her tunes, a vast repertoire, with unflagging vivacity. She can go from little-girl sweetness to a driving, rasping noise. She can make any sound that she wants to, including a saxophone, with all stops and mutes out and a full, rich timbre. Musicians have vacillated between calling her the greatest who ever lived and, still mindful of Billie, the greatest living. Once in a while someone says Carmen McRae is the greatest. But most say it's a draw between Ella and Sarah.

PART FOUR

How Long Has This Been Going On?

Living Icon, 1966–80

"She can not only hit whatever note she wishes, bending and coloring it at will, but she knows just the right note to select from the dizzying possibilities flying past her in the heat of a jazz improvisation. The way she can shade a pitch, or slither up and down a chromatic scale, or pick out the most piquantly expressive note in a chord, reveals a consummate musician, however informal her training."
—John Rockwell, *New York Times,* 1986

Ella achieved stardom with the appearance of her songbooks in the 1950s. She spent the 1960s solidifying her eminent career. By the 1970s she earned more per concert than any other jazz singer as she made the rounds of the world's concert stages, reaping standing ovations and honors.

Typically, she presented a strong, charming front. Through all her successes, however, she did not have an easy time of it. Ella had been felled as early as 1957 by an abdominal illness, reported in the papers as an abscess that required an operation, soon after she had opened at the New York Paramount. During her later years, eye problems, heart disease, and diabetes had more of an impact. She had suffered from a cataract in one eye and hemorrhaging blood vessels, a complication of diabetes, in her other eye that was corrected by surgery. Eventually she had 20–20 vision in her left eye. She would undergo another cataract surgery. The glare of flashbulbs bothered her a great deal, and after she repeatedly told one photographer to quit flashing his lights in her eyes and he refused to oblige her, she tried to hit him. Afterward, she said, she felt sorry because she knew he hadn't meant any harm, but he had been blinding her.—*LG*

ELLA FITZGERALD: A SUPREME MOMENT
Daily Star (Toronto), 1966

From this review, one can sense what it must have been like to a member of the audience that night. Ella often gave momentous performances exactly like this one.—LG

Jazz has its supreme moments. Usually they come spontaneously, when the excitement of the audience inspires the artists to new heights.

When these moments arrive, even superlatives fail to describe them adequately. But jazz fans who have experienced them just know.

A capacity audience at Massey Hall experienced several of them last night.

One of them came when Ella Fitzgerald reached the peak of expression and excitement almost at the start of a 75-minute performance. It came, in fact, during her fifth number of the evening, when she sang chorus after inspiring, thrilling chorus of "Let's Do It." It was almost frightening, because anything that followed should have been an anti-climax.

But Ella settled down into a comfortable niche, singing warm ballads like "Shadow of Your Smile," "Once in a While" and "Yesterday," restoring calm and order to the dedicated thousands.

And then she did it again. First she gave a goofy take-off on the Beatles' "Hard Day's Night" and followed it with a roaring "Mack the Knife." She had the audience howling for more.

The applause that greeted her at the close of her act was deafening, and she came close to pleading with the audience—in a clever "I Could Have Sung All Night" parody—before she made her way off stage.

Ella proved again last night that she is completely worthy of her title, The First Lady of Song. On stage, in the spotlight, her trustworthy pianist Jimmy Jones behind her (and former Oscar Peterson drummer Ed Thigpen providing the beat), Ella was in the world she ruled. She sang 20 songs in all, not every one a Fitzgerald classic, but she gave every person in that audience his money's worth.

ELLA
In The Great American Popular Singers, 1974

A particularly erudite critic with a thorough understanding of the elements of classical as well as jazz and popular singing, Henry

Pleasants has written a fascinating analysis of Ella's vocal equip-
ment and techniques, including her nearly three-octave range and
her method for moving from chest to head voice. He also correctly
defines all the virtues that lifted her above other singers, many of
whom had or have warm voices, or great rhythmic sense, or per-
fect intonation, or great creativity, or versatility in their reper-
toires. Ella had all these attributes, and in Ella they were stronger
than in any other singer.

For his understanding of Ella's artistry, Pleasants is required read-
ing.—LG

Gerald Moore, the English accompanist, tells about the time Dietrich
Fischer-Dieskau, following a matinee recital Moore and the German
Lieder singer had given together in Washington, D.C., rushed to the
National Airport and took the first plane to New York in order to hear
Duke Ellington and Ella Fitzgerald at Carnegie Hall.

"Ella and the Duke together!" Fischer-Dieskau exclaimed to Moore.
"One just doesn't know when there might be a chance to hear that again!"

The story is illustrative of the unique position that both Ella Fitzgerald
and Duke Ellington occupy in the musical history of our century. More
than any other artists working in the Afro-American idiom, they have
caught the attention and excited the admiration of that other world of
European classical, or serious, music.

Ella's achievement, in purely musical terms, is the more remarkable of
the two, if only because she has never ventured into the no-man's-land of
semiclassical or third-stream music separating the two idioms. Duke
Ellington is a familiar figure on the stage at symphony concerts, as both
pianist and composer, in his jazz-flavored symphonic suites. Ella has
ranged widely between the ill-defined areas known as "jazz" and "popular," but not into classical, although she has sung the songs of the great
American songwriters—Arlen, Gershwin, Porter, Rodgers, for example—
with symphony orchestras. Many classical singers, however, like Fischer-
Dieskau, are among her most appreciative admirers.

Unchallenged preeminence in her own field has had something to do
with it, along with consistent performance throughout a career that has
already extended over nearly forty years. Although she has never been, in
her private life, a maker of headlines, her honors have been so many that
word of them has filtered through to many who never saw a copy of
Billboard or *Down Beat* and never will.

To enumerate those honors would be tedious. Suffice it to say, citing the entry under her name in Leonard Feather's *New Encyclopedia of Jazz,* that, between 1953 and 1960 alone, she was placed first in *Metronome, Down Beat* and *Playboy* polls in either the "jazz singer" or "popular singer" categories, or both, no fewer than twenty-four times. She had been a poll winner long before that—she won the Esquire Gold Award in 1946—and she is heading the polls in both categories to this day.

With Frank Sinatra and Peggy Lee, she shares the distinction of having achieved a nearly universal popularity and esteem without sacrificing those aspects of her vocal and musical art that so endear her to fellow professionals and to the most fastidious of critics and lay listeners. Not even Frank and Peggy are admired so unanimously. The refinements of their art often fall on unappreciative or hostile ears. But with Ella, the exclamation "She's the greatest!" runs like a refrain through everything one reads or hears about her. One is as likely to hear it from an opera singer as from Bing Crosby ("Man, woman and child, Ella Fitzgerald is the greatest!").

Of what does her greatness consist? What does she have that other excellent singers do not have? The virtues are both obvious and conspicuous, and there is general agreement about them. She has a lovely voice, one of the warmest and most radiant in its natural range that I have heard in a lifetime of listening to singers in every category. She has an impeccable and ultimately sophisticated rhythmic sense, and flawless intonation. Her harmonic sensibility is extraordinary. She is endlessly inventive. Her melodic deviations and embellishments are as varied as they are invariably appropriate. And she is versatile, moving easily from up-tempo scatting on such songs as "Flying Home," "How High the Moon?" and "Lady Be Good" to the simplest ballad gently intoned over a cushion of strings.

One could attribute any one, or even several, of these talents and attainments to other singers. Ella has them all. She has them in greater degree. She knows better than any other singer how to use them. What distinguishes her most decisively from her singing contemporaries, however, is less tangible. It has to do with style and taste. Listening to her— and I have heard her in person more often than any other singer under discussion in these pages—I sometimes find myself thinking that it is not so much what she does, or even the way she does it, *as what she does not do.* What she does not do, putting it as simply as possible, is anything wrong. There is simply nothing in her performance to which one would want to take exception. What she sings has that suggestion of inevitability that is always a hallmark of great art. Everything seems to be just right. One would not want it any other way. Nor can one, for the moment, imagine it any other way.

For all the recognition and adulation that has come her way, however, Ella Fitzgerald remains, I think, an imperfectly understood singer, especially as concerns her vocalism. The general assumption seems to be that it is perfect. That she has sung in public for so many years—and still, when on tour, may do two sixty-minute sets six or seven nights a week—with so little evidence of vocal wear and tear would seem to support that assumption. Her vocalism is, in fact, as I hear it, less than perfect. "Ingenious" and "resourceful" would be more appropriate adjectives.

She has, as many great singers in every category have had, limitations of both endowment and technique. But, also like other great singers, she has devised ways of her own to disguise them, to get around them, or even to turn them into apparent assets. Ella's vocal problems have been concentrated in that area of the range already identified in the case of earlier singers as the "passage." She has never solved them. She has survived them and surmounted them.

She commands, in public performance and on record, an extraordinary range of two octaves and a sixth, from the low D or D flat to the high B flat and possibly higher. This is a greater range, especially at the bottom, than is required or expected of most opera singers. But there is a catch to it. Opera singers, as they approach the "passage," depress the larynx and open the throat—somewhat as in yawning—and, focusing the tone in the head, soar on upward. The best of them master the knack of preserving, as they enter the upper register, the natural color and timbre of the normal middle register, bringing to the upper notes a far greater weight of voice than Ella Fitzgerald does. Even the floated *pianissimo* head tones of, say, a Montserrat Caballé should not be confused with the tones that Ella produces at the upper extremes of her range.

Ella does not depress the larynx, or "cover," as she reaches the "passage." She either eases off, conceding in weight of breath and muscular control what a recalcitrant vocal apparatus will not accommodate, or she brazens through it, accepting the all too evident muscular strain. From this she is released as she emerges upward into a free-floating falsetto. She does not, in other words, so much pass from one register into another as from one voice into another. As Roberta Flack has noted perceptively: "Ella doesn't shift gears. She goes from lower to higher register, the same all the way through."

The strain audible when Ella is singing in the "passage" contributes to a sense of extraordinary altitude when she continues upward. In this she reminds me of some opera tenors who appear to be in trouble—and often are—in their "passage" (at about F, F sharp and G) and achieve the greater impression of physical conquest when they go on up to an easy, sovereign B flat. The listener experiences anxiety, tension, suspense, relief and amazement. It is not good singing by the canons of *bel canto*, which reckon any evidence of strain deplorable. But it is exciting, and in the performance of a dramatic or athletic aria, effective.

Both this sense of strain in that critical area of Ella's voice, and the striking contrast of the free sound above the "passage" may help to explain why so many accounts of her singing refer to notes "incredibly high." Sometimes they are. The high A flat, A and B flat, even in falsetto, must be regarded as exceptional in a singer who also descends to the low D. But more often than not they sound higher than they are. Time and again, while checking out Ella's range on records, I have heard what I took to be high G or A flat, only to go to the piano and find that it was no higher than E or an F. What is so deceptive about her voice above the "passage" is that *sound* is high, with a thin, girlish quality conspicuously different from the rich, viola-like splendor of her middle range. It is not so much the contrast with the pitches that have gone before as the contrast with the sound that has gone before.

In purely vocal-technical terms, then, what distinguishes Ella from her operatic sisters is her use of falsettto; what distinguishes her from most of her popular-singer sisters is her mastery of it. One may hear examples of its undisciplined use in public performance and on records today in the singing of many women, especially in the folk-music field. With most of them the tone tends to become thin, tenuous, quavery and erratic in intonation as they venture beyond their natural range. They have not mastered falsetto. Ella has. So has Sarah Vaughan. So has Ella and Sarah's admirable virtuoso English counterpart, Cleo Laine.

The "girlish" sound of the female falsetto may offer a clue to its cultivation by Ella Fitzgerald, and to some fundamental characteristics of her vocal art. It is, for her, a compatible sound, happily attuned to her nature and to the circumstances of her career. She entered professional life while still a girl. Her first hit record, "A-Tisket A-Tasket," was the song of a little girl who had lost her yellow basket. The girl of the song must have been a congenial object of identification for a young singer, born in Newport News, Virginia, who spent her childhood first in an orphanage, later with an aunt in Yonkers, New York, who drifted as a young dancer into Harlem clubs, and who fell into a singing career in an amateur contest at the Harlem Opera House when she was too scared to dance.

"It was a dare from some girl friends," she recalls today. "They bet me

I wouldn't go on. I got up there and got cold feet. I was going to dance. The man said since I was up there I had better do something. So I tried to sing like Connee Boswell—'The Object of My Affection.'"

According to all the jazz lexicons, Ella was born on April 25, 1918, and entered that Harlem Opera House competition, which she won, in 1934, when she would have been sixteen. She became vocalist with the Chick Webb band the following year, was adopted by the Webb family and, following Chick's death in 1939, carried on as leader of the band until 1942. She would then have been all of twenty-four, with ten years of professional experience behind her.

According to Norman Granz, who has been her manager throughout the greater part of her career, she was younger than that. Granz says that she was born in 1920 and had to represent herself as older, when she first turned up in Harlem, to evade the child-labor laws. She was adopted by the Webbs because a parental consent was a legal prerequisite for employment.

It should hardly be surprising, then, that her voice, when she began with the Chick Webb band, and as it can be heard now on her early records, was that of a little girl. She was only fourteen. She was a precocious little girl, to be sure, and probably matured early, as other black entertainers did—Ethel Waters and Billie Holiday, for example—who grew up in the tough clubs and dance halls of Harlem while other girls were still in secondary school. What mattered with Ella, however, and affected her subsequent career, was that the little girl could also sound like a young woman—and was irresistible.

The sound worked, and so did the little girl. Ella has never entirely discarded either the girl or the sound. She was, and has remained, a shy, retiring, rather insecure person. To this day when, as a woman of matronly appearance and generous proportions, she addresses an audience, it is always in a tone of voice, and with a manner of speech, suggesting the delighted surprise, and the humility, too, of a child performer whose efforts have been applauded beyond her reasonable expectations.

Nor has Ella ever forsaken her roots in jazz. George T. Simon, in *The Big Bands*, remembers watching her at the Savoy Ballroom in Harlem when she was with Chick Webb:

> When she wasn't singing, she would usually stand at the side of the band, and, as the various sections blew their ensemble phrases, she'd be up there singing along with all of them, often gesturing with her hands as though she were leading the band.

The fruits of such early enthusiasm and practice may be heard today in Ella's appearances with the bands of Count Basie and Duke Ellington, when one or more instrumental soloists step forward to join her in a round of "taking fours," with Ella's voice assuming the character and color of a variety of instruments as she plunges exuberantly into chorus after chorus of syllabic improvisation (scatting).

Ella owes at least some of her virtuosity in this type of display, or at least the opportunity to develop and exploit it, to Norman Granz, and her many years' association with his jazz at the Philharmonic tours. Benny Green, the English jazz critic, thus describes the importance of this association to the shaping of Ella Fitzgerald's art and career:

When Ella first began appearing as a vocal guest on what were, after all, the primarily instrumental jazz recitals of Norman Granz, it might have seemed at the time like imaginative commercial programming and nothing more. In fact, as time was to prove, it turned out to be the most memorable manager-artist partnership of the post-war years, one which quite dramatically changed the shape and direction of Ella's career. Granz used Ella, not as a vocal cherry stuck on top of an iced cake of jazz, but as an artist integrated thoroughly into the jam session context of the performance. When given a jazz background, Ella was able to exhibit much more freely her gifts as an instrumental-type improviser.

Elsewhere, reviewing an appearance by Ella with the Basie band in London in 1971, Green has described as vividly and succinctly as possible the phenomenon of Ella working in an instrumental jazz context:

The effect on Ella is to galvanize her into activity so violent that the more subtle nuances of the song readings are swept away in a riot of vocal improvisation which, because it casts lyrics to the winds, is the diametric opposite of her other, lullaby, self. And while it is true that for a singer to mistake herself for a trumpet is a disastrous course of action, it has to be admitted that Ella's way with a chord sequence, her ability to coin her own melodic phrases, her sense of time, the speed with which her ear perceives harmonic changes, turn her Basie concerts into tightrope exhibitions of the most dazzling kind.

I was her activity with Jazz at the Philharmonic that exposed and exploited the singular duality of Ella Fitzgerald's musical personality. Between 1942, when her career as a band leader came to an end, and

1946, when she joined Granz, she had marked time, so to speak, as an admired but hardly sensational singer of popular songs. With Jazz at the Philharmonic, she was back with jazz.

The timing was right. Bop had arrived, and Ella was with it, incorporating into her vocal improvisations the adventurous harmonic deviations and melodic flights of Dizzy Gillespie and Charlie Parker. Indeed, according to Barry Ulanov, in his *A History of Jazz in America*, the very term "bop," or "bebop," can be traced to Ella's interpolation of a syllabic invention, "rebop," at the close of her recording of "'T'ain't What You Do, It's the Way That You Do It" in 1939.

She has cultivated and treasured this duality ever since, and wisely so. Singers who have adhered more or less exclusively to an instrumental style of singing, using the voice, as jazz terminology has it, "like a horn," have won the admiration and homage of jazz musicians and jazz critics, but they have failed to win the enduring and financially rewarding affections of a wider public. Others have stuck to ballads and won the public but failed to achieve the artistic prestige associated with recognition as a jazz singer. Ella, more than any other singer, has had it both ways.

Norman Granz, again, has had a lot to do with it. When Ella's recording contract with Decca expired in 1955, she signed with Granz's Verve label and inaugurated, in that same year, a series of Song Book albums, each devoted to a single songwriter, that took her over a span of twelve years through an enormous repertoire of fine songs, some of them unfamiliar, by Harold Arlen, Irving Berlin, Duke Ellington, George Gershwin, Johnny Mercer, Cole Porter and Richard Rodgers.

These were the first albums to give star billing to individual songwriters, and they served the double purpose of acknowledging and demonstrating the genius of American composers while providing Ella with popular material worthy of her vocal art. "I never knew how good our songs were," Ira Gershwin once said to George T. Simon, "until I heard Ella Fitzgerald sing them."

As a jazz singer Ella has been pretty much in a class by herself, and that in a period rejoicing in many excellent ones, notably Billie Holiday, Peggy Lee, Carmen McRae, Anita O'Day, Jo Stafford, Kay Starr and Sarah Vaughan, not to overlook, in England, Cleo Laine. I am using the term "jazz singer" here in the sense that jazz musicians use it, referring to a singer who works—or can work—in a jazz musician's instrumental style, improvising as a jazz musician improvises. Ella was, of course, building on the techniques first perfected, if not originated, by Louis Armstrong, tailoring and extending his devices according to the new conventions of bop.

There is a good deal of Armstrong in Ella's ballads, too, although none of his idiosyncrasies and eccentricities. What she shared with Louis in a popular ballad was a certain detachment—in her case a kind of classic serenity, or, as Benny Green puts it, a "lullaby" quality—that has rendered her, in the opinion of some of us, less moving than admirable and delightful. In terms of tone quality, variety and richness of vocal color, enunciation, phrasing, rhythm, melodic invention and embellishment, her singing has always been immaculate and impeccable, unequaled, let alone surpassed, by any other singer. But in exposing the heart of a lyric she must take second place, in my assessment, at least, to Frank Sinatra, Billie Holiday, Peggy Lee and Ethel Waters.

This may well be because she has never been one for exposing her own heart in public. She shares with an audience her pleasures, not her troubles. She has not been an autobiographical singer, as Billie and Frank were, nor a character-projecting actress, as Ethel Waters and Peggy Lee have been, which may be why her phrasing, despite exemplary enunciation, has always tended to be more instrumental than oral, less given to the rubato devices of singers more closely attuned to the lyrical characteristics of speech.

What she has offered her listeners has been her love of melody, her joy in singing, her delight in public performance and her accomplishments, the latter born of talent and ripened by experience, hard work and relentless self-discipline. Like Louis, she has always seemed to be having a ball. For the listener, when she has finished, the ball is over. It has been a joyous, exhilarating, memorable, but hardly an emotional, experience.

Also, like Louis, she has addressed herself primarily to a white rather than a black public, not because she has in any sense denied her own people, but rather because, in a country where blacks make up only between 10 and 20 percent of the population, white musical tastes and predilections are dominant. They must be accommodated by any black artist aspiring to national and international recognition and acceptance. In more recent years, younger whites have tended to favor a blacker music. A B. B. King has been able to achieve national celebrity where a Bessie Smith, fifty years earlier, could not. When Ella was a girl, what the white majority liked was white music enriched by the more elemental and more inventive musicality of black singers and black instrumentalists.

Ella's singing, aside from the characteristic rhythmic physical participation, the finger-popping and hip-swinging, and the obviously congenial scatting, has never been specifically or conspicuously black. It represents rather the happy blend of black and white which had been working its way into the conventions of American popular singing since the turn of the century, and which can be traced in the careers of Al Jolson, Sophie Tucker, Ethel Waters, Mildred Bailey and Bing Crosby.

When Ella was a girl, black singers—those in organized show business, at any rate—were modeling themselves on the white singing stars of the time, and many white singers were modeling themselves on the charmingly imperfect imitation. It is significant that Ella's first model was Connee Boswell. A comparison of the records they both made in the late 1930s shows again how perceptive an ear Ella had from the first. But it is just as significant that Connee Boswell belonged to a generation of jazz-oriented white singers—others were Mildred Bailey and Lee Wiley—who had been listening to Bessie Smith and, above all, to Ethel Waters.

Again like Louis Armstrong, Ella Fitzgerald has achieved that rarest of distinctions: the love and admiration of singers, instrumentalists, critics and the great lay public. But while she may be for the jazzman a musicians' musician, and for the lay public the First Lady of Song, she has always been more than anything else a singers' singer. Jon Hendricks, of Lambert, Hendricks and Ross fame, has put it well, responding to an Ella Fitzgerald record on a *Jazz Journal* blindfold test:

Well, of course, she's my favorite—she's tops! I just love her. She's Mama! I try and sing my ballads like she does. I was working in a hotel in Chicago, and Johnny Mathis came in to hear me. I had just finished singing a new ballad I was doing at the time, and he came up to me and said, "Jon, you sure love your old Fitzgerald, don't you?"

"Yes," I replied, "and don't you, too?"

"We all do!" he said.

And that's it. Everyone who sings just loves little old Fitzgerald!

ERNEST DUNBAR
ELLA STILL SINGS JUST THIS SIDE OF THE ANGELS
New York Times, 1974

Ernest Dunbar, who wrote this piece as a freelancer for the Times, *had a special affection for jazz and for Ella Fitzgerald. He was privy to a rare interview with Ella when she was rehearsing for a performance in upstate New York, and he also was able to get her longtime accompanist, Tommy Flanagan, to describe the way he and Ella worked together. By this time, at the age of fifty-six, she had already undergone two cataract operations and said she was blind in one eye. Yet she neither indulged in self-pity nor succumbed to the pressures of her illnesses. She was chatty and friendly during her interview sessions with Dunbar; the resulting piece shows Ella at her relaxed, gregarious best, grateful for the public's adulation. They discuss Duke Ellington, Ella's attitudes toward Bop, and her singing style, and Dunbar demonstrates his understanding of singing and singers.—LG*

In the darkened amphitheater of the Nanuet Theater-Go-Round in suburban Spring Valley, N.Y., late one recent afternoon, Ella Fitzgerald sat brooding in a front-row seat. Squatting silently on the circular stage before her, bathed in the orange glow from a pair of muted spotlights, were a piano and a set of drums with transparent skins. Ella was waiting to begin rehearsal for her appearance at the club that night. I was there to watch her and talk with her about her forthcoming Great Performers Series concert at Avery Fisher hall. That event, this Friday night, will mark the return of the First Lady of Song to the New York concert stage after an absence of more than a year.

The rehearsal was late getting started. Drummer Bobby Durham was on hand, but the other two-thirds of Ella's accompanying trio—pianist Tommy Flanagan and bassist Keter Betts—inexplicably had not arrived. Ella, in an open-necked blouse, brown suede jacket, and beige knit skirt, stood pushing at the thick, deeply tinted glasses she now wears. "It's not like Keter to not show up," she said to no one in particular. "It's never happened before. I wonder if he's had an accident?" Keter Betts has accompanied Miss Fitzgerald for more than five years; Tommy Flanagan for more than 15. Like an anxious mother awaiting her tardy schoolchildren, she looked at her watch, strained another worried glance into the darkness of the huge arena.

Finally, Flanagan arrived, fortyish, dapper in flared trousers, his balding head topped with a Leninesque leather cap. While he was still making his explanations, a puffing Keter Betts joined them lugging his bass's amplifier. The tension subsided.

Ella mounted the round stage and launched into the 1940's era blues rocker, "Why Dont'cha Do Right?" as technicians adjusted microphone levels for her voice. The musicians followed her flawlessly, chuckling now and then over bits of vocal "business" she threw in to enliven a tune she'd performed hundreds of times before.

Ella Fitzgerald's voice is not big. At times it's even a little raspy, though not unpleasantly so. She doesn't overpower you with sheer volume like Aretha Franklin or dazzle you with the highly mannered approach of a Barbra Streisand. She just sings the hell out of a song, fleshing out the melody, caressing each note, extending the harmonies and inserting nuances that the songwriter might have written if he'd possessed her musicianship.

After 40 years in the music business, Ella has lost none of the qualities that made her one of the great performers of her generation. After a recent engagement in Detroit, a critic described her as "still the best in her field—which is just this side of the angels." The noted English jazz critic Benny Green recently called her "the best-equipped vocalist ever to grace the jazz scene, having a freakishly wide vocal range, literally perfect intonation and an acutely sensitive ear for harmonic changes. . . . There is to her voice a lilting lullaby quality which renders even commonplace material moving."

Completing "Why Dont'cha Do Right?" she throttled back into a low-keyed ballad, "Jim." At times her voice seemed that of a young girl; at other moments she produced the ripened tones of a mature woman.

After pausing to debate the choice of songs with Flanagan, Ella ripped into an up-tempo version of "Cherokee," scatting riffs from "Indian Love Call" and the Swing Era classic, "Big Noise From Winnetka," along the way. Flanagan, Betts and Durham put down a melodic cushion for Fitzgerald improvisations to soar over, around and under. Although she was performing in low gear in rehearsal, it was clear the Fitzgerald magic remains potent.

Later, Flanagan, a small professorial looking man with solid jazz credentials, talked with me about the way a Fitzgerald number develops. "Sometimes, Ella comes up with a tune she's heard somewhere, or I may send her a song that I feel is especially for her. Then we get together to find the key she's comfortable in. She tells me how she feels this piece should be done—serious or playful and humorous—the kind of mood it communicates to her. I then work up an orchestration that embodies her ideas and my own and we try it together. But an arrangement for Ella is only a framework within which to move. She will still do all kinds of things within that framework. Often, she'll add a new twist or improvisation, even when we're actually on the stage performing. She may lag behind the beat a bit or move ahead of it, but she always knows exactly what she is doing. What would be musically risky for some singers, she pulls off easily. She rarely sings a song exactly the same way she did it last. But we've all played together for so long that no matter what she does, we are all right there together."

That night, as Ella, swathed in a voluminous pleated blue gown, took to the Nanuet stage, a mostly white, mostly over-30 audience rose to give her an extended ovation, one of several she would receive during the evening. She gave a characteristically eclectic performance, spanning decades, styles and composers: Ellington, Bacharach, Carole King, Cole Porter, Gershwin, Randy Newman and Stevie Wonder. Swing, bop, pop, bossa nova, Broadway musicals and soul . . . all done in the impeccable Fitzgerald style.

At the end of the performance, the revolving stage came to a halt, with Ella 180 degrees opposite the point where she was supposed to exit. After a bit of good-natured grumping ("How do you get off this thing?"), she found her way to the ramp, virtually invisible in the darkened auditorium. The awkward moment dissolved as two teen-age attendants led her from the stage.

Ella is an early riser. I dropped in on her suite at the Spring Valley Holiday Inn the next morning to talk about her Friday concert at Avery Fisher Hall—and about new developments in her long career.

She met me at the motel room door, wearing a brown print dress and a gold necklace with a peace symbol. She remains a shy, gentle woman, despite her years in show business. Pushing at her horn-rimmed glasses, lowering her lids, she settled into a pseudo-Spanish chair and talked about the way it is now.

Last month at its Princess Anne branch, the University of Maryland dedicated the Ella Fitzgerald School of Performing Arts, a $1.6-million building serving some 1,200 students, the first such structure in the nation to be named for a black artist. For Ella Fitzgerald, it is another milestone in a career that began when she was discovered in 1934 by the late drummer-leader Chick Webb after he saw her win a talent contest at Harlem's Apollo Theater. Webb hired the gangly 16-year-old orphan to sing with his band; he became her legal guardian and honed her innate musical gifts to professional perfection.

Webb died in 1939 of spinal tuberculosis, but not before Ella had recorded "A-Tisket, A-Tasket," a tune she had written in 1938 to amuse him during his waning days in the hospital. That record, based on a nursery rhyme, launched her on a career that saw her win the *Down Beat* magazine award as Best Female Singer for 18 consecutive years as well as four Grammy awards. Yet after more than 100 albums and over 25 million records sold, the University of Maryland honor is still something special to Ella: "Every night when I say my prayers I just thank God for the beautiful thing that happened to me and that I am here to see it. You know, so many things happen after people have passed, but here I'm seeing it. I just couldn't believe it."

Ella's gratitude for being able to see the ceremonies honoring her reflect more than just a recognition of life's brevity. She has been beset with serious eye problems and has had two operations for cataracts. "When something like this happens," she says, "it makes you stop and say to yourself: 'Where am I going? What am I doing—for myself and for others?' It kind of makes you think. So I say to myself, 'Well, I'm really only seeing out of one eye now, but God gave me a voice. He gave me something with which to make other people happy. There must have been a reason.'"

After undergoing eye surgery in 1971 and 1972, Ella began to take life easier. "I used to work 48 weeks a year, but now we do 36 weeks, and even that is split up frequently so that we can spend more time at home. The fellows in my group like it this way—they get to spend more time with their families—and I get to spend more time watching my 13-year-old niece grow up." The niece and a pair of servants share the 13-room home she owns in Beverly Hills. Ella's second marriage, to bassist Ray Brown, ended in divorce in 1953. A son from that marriage, Ray Brown Jr., 25, lives in Spokane, Wash.

Ella Fitzgerald's friends tend to be a few women she's known for many years, such as Mrs. Louis Armstrong, and vocalists Sarah Vaughn, Carmen McRae, Peggy Lee, as well as the men from the Duke Ellington and Count Basie orchestras. "Those were the bands that I used to hang around with the most," she says with a fond smile, "so I guess we're the closest."

Ella was deeply affected by the death of Ellington, whom she had known since her days as a teen-age vocalist with Chick Webb's band. At his funeral in New York's St. John's Cathedral, she sang a dirge-like version of Ellington's "In My Solitude" and the moving spiritual "Just A Closer Walk With Thee," that brought tears to the eyes of virtually everyone present. "I don't know what I was singing," she says now. "I have the feeling I was singing the wrong words but all I knew was that from where I was standing I could look right across at his body and I was sort of frozen. You knew his death had to come sometime, I guess, but I'd known him ever since I was a girl. He used to tell me a lot of things that made a lot of sense. Once I had a big problem with a love affair when he and I were working in the same theater and I turned to him for advice. He told me, 'Ella, it's like a toothache. If it hurts bad enough, you get rid of it. You miss it for a while, but you feel better afterwards.' Some musicians put other performers down, but Duke never had anything bad to say about anyone. I don't think people realize even yet how great the man was."

These days Ella Fitzgerald frequently sings to the accompaniment of symphony orchestras, in places like Spokane, El Paso, Ft. Worth, Toronto, Cincinnati, and Jackson, Miss. "It's just beautiful," she says, "it gives me a chance to do some of the tunes we've recorded but don't usually have a chance to perform in nightclubs, things with lush strings and horns."

But can a cumbersome symphony swing?

"Oh, yes," Ella replies with a laugh. "Take Fort Worth, they've got a jazz band within the symphony orchestra, people who play both kinds of music. They've got a great young trumpet player that we would have stolen if we could, but he's still in school!"

Since the mid-1950's Miss Fitzgerald has been managed by jazz impresario Norman Granz. "He's a good friend as well as my manager. I had gotten to the point where I was only singing bebop. I thought that bop was IT! That all I had to do was go some place and sing bop. But it finally got to the point where I had no place to sing. I realized then that there was more to music than bop. Norman came along then and he felt that I should do other things, so he produced the Cole Porter Songbook with me. It was a turning point in my life."

"I was in Chicago recently doing a number with a lot of boppin', scat-singing, and when I got through everybody applauded. But one woman just sat there looking unhappy. So I went up to her, forgetting that I had the 'live' mike in my hand, and said, "You look so unhappy, what's the matter?' She said, 'I don't *understand* what you're singing!' Everybody in the place broke up! So I sang a ballad then, and she was happy. What I try to do in my act is to satisfy everybody. Country and Western or what-ever—it's all music.

"We don't have the Cole Porters and the George Gershwins anymore, but we do have the Bert Bacharachs, Stevie Wonder and people like Paul Williams. I dig his lyrics. I also dig Marvin Gaye. When I sang his 'What's Goin' On?' some people said 'Why are you doing that? It's a protest song!' I told them, 'I don't find it that way. To me, it's good music.'"

What's ahead for Ella Fitzgerald? "Well, I'd like to do an album for children." She paused. "Then, who knows? Meanwhile, there's the Great Performers Concert to do at Avery Fisher Hall. Ummmm, I think maybe I'd better go out and get me a new gown!"

JOHN S. WILSON
"ANGEL EYES" IS TRIUMPH FOR ELLA FITZGERALD
New York Times, 1978

Here is another rave review that Ella typically inspired. John S. Wilson, who for many years was tantamount to the dean of American jazz critics for his perspicacity and his position on the influential New York Times, sometimes found fault with even the greatest jazz stars. But Ella seemed to win his praise all the time.

Wilson never wrote books and didn't even review them. He built his entire vaunted reputation on his excellent criticism for newspapers.—LG

Less than three weeks after appearing before a cheering, overflow audience at Avery Fisher Hall, Ella Fitzgerald was back in town Saturday evening at Carnegie Hall as part of the Newport Jazz Festival. The closeness of the two engagements, caused when her Avery Fisher Hall concert scheduled for mid-March was postponed until June because of her illness, did not seem to diminish her Newport Festival appearance in the slightest. The hall was packed and the audience was on its feet cheering at her first entrance.

If her reception at Carnegie Hall was a virtual rerun of that at Avery Fisher, Miss Fitzgerald's program, from the throwaway opening with "Too Close for Comfort" to the encore of "How High the Moon" with its virtuosic, extended exploration of vocal exercises and quotes from pop songs and show tunes, was only slightly different. Once again she brought out the melodic charm of Cole Porter's "Dream Dancing," eased her way through "Ain't Misbehavin'," breathed new life into "St. Louis Blues" and traded swinging "Fours" with Tommy Flanagan's piano on "One Note Samba."

But some of her finest moments came in songs she had not sung at Avery Fisher. There was an "I Cried for You" that started out with a smooth, swinging drive, lifted to a trumpetlike cry in the second chorus and, finally, went out on an extraordinary chorus (especially for Miss Fitzgerald) that was rugged, swaggering and jubilant.

Her special triumph, however, was "Angel Eyes," sung with a depth of feeling that one has not expected from Miss Fitzgerald in the past, projected with the purest of her rich, warm tones and developed with great sensitivity for the mood. It brought the audience roaring to its feet in one of the biggest demonstrations of the evening, and Miss Fitzgerald, tearing through her glasses, remarked happily, "I'd better keep that one."

ANGELA TAYLOR
ELLA FITZGERALD, IN TUNE AT HER OWN PARTY
New York Times, 1980

This piece contrasts with Joel Siegel's "Ella at 65," later in the book. In this story by a reporter who often writes about the stylish and famous people who seem out of the reach of mere mortals, Ella the person recedes into the distance, and Ella the celebrity, the paragon of the best in popular jazz singing, is on display. True, she does sing with her old friend Jon Hendricks and stuns the crowd. Most of all, this piece portrays Ella as a darling of the rich and famous, both a royal bauble and royalty itself—a very different person from the desperate adolescent who escaped by the skin of her teeth from reform school.—LG

It's been a very busy week for the folks who love to get all dressed up and go to parties where they see many of the same friends they kissed delightedly the night before. What with Pierre Cardin's party at the Metropolitan Museum of Art on Monday and Altman's dinner to benefit the New York Public Library on Tuesday, one would think that Lord & Taylor might have had to scrounge for its guests on Wednesday night.

But it was no problem—the store had an attraction few people would pass up. Her name is Ella Fitzgerald and she is the natural successor to the title of America's Sweetheart, now that Mary Pickford is no longer among us. Miss Fitzgerald was presented (by Joseph E. Brooks, the store's chairman) with the Lord & Taylor Rose Award. The award, a store executive explained, is given yearly to the "person whose outstanding contribution in their field has enriched all our lives."

Nothing short of a broken leg would have kept a guest away from the possibility that Ella might sing. Not even Edward Villella, the dancer, who arrived on a crutch and with his wife, Linda, a former Canadian figure skater. Mr. Villella explained that he was recovering from back surgery, but was doing nicely, thank you, and proceeded to do a dance step to prove it.

There were any number of repeaters from earlier parties: Lee Radziwill, in Bill Blass's one-shouldered white sheath; Pat Kennedy Lawford, in glitter; the T. Suffern Tailers (Jean Tailer's new slender figure much admired in a red mermaid number), and Estée Lauder in black chiffon. Mrs. Lauder noted that the receiving line was at the Clinique counter, so it was all right if the guests had their drinks at Elizabeth Arden or Revlon in the cosmetics department, which had been transformed with flickering candles.

Warm Greetings from Friends

Ella was kissed and hugged by hundreds of her old friends: Eubie Blake, looking frail but grinning from ear to ear; Ruth Ellington Boatwright (Duke's sister), in clouds of blond hair.

The musical crowd: Jule Styne and Sammy Cahn, the Adolph Greens (she's Phyllis Newman), the Robert Sarnoffs (Anna Moffo) and Marion McPartland.

The theater: Cicely Tyson, her hair done up in a fascinating arrangement of braids, came with Arthur Mitchell of the Dance Theater of Harlem; Celeste Holm in black velvet; Jane Alexander with her husband, Edwin Sherin, artistic director of the Hartman Theater Company in Stamford, Conn.; Anne Jackson and Eli Wallach.

Fashion: Calvin Klein, Pauline Trigere, Mollie Parnis and Donald Brooks. Publishing: the Clifton Daniels; Osborne Elliot, former editor of *Newsweek*, and Thomas Guinzburg of Viking Press, who escorted a ravishing young woman named Ching Cruz.

The Richard Salomons (he's chairman of the New York Public Library Board of Trustees) had, of course, been at the Altman party the night before.

"We're getting out a lot these nights," he said. Gordon J. Davis, the Parks Commissioner, was with his wife, Peggy, who started out to be a jazz singer but went on to Harvard Law School and became a Criminal Courts judge instead. He said they hadn't been to a party in years, adding, "The last time we went, the guest of honor was a car."

Barbara de Portago, wearing black velvet breeches by Don Sayres, was excited. "I hope Ella sings," she said, "I've never heard her except on records."

And Ella did sing. First, on some film clips with a narration by Douglas Fairbanks Jr. ("He gets handsomer and more British all the time," remarked a guest.) On the screen, a young Ella sang "A-Tisket, A-Tasket" and the crowd, which had now moved up to the store's penthouse for dinner, went wild.

And then Jon Hendricks, who was part of the team of Lambert, Hendricks and Ross, surprised the guest of honor, first with a medley of her songs and then with a challenge to "scat" with him. She did, and for a full 10 minutes the pair did every variation on scat anyone had ever dreamed of.

"Where did you go?" Schuyler Chapin, dean of Columbia's School of the Arts, asked his wife, Jean, when she disappeared from the table even before dessert. "To kiss Ella, of course," she replied. That was probably the 200th kiss planted on her smiling cheeks, and the evening wasn't over.

LEN LYONS
BEBOP AND MODERN JAZZ: THE EARLY STYLES
In The 101 Best Jazz Albums, 1980

The exceptionally knowledgeable, insightful jazz writer Len Lyons praises The Complete Ella in Berlin: Mack the Knife *(Verve, 1960) and other albums. In his article "Ella Fitzgerald," included later in the book, Leonard Feather expands on the comparisons Lyons makes here.—LG*

Ella Fitzgerald, Sarah Vaughan, and Carmen McRae communicate very different emotions through a song; yet they share a common heritage in the style of jazz singing established by Bessie Smith and Billie Holiday. Their rhythmic feeling, instrument-like voice quality, and preference for improvising within bebop's boundaries place them in the mainstream of the music. They have also accepted the big band's singers' repertoire of popular ballads, occasionally varied by jazz compositions. Their major departure from Bessie and Billie has been twofold: They are less tied to the blues (in Billie's case, blues feeling—in Bessie's, the blues form) and more inclined to use their voices flexibly, interacting freely with other instruments in the band.

Ella Fitzgerald was born in 1918 and began her career in Chick Webb's band of the 1930's. One can still hear in the full-blown dynamic style and the rhythmic punch of "Mack the Knife" that she has not left the swing era too far behind. Her first hit record with Webb in 1938, "A-Tisket, A-Tasket," is available on MCA's two-disc set *The Best of Ella Fitzgerald,* but it by no means represents her mature work, which began when she signed with Norman Granz's Verve label in 1955. The first products of this union were the famous *Songbooks* of George Gershwin, Cole Porter, and Rodgers and Hart, all available on two-disc sets. While these orchestral sides are pretty and sensitive, they are quite short on jazz content. (The best album of that series, which is devoted to Ellington's music and arranged by Duke for Ella and his 1956 orchestra, was reissued by Verve in February 1980; it is highly recommended.) The feeling is much looser on a series of sessions with Louis Armstrong, collected on Verve's *Ella & Louis.* Ella and Louis are backed here by the Oscar Peterson trio plus Herb Ellis on guitar, a group that unleashes Fitzgerald's rhythmic verve and imagination. She and Louis Armstrong communicate with genuine affection and spontaneity, making this one of three essential Fitzgerald collections. The second, *Ella & Duke at the Côte D'Azur,* documents an exciting 1966 live performance by both Fitzgerald and Ellington's orchestra. The band's drive becomes a reservoir of energy for Ella, who sings on fewer than half the tracks.

"Mack the Knife" is unsurpassed for energy and consistency. Ella is obviously at home with the band, a copy of the earlier Peterson combo. "How High the Moon" is a tour de force. Its six improvised choruses end on a note it is hard to imagine her hitting after her marathon scatting performance. Ella's infallible pitch and the clarity of her voice allow for an instrumentalist's degree of flexibility, as one hears on the up-tempo improvisations like "Gone with the Wind" and "The Lady Is a Tramp." Ella makes masterful use of melodic embellishments. Although she lacks the sense of tragedy that wells up so frequently in the work of Bessie Smith and Billie Holiday, she replaces it with imagination, warmth, and an uplifting rhythmic feeling. These qualities emerge equally on ballads like the gracefully improvised "The Man I Love," and on swinging romps like "Mack the Knife," for which she found herself improvising words as well as music. The spontaneity of this concert album, along with her bold and flawless performance, reveal Ella's major asset—the ability to communicate joy and exhilaration.

Gary Giddins, the veteran critic for the Village Voice, *was using the word* icon *to describe Ella's status by the time he wrote this overview of her career and accomplishments.—LG*

Ella Fitzgerald is one of a handful of preeminent jazz performers who have become public monuments, emblematic of an unquestioning national pride. She embodies jazz as a positive force even for those who pay no attention to jazz. Yet not unlike Kate Smith's or Mahalia Jackson's, her enduring authority may have more than a little to do with an image of youthless (which is to say ageless) maternalism, sturdy and implacable. Large-boned women tend to intimidate their potential detractors. Unlike Smith, whose voice was without direction or artistry, or Jackson, whose euphoric artistry was narrowly directed, Fitzgerald is principally an inspired and readily accessible entertainer—robust and swinging, if rarely cathartic. She is often exhilarating (her voice still has much of its girlish purity, stretching over a perfect two-octave midrange, and her rhythms are irresistible), but one attends her performances expecting to be moved less by introspective drama than by the contagiousness of her joy in singing.

Fitzgerald's long career is a tangle of paradoxes. The pop and song-book records notwithstanding, she is determinedly a jazz singer, yet she cannot sing the blues and tends to embroider them into banality. She is an irreproachable connoisseur of ballads, but has little talent for histrionics: The stilted Bess she presented to Armstrong's effulgent Porgy is a case in point. She is a product of the Swing Era ("A-Tisket, A-Tasket," recorded with her mentor Chick Webb, remains the biggest hit of her career) who became associated in the public's mind with bebop-inflected scat singing. (Although she makes melodic references to bop, her time and phrasing have more in common with the even 4/4 rhythms of swing players like Lionel Hampton, Coleman Hawkins, and especially Roy Eldridge, whose cross-octave improvisations may well have influenced her.) She is a black singer who names the white Connee Boswell as her primary model. She is a peerless "straight" interpreter of pop songs, and also a willful embell-isher who can attack songs as though their lyrics had no more significance than scat syllables. She does not make hit records, but she works exclu-sively in the world's great concert halls.

In recent years, she has been ill, and her voice has lost some of its luster, its purity. The plush falsetto, once as solid and flexible as mercury, has been raked by time. At several concerts, I found myself growing impatient and leaving early. So I was caught entirely off guard by her stupendous performance at a Pablo Jazz Festival concert at Carnegie Hall last weekend. The material was without exception superb, and the asides brief and charming. The ballads were thoughtful, the swingers galvanizing, and the voice was brighter than I'd heard it in several years. On a recklessly fast "Lover, Come Back to Me," she chugged along like a well-oiled engine, roaring into a high-note conclusion with a majestic aplomb that all but announced, renascence.

You expect to hear her in optimum circumstances—in Tommy Flanagan's trio, she has the best accompaniment in the business. But she was additionally inspired by the presence of the Count Basie band (without Basie). The nasal entrance of the reeds on "My Old Flame" goaded her, and on "Mr. Paganini" (how she makes that musty war-horse hustle!) she traded fours with Jimmy Forrest and Al Grey, holding her own with tremendous wit and assurance. She affected Grey's plunger sound and Forrest's grit, matching their every conceit, and when all three began riffing in tandem and the orchestra added gleaming staccato exclamations, the Swing Era seemed fully and unequivocally revived. There were quieter moments, too—gentle duets with guitarist Joe Pass, as well as selections with the trio, including two elegant and overlooked gems by Benny Carter ("When Lights Are Low") and Duke Ellington ("I Ain't Got Nothing But the Blues," which, of course, is not a blues). When Fitzgerald is at her most monumental there is nothing of the monument about her.

In the beginning, no one would have thought to characterize her as, or predict for her the status of, an icon. She was too much the lively young girl, precocious but vulnerable, looking for her little yellow basket. Fitzgerald's performing venues and salary didn't begin to reflect her cross-generational prominence until the mid-1950s, when she left Decca Records after a 20-year association and—under the tutelage of her manager and producer, Norman Granz—embarked on a series of lushly orchestrated *Songbooks*, each devoted to a single songwriter, for Verve. She insisted on being recognized as an artist who sang jazz and pop, as opposed to a jazz singer who sublimated pop to jazz biases. Some critics faulted her versatility, complaining that she lacked Billie Holiday's uncompromising *Angst*. But if she transcended the jazz audience, she never abandoned jazz principles. The main reason the songbooks stand up so well is the rhythmic lilt and telling embellishments with which she intuitively edits the material.

It would be a mistake, however, to assume that the more than 300 sides she cut for Decca (about 40 of them as the vocalist with Chick Webb's orchestra) were more rigidly conceived within the jazz idiom. Indeed, the Deccas were the most commercially designed recordings of her career, save the dim exploitation albums of the late '60s and after, made for Capitol and Warners (i.e., Ella sings country, Ella sings the Beatles). The first half of her career is a reflection of the prevailing attitudes—the imaginative strengths and limitations—of the producers who operated Decca, as well as her extraordinary rapport with the musical climate of the Depression and war years. Fitzgerald became the most popularly acclaimed jazz singer of all time during the age of Eisenhower, but it was during the era of Little Orphan Annie that she scored her biggest hit record.

The Fitzgerald story has been told often, if elliptically. Briefly, she was born in Newport News, Virginia, in 1918, and taken to an orphanage in Yonkers, New York, after the death of her mother in the early 1930s. (Considering her renown, one can only be astounded at how little is known of Fitzgerald's early years. Her ability, shared by Armstrong and Ellington, to control the dissemination of biographical material is perhaps the one advantage to the invisibility syndrome addressed by Ralph Ellison.) In 1934, Benny Carter heard her at an amateur contest at Harlem's Apollo Theater and recommended her to several influential men in the music business, including Fletcher Henderson and John Hammond, who were unimpressed. Drummer and bandleader Chick Webb, a dwarfed hunchback, agreed to give her a try and soon assumed total responsibility for her. He became Ella's legal guardian even as he reorganized his trailblazing orchestra around her unfledged 17-year-old voice. His faith paid off three years later when her adaptation of a nursery rhyme, "A-Tisket, A-Tasket," put them on top of the heap. During the summer of 1938, that recording was omnipresent. When Webb died the following summer, Fitzgerald confirmed her loyalty by fronting the orchestra—she kept at it for three years, before going out as a single.

Except for a couple of sessions with Teddy Wilson and Benny Goodman, all the records she made between 1935 and 1955 were for Decca, a label subsequently assimilated by MCA, which allows all but a handful of its treasures to repose in its vaults.* Decca's base commercialism was typified when it induced Jascha Heifetz, during his brief sabbatical from RCA, to cover "White Christmas," the label's all-time bestseller as recorded by Bing Crosby. It was Decca's policy to integrate jazz and pop—prefiguring the present crossover cancer. The results were often charming, and just as often detestable. Fitzgerald's sessions were frequently burdened with contemptible material and banal vocal choirs, which may be why they are no longer deemed worthy of reissue. But that wouldn't explain why the superior sides, which are numerous, are also unavailable.

It's tempting to speculate about the kind of records Ella might have made for Columbia in those years, when John Hammond's policy was to present Billie Holiday in small instrumental groups consisting of the most accomplished jazz musicians of the day, usually under the leadership of Teddy Wilson. Early in 1936, Fitzgerald did record two sides with Wilson. "All My Life" is a pleasantly nostalgic ballad, enunciated with a clarity worthy of Ethel Waters, even if the sensibility is relatively naive; "My Melancholy Baby" swings steadily on the beat and is enhanced by good-natured improvisatory touches. Whereas Holiday personalized a song by inflecting every phrase, Fitzgerald conveyed a purer approach, less idiosyncratic and sometimes less discerning. Benny Goodman was so impressed with her that he used her as a replacement for Helen Ward in June of that year. She gave "Goodnight, My Love" a well-phrased but formal, even stiff, reading; "Take Another Guess" unveiled the girlish, swinging Ella, though her vocal quality was thick and clouded, not yet fully formed. In those years, she accented long-vowel sounds with increased vibrato and broke words into staccato syllables to stress rhythmic impact. She had more faith in melody and rhythm than in lyrics.

By the end of 1936, she was emerging as the definitive voice of swing, performing many tunes with the words *swing* or *swinging* in the title. One of them, "Organ Grinder's Swing," was recorded at the first session under her own name—accompanied by the Savoy Eight, a contingent from the Webb band—and proved to be prophetic. It was a novelty with a childhood theme that led to several others, including "Betcha Nickel," "Chew-Chew-Chew," and, of course, "A-Tisket, A-Tasket." Of greater importance, it showed her off for the first time as an aggressively deft scat singer. In the final chorus, she riffs the phrase "Oh, organ" and outswings the band. At her third session, Decca characteristically teamed her with the popular Mills Brothers, an indication of the company's confidence in her growing success. She was still only 18.

Her voice matured greatly during the next couple of years, though her naive, on-the-beat determination abided. More often than not, the material was pitiably weak, but if Fitzgerald could not transcend it like Holiday, she could uplift it with her expressive, trumpetlike delivery—for example, "If You Should Ever Leave" or "Dipsy Doodle." On the latter, she sounds entirely oblivious to the song's abysmal lyric. She could raise temperatures on a worthy swinger like Irving Berlin's "Pack Up Your Sins and Go to the Devil," or fashionable band numbers like "If Dreams Come True" and "Rock It for Me," but she also betrayed awkwardness in those years—a bumptious quality undoubtedly exacerbated by the dire novelties that threatened to become her trademark.

The sensual lilt in her voice became more pronounced in 1939, in such memorable readings as "Don't Worry About Me" and "If I Didn't Care." With "Stairway to the Stars," her characteristic approach to ballads was codified: The first chorus was reasonably straight and the second was an exercise in swingtime, as she transfigured the key melody into a contagiously rocking riff. Yet her improvisations remained fairly predictable, and you can get a fair idea of how much she grew by comparing "Stairway" with "Soon," recorded in 1950. Once again, a forthright chorus is followed by a rhythmic one, but the voice has flowered into the very embodiment of swing phrasing—luscious and effortless.

The 1940s were undoubtedly the period of Fitzgerald's most uneven recordings, a reflection of an in-between dilemma that defined the era. Swing was losing its magic, and bop was little more than a underground workshop. Decca presented her in a series of encounters with the label's black artists—Louis Armstrong, the Ink Spots, Louis Jordan, the Delta Rhythm Boys, Sy Oliver, Bill Doggett, the Mills Brothers (again), and others. These accounted for some of her most successful records of the decade, musically as well as commercially, especially when compared with the numerous ballads she was asked to sing in collusion with lumbering string orchestras and vocal choirs under the direction of Gordon Jenkins. Fitzgerald is frequently miraculous despite the overblown settings, but the dim arrangements engulf her in a period flavor. Her thick delivery had now metamorphosed into a light and pristine style, fully at home in the greater spaciousness of her range. But it wasn't the kind of voice that could always turn dross into gold. Too often, a superficiality set in that matched the material and made her seem a brilliantly equipped hack.

Yet in many scintillating deviations from the stock ballad settings, a mature Fitzgerald was emerging—the queen of scat, the first lady of song. Her 1945 "Flying Home" was an all-scat performance that established her among the jazz modernists. She wasn't born of bop, like Sarah

Vaughan, but she was thoroughly accepted into the fold. With her ear and technique, Ella was not likely to be intimidated by a flatted fifth; on the contrary, she was still in her 20s, and the new sounds of Charlie Parker and Dizzy Gillespie were a welcome source of inspiration. She thrived on it, roaring through a lexicon of bop licks on "Lady Be Good," which became one of her most requested and enduring showpieces, and on the more imaginative "How High the Moon," where she followed a straight chorus with a vigorous variation compiled equally of phrases from swing and bop.

Fitzgerald's ballads, too, reflected her enhanced improvisational powers. She displayed a penchant for altering the character of a dull phrase by raising a key note the interval of a sixth. She continued to develop her mastery of portamento, with which she would rise or fall to the proper note or, more intriguingly, begin with the written note and slide into a more colorful interval. She meshed beautifully with the Mills Brothers on a serene and enticing "I Gotta Have My Baby Back"; displayed wonderfully airy highs on "I've Got the World on a String"; exhibited the purest voice ever applied to scat on the extended novelty, "You'll Have to Swing It." It's not at all surprising, given the fullness of her recording regimen, that Fitzgerald could be drearily impersonal even with attractive material (as on "I Wished on the Moon," 1954), but when she was committed to a song ("It Might as Well Be Spring," 1955), she was luminous.

Fitzgerald recorded exclusively for Decca until 1955. The 20 sides she recorded with pianist Ellis Larkins (eight Gershwin titles in 1950, and a mixed bag in 1954) represent the culmination of that long episode in her career. I've heard singers argue that she never surpassed the collaboration with Larkins, and to be sure she achieves a sensuousness and command of the material that is, note for note, enthralling. Her voice had never sounded quite as resplendent before. Few interpretations of popular songs can match her readings of "Soon," "Someone to Watch over Me," "I've Got a Crush on You," and "How Long Has This Been Going On?" although their very excellence heightens the exasperation generated by a survey of her entire output in those years. The Gershwin sides (just enough for a 10-inch album) prefigured the hugely popular if less compelling *Cole Porter Songbook* in 1956.

The gloried monument of popular song that Fitzgerald became after she signed with Verve records coincided with the rise of TV and hi-fi, both of which repeatedly underscored her renown. The successes included eight songbooks (the Ellington, Berlin, Arlen, Gershwin, and untypically concise Mercer are especially fine); a triumphant appearance in Berlin (she wore a blonde wig); collaborations with Armstrong, Ellington, and Basie; a few movie roles and frequent guest spots on television; and dozens of albums with large ensembles or intimate jazz combos. She has enjoyed an association of nearly 10 years with the outstanding pianist Tommy Flanagan. A misguided 1963 recording with her old friend Roy Eldridge (*These Are the Blues*) demonstrated her ongoing detachment from the funk and drama of the blues. But by then, blues were the last thing anyone associated with the First Lady of Song.

Notes

*European and Australian companies have done wonders with the Decca catalogue, but in this country MCA has been content to do little more than reissue the same best-of compilations that have been available for more than three decades. Its initial attempt at a new CD series was disastrous, trumping even Sony and Bluebird in the awfulness of the digital sound. You'd think Fitzgerald would have sold enough records to inspire the company to do something worthy of the many great performances in its possession. That responsibility has been assumed elsewhere. A reissue series called Classics, manufactured in France and distributed here by Qualitron Imports, Ltd., has turned up in local stores. They've issued four CDs thus far in a series called *The Chronogical* [*sic*] *Ella Fitzgerald*, tracing her career from the first recording with Webb in 1935 through the June 29, 1939, session at which she took over the reigns of the orchestra after Webb's death. Excepting "Wake Up and Live" and an alternate take of "I Want to Be Happy," every record she made in that period (including the Teddy Wilsons and Benny Goodmans on Columbia) is here, with the promise of successive volumes to follow. The sound is acceptable—better, in fact, than the MCA Deccas. Grab them while you can.

JOEL E. SIEGEL
ELLA AT 65
Jazz Times, 1983

Joel Siegel teaches film writing and literature at Georgetown University. In 1993 along with Buck Clayton and Phil Schaap, he won a Grammy for writing the liner notes for The Complete Billie Holiday on Verve. *He writes about film and music for the* Washington, D.C., City Paper.

This article brings Ella to life on the printed page, with some of the high-voltage charm and energy that she presented onstage before the public. Talkative and self-revelatory, with none of the self-consciousness that plagued her earlier years, Ella was growing older with grace, stepping off the pedestal from which she had conducted many of her mid-career interviews. The conversation is far-ranging, starting with her mother's influence and running through her songbook recording experience, her confrontations with racial prejudice, her benefit work, and her experiences as a grandparent.—LG

More than 50 years ago on a street in Yonkers. N.Y., Ella Fitzgerald's mother taught her a lesson in practical humility that she hasn't forgotten. "I had just appeared in a junior high school play," Ella recalls, "and everybody thought I'd been pretty good. Well, I was walking with my mother and somebody from school spoke to me. I turned my nose up. You know how you get when you're young and think you're so great. My mother turned and slapped me so hard that I saw stars, right there on the street. She said 'Don't you ever go around where you don't speak to somebody, because someday that might be the very person who could be in a position to help you.' That's something I've always kept in my mind. No matter who it is or what they are, you speak because that's a person who could help you some other time."

Half a century later, the memory of that slap can still be felt in Ella's gracious manner and surprising lack of self-importance. Today, surely, the friendliness exists for its own sake. Obviously, Ella is not a woman who has to worry about ever needing help from anybody. She is the most honored living singer of jazz and popular music, winner of countless music awards and jazz polls, recipient of more Grammies than other singers even dream of, bearer of more than a dozen honorary degrees from schools like Dartmouth, Howard, Boston University and Washington University in St. Louis, and one of the handful of artists to be honored with a Kennedy Center Award for her contribution to American culture. Her recordings, concert and club appearances and television commercials (Memorex tapes, Kentucky Fried Chicken) have made her a very wealthy woman, thanks to the efforts of her manager Norman Granz, the impresario and record producer with whom she has been associated for 30 years.

It's almost unimaginable that a woman of such talent, wealth and celebrity could remain so modest about herself and her accomplishments. But when Ella expresses doubt about whether the audience at an upcoming concert will like the program she's prepared, or confesses to how inadequate she feels comparing her limited formal musical knowledge with that of better-trained singers like Sarah Vaughan and Cleo Laine, or interrupts herself to ask an interviewer whether she's talking too much, her manner is so direct and unaffected that one has to believe her. After years of exposure to TV talk show false modesty and synthetic show-biz self-effacement, it's easy to recognize the real thing.

* * *

I talked with Ella in Baltimore in early June. She had arrived to accept her most recent tribute, an honorary degree from the Peabody Conservatory. Before her visit, she had completed an arduous eight weeks on the road, and put the finishing touches on an album of Gershwin songs backed by André Previn and the brilliant Danish bassist Niels-Henning Orsted Pedersen. Several nights earlier, she had performed in New York at the Friar's Club dinner for Elizabeth Taylor (at Liz's personal invitation) where she shared the dais with Frank Sinatra, Dinah Shore, Joe Williams and other stars. Immediately following the Peabody ceremony, she flew home to Beverly Hills for several days of rest, then turned around and jetted back to Washington D.C. to open the 1983 Kool Jazz Festival at the Kennedy Center Concert Hall. It's understatement to observe that not a mote of dust is settling on this 65-year-old lady.

Sitting straight-backed on a sofa in her suite at the country-clubby Cross Keys Inn, she looks at least a decade younger than her age, much younger than her photographs. Unnecessarily apologizing for her appearance—she looks very smart in a blue suit with a blue, green and purple blouse—she is trimmer than she has been at any time since the Thirties. Her long battle with the bulge seems to be in its final campaigns.

Initially, she isn't an easy person to interview. She speaks very carefully and somewhat guardedly, stopping to correct the rare mispronunciation or grammatical slip-up. Her speech is formal; she refers to *Miss* Billie Holiday and *the late* Chick Webb. In telling anecdotes, she uses the first person plural. Not a royal "we" but rather to avoid what might strike the listener as an immodest repetition of "I."

Some of her uneasiness is justified by past experience. "One time when we were in Washington, the man who was supposed to interview me went on vacation and they sent a sports writer. He had to cancel a fishing trip, so he was angry even before he walked in the door. We *really* didn't get along. He didn't know anything about what I did, and kept asking me what kind of music I sang and whether I had made any records. I guess he thought I was the worst person in the world, but then I got worried for him because he didn't know any questions to ask me.

"Sometimes people think that I don't like interviews, but you can imagine what it's like when every day you have to repeat how you got your start and tell the names of your favorite singers. You start feeling that people have read the same things so often that they'd like to know some new things about you. Oh, gosh, I want to talk. Sometimes, when I find somebody who asks some different questions, I talk like all women. I never stop!"

As she speaks, she begins to feel more comfortable. Some of the "we's" turn into "I's." After an hour, she's laughing about learning disco dances from her nieces and nephews, and passing around color photographs of her 7-month-old grandnephew's christening.

* * *

Ella was born on April 25, 1918 in Newport News, Virginia. She never knew her father. As an infant, she moved with her mother and Portuguese stepfather to Yonkers. Recently, she's learned from an aunt that her father played guitar, a possible hereditary clue to her musical gifts. Her mother liked to sing, classical music mostly, but she also had records by blues singer Mamie Smith, the Mills Brothers (with whom Ella subsequently recorded) and Connee Boswell, the singer who was Ella's inspiration.

As a child, Ella was impressed by a rubber-limbed dancer named Snakehips Tucker. "People in Yonkers thought I was a good little dancer, so that became my ambition. They used to tease me and call me Snakehips Ella. I entered an amateur contest at the Apollo as a dancer, but when I got out on stage and saw all the people and the lights, I guess I lost my nerve. The guy said 'You're up here, do something!' The first thing that came to my mind was Miss Connee Boswell. I knew her record of "The Object of My Affection" and "Judy," so I sang those songs and won the contest by imitating her. Something about her sound and timing appealed to me; she didn't sound like all the others.

"When I was young, I never paid much attention to music. In school,

I took just enough music to earn my half-credit. I used to run up and down the stairs screaming and sang for a while in the Westchester-White Plains choral group. My mother hired a man to teach me piano. The lessons cost $5.00 and we were poor. The teacher had slit the skin between his fingers so that he'd have a wider reach. I was so fascinated listening to him talk and play that I hardly learned a thing. I regret it, because if I had learned to play, it would have meant a whole lot now.

"I spent most of my time around the neighborhood. It was a mix-ture—Italian, Spanish, Portuguese. In the summer, everybody was up on the roof and we'd have block parties during the Italian festivals. It was all family. If a mother was going out, she'd throw her child in bed in some-body else's house. We never thought whether it was right or wrong. Everybody was happy.

"My mother worked first as a caterer, then at a laundry. My old man dug ditches and tried to be a chauffeur at night. We didn't have much. People laugh at me today when I tell them that I used to go to school with bread and a banana for lunch.

"My mother was part-Indian, a very lovable person. There was a lit-tle Italian boy in the neighborhood who loved her so much. If he did some-thing bad, his mother had to bring him to our house and my mother would scold him. He wouldn't listen to anybody but her, and he had to go with her wherever she went. One day she went out driving with my cousin and took that little boy along. My cousin, who wasn't a good driver, had an accident. Mother grabbed the boy to protect him and struck her head on an iron bar. The injury never healed inside and she died not too long afterwards. I like to think that she's somewhere approving of what's hap-pening to me. I would love to have been able to give her homes or what-ever she wanted. I feel that through my aunt, who brought me up, I've been able to do some of the things that I'd have liked to have done for my mother."

The first time Ella won an amateur contest, alto saxophonist Benny Carter was in the audience. He took her to sing for bandleader Fletcher Henderson who was not terribly impressed. Tiny Bradshaw offered her a job with his band but she had to turn it down; without the permission of a legal guardian, she was not permitted to travel. In 1935, at age 16, she was able to join Chick Webb's band after the drummer and his wife agreed to become her guardians.

Ella credits Webb with helping her to forget Connee Boswell and forge her own vocal style. "I began trying to sing ballads, and he took the tem-pos down gradually without my even noticing it. I had never really studied music, so whatever came out of me, that's the way it was. I'm not a musician or anything like that. What I know, I've learned from the bands I've worked with—Count Basie, Duke Ellington, Dizzy Gillespie. If the musicians like what I do, then I feel I'm *really* singing. They say that I have a good ear, which was enough to start me. Then I had to experience different things, to learn how to tell songs like stories."

While with the Webb band, Ella married a man on a dare; he bet that she wouldn't do it, and she took him up on the wager. The marriage was subsequently annulled. (In 1948, she married bassist Ray Brown and adopted a son, Ray Jr., who now plays drums and guitar with a band in Seattle. Brown and Ella were divorced in 1952 and she has not remarried.) Her 1938 hit record "A Tisket, A Tasket," cut with the Webb band just after her 20th birthday, brought her national recognition. Bandleader Jimmy Lunceford offered her a $60 weekly raise if she'd join his orchestra, bringing her salary all the way up to $75. But Ella remained with Webb, who ended up paying her $125. She says, "I would never have left that band. It was like my family; I wouldn't have felt secure with another band."

When Webb died suddenly in 1939, Ella became the band's nominal leader, though in fact it was directed by others. ("They'd let me conduct one number each show to make me feel I was the leader.") Then war broke out and more band members were drafted than could be adequately replaced. The Webb band was dissolved in 1941. Ella then toured with the Ink Spots vocal group before going out as a single. Her pianists over the years have included Don Abney ("He's now living in Japan where he's a big star"), Hank Jones ("Hearing his chords each night was like ear training") and Tommy Flanagan ("He really started getting me singing what I heard inside and wanted to get out.")

"I learned scat singing from Dizzy Gillespie while I was on a tour with his band. Listening to Dizzy made me want to try something with my voice that would be like a horn. He'd shout 'Go ahead and blow!' and I'd improvise. We did "Lady Be Good" on the Make Believe Ballroom radio show; the people at Decca heard it and had me record it. Dave Garroway, God bless him, played that record so often on his radio program in Chicago that I got to work every theatre in the city. Bopping was a different thing and everybody wanted to hear it."

Norman Granz, impresario of the touring Jazz at the Philharmonic packages, admired Ella's bopping and, in 1950, invited her to join his all-star jazz caravan. As things turned out, he changed the entire course of her life. "Norman felt that there was more to my singing than just bopping.

He got the idea of the Songbook albums—Cole Porter, Rodgers and Hart, Ellington, Berlin, Gershwin, Arlen and Kern. It was a new beginning for me. Now, in addition to the jazz singing, I had something to offer people who wanted to hear the pretty songs. I was learning something new and becoming someone else. Norman picked all the songs; I hardly knew what I was going to be singing till I got to the studio. I can read music a little bit, but I'm not the world's greatest reader. Sometimes it's fun to record like that, but often you wish that you knew the songs a little bit better. When you hear the final recording, you think 'If I had really known the song, I would have tried this, or I would have done that.'

"I don't think we ever stop learning in music. In the past few years, I've done an album with Brazilian musicians where I sang in Portuguese, and in Europe I did a little country-and-western thing with "Old MacDonald's Farm" and you wouldn't believe how popular it was. Norman has just released a concert album that I did in Nice and on it I sing a bit of everything—ballads, bop, pop songs, Brazilian music."

Although she and Granz have had their disagreements over the years, Ella is grateful to him for more than music. "He really had to fight for lots of things he believed were right. He broke down barriers. Once in Ohio, there was a hotel that didn't want racial mixing in the rooms. Norman had everybody paired up, Oscar Peterson with Buddy Rich, and so on. When the guy said that he didn't have any rooms for us, Norman went right to the NAACP and got the story on the front page of the newspaper. The hotel let that manager go because they didn't want any more bad publicity."

In a segregated auditorium in South Carolina, Granz hired a girl to come down from New York to sell tickets and, covertly, arrange for mixed seating. Ella recalls, "When the show started, the people were all staring at each other and so afraid that they couldn't even applaud. We got away with it, even though they ran us out of town after the show." In yet another Southern town, the JATP musicians switched white and colored rest room signs in bus stations, implementing instant desegregation.

"Let's face it, there were lots of things back then that you either had to overlook or you got angry and cried about. That's why we should have a Martin Luther King day in this country. He did so much, not just for one group but for everybody; he turned the world around. You'd be surprised how in different countries people still sing the songs that were heard during the March. He made it so that instead of fighting, people now talk, and it's so much easier."

In 1971, following a cataract operation on her left eye, Ella's right eye began hemorrhaging, kicking off a series of health problems that nearly took her sight away. She was in Nice at the time, at the end of an exhausting tour that had taken her from L.A. to N.Y. to South America to Lebanon. She had not fully recovered from the operation, and all the travel and time changes, along with an incipient diabetic problem that she was unaware of, culminated in the hemorrhage.

"I was off for eight months, but after operations and good medical care, I managed to pull through it. I'm reading 20-20 with my left eye now. I'm only bothered when there's lots of smoke and when they use flashbulbs. Then I fell like I've been punched in the eye and can only see spots. When I first returned to work, I was afraid that people would laugh at me for wearing glasses on stage. But nobody paid the slightest bit of attention, so it was o.k."

While recovering from eye surgery, Ella studied French, mostly to keep busy. She was making good progress with a teacher in L.A., but slowed down when she went back on the road. "My teacher in San Francisco was *so* handsome, I didn't learn a thing. He'd walk in with the simpatico look. Then we'd have sandwiches and Napoleon brandy, and before I knew it the lesson was over." She knows some Spanish and Italian from her childhood, and learned Danish during the three years she lived in Denmark. She hopes to record albums in Spanish and Italian for her European and South American audiences.

* * *

These days, Ella tours less than half the year, but grows restless after a few weeks at home. She's a soap opera addict, and has an extensive library of international cookbooks. She used to cook for her son and the three nieces she raised ("my guinea pigs") but feels that cooking for one is uninspiring.

Her biggest interest apart from music is charity work. "I'm a glutton for anything that involves kids. I donated three nights of performances to benefit a nursery school in Watts that's named after me. Oscar Peterson and Basie did the same, and Henry Fonda, God bless him, made some beautiful pictures that were sold for the school. We raised enough to construct the building, and each year they add to it."

The Ella Fitzgerald Child Care Center is free for the children of working mothers. Teachers donate their time, offering classes in languages, music, dance and drama to students aged 2–12. A second school has opened in the Los Angeles area. Ella feels very strongly about such schools. "In Europe, they have them just about everywhere for working mothers and their kids. How else can children learn and enjoy life? It's sad to read that child care centers are being closed in this country because they are so necessary."

She would also like to record a children's album and do the soundtrack for a TV cartoon series that she'd like to call Auntie Ella. She enjoys reading to her nieces and nephews, though she admits "nowadays kids are so hip to everything that there aren't many stories you can read them." In South Carolina, she recently performed for an audience of 13,000 children. Afterwards, one little boy told her that he was disappointed that she didn't break the glass. "I realized that to all these kids, I wasn't Ella Fitzgerald but the lady who shatters the glass on TV. In Germany, there was a 12 year old girl who ran up on stage after each song and gave me a flower. By the end of the concert, I had a whole bouquet. If I were ever to do anything but music, it would have to be around children."

Something Duke Ellington once told her helps to explain the sweetness and serenity of Ella's attitude towards life. "He said 'If something hurts, think of it like a toothache. When a tooth hurts, you pull it out. You miss it, but you feel better.' Thinking of that expression relaxes me. When something upsets me, I've learned to walk away from it. I think of something else and I begin to feel better. I used to pout a lot. Norman would holler at me and I'd cry, cry, cry all the time. I was making me very self-conscious. Now I'm at the point where I try to do the best that I can, and beyond that I can't worry. And when I'm angry, instead of keeping it inside, I now speak my mind and then forget about it."

Although some reviewers disagree, Ella feels that aging has not taken too great a toll on her vocal equipment. "Of course," she admits, "as you get older, you start worrying about your vibrato and all that. But by having my trio—Paul Smith on piano, Keter Betts on bass, Bobby Durham on drums—take some of my songs down a tone or two, I can sing a full show without straining. And over the past few years, I've developed some low tones that I never had before."

Otherwise turning 65 has not affected her in the slightest. "It used to be that when a woman turned 40, she started knitting and crocheting. People don't do that any more and it's beautiful. Doctors say that as long as you feel like doing something, you should do it. I love to dance, and I don't care who says 'Look at that old lady doing the disco dance,' I'm gonna do it because I love it!"

Ella Fitzgerald is not a sophisticated woman in any conventional sense. The things she cares about are the common concerns of most people— children, food, living a useful, peaceful life. But she's got the special wisdom that comes from knowing who and what you are. "I always was taught that you're only as great as the people make you. When you get to feeling that you know you're great, the heart goes out of things. I have to feel what I'm singing, and if I just walked out on stage and said 'Here I am. Take me!,' it wouldn't be right.

"I enjoy what I'm doing now more than I ever have. Let's face it, after all these years, most people have stopped singing. Some of them are popular this month, next month you don't hear anything about them. I feel I have a lot to be grateful for."

LESLIE GOURSE
TALES OF MEL LEWIS AND WALTER GIL FULLER
Late 1980s

To expose readers to various sides of Ella Fitzgerald, I reprint here a few complaints about her that I have heard in the course of my interviews with jazz world veterans over the years. The First Lady of Song wasn't perfect, a few people said. One must be mindful of the stresses and demands on her, but she could be downright cranky and mercurial at times. The diva in her soul—at least as it was recalled by other people—adds a bit of spice to her life story. The only thing missing is Ella's side of these tales. There are undoubtedly people who will pop up and say, "That sounds just like her," and others who will say, "It's impossible." I am telling you the stories the way I heard and taped them.—LG

Drummer Mel Lewis, whose father was a drummer in the Buffalo area, recalled a period when his father came home nights from a job accompanying Ella Fitzgerald in a local club. Ella was driving the drummer and others in the group crazy with her complaints about their support—probably in the 1940s; she felt she was giving terrible performances, and she blamed everyone in the group. Actually the group was fine, and she was putting on good shows, Mel's father told him, but she just didn't know it. And Mel's father was delighted when she left town.

Arranger Walter Gil Fuller was hired by Ella to write some charts for an upcoming performance by Ella with Duke Ellington's band. Fuller waited and waited for Ella to appear in his midtown Manhattan office with the music she wanted him to arrange. She finally showed up a day before the scheduled performance and expected him to make a miracle. He felt she had no appreciation of the task ahead of him; he had to stay up all night, writing as fast as his hands and mind could go. Fuller, who had worked as an arranger and musical director for Dizzy Gillespie, had moments when he could be irascible himself, and this job for Ella gave him the opportunity to exercise his capacity for ire. He swore to himself that he would never work for her again, and he never did.

TED FOX
SHOWTIME AT THE APOLLO
1983

The legend of the Apollo was built on the legacy of great performers such as Ella Fitzgerald. When anyone wants to emphasize how great a place or a performance was, whether it was the Apollo, a tour, or a concert, all one has to do is invoke the name of Ella Fitzgerald. Her aura lifts the place or the event out of the ordinary. The Apollo gave Ella a forum when she was starting her career, but it was Ella (and Count Basie, Billie Holiday, and Lena Horne—performers of that caliber) who, in the long run, gave substance to the venerated reputation of the Apollo. To say that Ella played there was tantamount, in other circles, to saying that Abraham Lincoln slept in a particular hotel.—LG

"The Apollo had thirteen dressing rooms on four floors, and within their tacky, cold, painted cement walls beat the heart of the Apollo Theatre. There Louis Armstrong entertained guests and well-wishers in his underwear. James Brown held court. Ella Fitzgerald set out her usual spread of fried chicken, cold drinks and cut watermelon."

John Hammond: "The nicest thing at the Apollo this week isn't the rocking rhythm of that noble of rhythm—Count Basie. It isn't the slim, graceful bronze Jeni Le Gon. Nor is it even the swing-shouting of Jimmy

Rushing, despite the fact that he hung 'em from the rafters. The sensation of the show is the statuesque and effervescent Billie Holiday and braving controversy we dare to place her in a superior position to Ella Fitzgerald . . ."

"When performers hit the Apollo stage, no matter how celebrated they were, no matter how successful they were, they were nervous," said Bobby Schiffman. "When Ella Fitzgerald was ready to go at the Apollo, she was nervous as hell. Every performer was, but it keyed them up.

"The war years brought expectations in the black community that perhaps white people meant what they said. Black participation in World War II was thorough—nearly one million served. As in the First World War, when its nation called, the black community responded. The Apollo supported the men and women in uniform. Thirty-five tickets were set aside each day for the soldiers at the Harlem Defense Recreation Center. Also, headliners on each week's bill—Billie Holiday, Ella Fitzgerald, Bill Robinson, Lucky Millinder, Cab Calloway, Earl Hines, Willie Bryant, the Ink Spots, and Lena Horne—entertained and socialized with the servicemen, making Tuesdays at the U.S.O. Center 'Apollo Night.'

[The Ink Spots'] "first million-selling disc came in 1944 with 'Into Each Life Some Rain Must Fall,' performed with Ella Fitzgerald . . .

"No jazz show was successful unless it had a major female artist headlining," said Bobby Schiffman of the family that owned the theater. "If you had Sarah Vaughan, you had a successful jazz show. You had Nancy Wilson, then you could have Cannonball Adderley and any number of major attractions there. But you better have that vocalist, who is gonna express what they had to say in words—rather than on the horn—as the main attraction of the show. I have had some great pure-jazz shows with Miles Davis, Mongo Santamaria, Charlie Parker, Thelonious Monk, Errol Garner, or Dave Brubeck. But if you don't have Ella Fitzgerald, Sarah Vaughan, or Dinah Washington as the headliner, you can forget it."

GARY GIDDINS
CHILLED CLASSICS AND THE REAL THING
From Rhythm-a-ning: Jazz Tradition & Innovation in the '80s, 1985

Giddins critiques the latest releases of some of Ella's oeuvre, some never before issued.—LG

Polydor released the Ella Fitzgerald Gershwin box (Verve 2613 063) earlier this year (1983) and it remains a matchless feat of intelligent, articulate consistency; she never wrings a false emotion, and although she isn't a profound interpreter of lyrics either, she never subverts their meaning. For the Songbooks, Fitzgerald opted for definitive and respectful readings, shorn of any kind of self-conscious artiness. For Ella at her expressive best, however, her finest Gershwin interpretations are the eight wonderfully sensual performances she recorded in 1950 with pianist Ellis Larkins as her sole accompaniment: *Ella Sings Gershwin*, recently reissued (MCA 215), is one of the great records of that decade, and proof that she never needed all that fancy-dan arranging. Polydor has also just issued *The Ella Fitzgerald Set* (Verve 815 1471) as part of its Jazz at the Philharmonic Series, and although the sound is dire, these previously unissued concert performances from 1949 to 1954 are worthy additions to her admittedly sprawling discography. Hank Jones headed her trio in those years, but he was never much featured on her studio recordings, as he is here. All of the songs (including versions of "Later" and "Basin St. Blues" recorded shortly before the studio ones) are good except "Hernando's Hideaway," which she manages to salvage with irony.

LESLIE GOURSE
CELEBRATING ELLA
Jazz Times, 1991

Asked by Jazz Times *to fill in for Leonard Feather, I added my own words of praise to those of many great artists.*—LG

Although a variety of ailments have bothered Ella Fitzgerald for some time now, they haven't stopped her from winning a Grammy this year—her 13th—or from planning a tour this summer. Her health may be fragile, but, to quote Joe Williams, "she still can outswing anybody." So it seems a fitting time to reflect on Ella's remarkable career and invite some of her friends and colleagues to pay tribute to her great artistry and charm.

Nearly all singers describe Ella as a primary and lasting influence. Helen Forrest, recalling Ella's inspiration, once summed up the consensus:

> I started out copying Mildred Bailey and Ella Fitzgerald and Ethel Waters and the great blues singers of the early days. Billie [Holiday] had the purest jazz phrasing of any singer . . . Ella, of course, has a pure rich

sound and a great range . . . I listened to her—the greatest jazz singer—
and to Mildred Bailey from the time I was twelve . . .

Sarah Vaughan, singing for a week in 1943 at the Apollo Theatre as
the amateur night contest winner, remembered Ella's personal touch. Ella,
then the headliner at the theatre, generously stepped in to prevent Sarah
from signing the wrong contracts with the wrong agents. Nine years earlier, Ella had won the contest herself, when she was about sixteen years
old. (Her passport lists her birthdate as April 25, 1918.) Right away,
bandleader/drummer Chick Webb started guiding her career.

Little is known about Ella's life before Chick Webb and his wife
became her mentors and guardians. She had been born in Newport News,
Virginia and grew up under the care of an aunt in Nyack, New York.
While other great jazz singers, especially Armstrong and Waters, wrote
candid stories of their early lives, Ella's life has remained an intriguing
mystery. Yet her professional life, under jazz impresario Norman Granz's
canny management, has been bathed in brilliant light.

Her talent combines it all in one package: a peerless sense of rhythm
that allows her to move like quicksilver over the notes, perfect intonation,
a wide range, a sunny sound full of ease, authority and musical inventiveness. "No one in the world can beat Ella as a riff singer," Ethel Waters
exclaimed.

Among the countless singers impressed with Ella is Annie Ross, who
once said that ever since she heard one of Ella's earliest hits, "A-Tisket-A-
Tasket," "the musicality of Ella Fitzgerald appealed to me and has never
diminished one bit."

Rosemary Clooney agrees:

All sorts of people will say they love Ella, but I am one of the ones who
had a chance to know her, ever since my sister and I were with Tony
Pastor's band. Ella was one of the first persons we met with that degree
of national prominence. She was always childlike in her trust of people,
and she opens up immediately. She is personal; you learn a great deal
about her right away. There's no artifice. That warm sound, that perfect
vibrato, is a part of her, an extension of her personality. It's engaging and
moving, because she's open and childlike. Add to that musicality, and it's
an explosion.

To critic Leonard Feather, a personal friend of Ella,

she's the definitive jazz singer. She lost time recording dumb songs at
Decca [beginning in 1935]. Some of those songs were the worst things

that ever happened to her. The best that ever happened to her was Norman Granz. He guided her to do commercially salable albums of the music of Cole Porter, Duke Ellington and Irving Berlin. And she did a great job with the songs, of course, with great accompaniment, strings and orchestral settings [on Granz's Verve label beginning in 1955]. She never sacrificed her validity as a jazz artist.

She's also a very sweet person, incredibly modest. She doesn't realize that's she's as important as Frank Sinatra. If she hears that Tony Bennett is going to be some place, she says, 'Oh, Tony Bennett will be there.' She has less ego than anyone and has never gone off in the wrong direction. Perhaps it's because she's so insecure and shy and so impressed with others that she has been so successful.

Pianist Jimmy Rowles, who spent years as her accompanist, offers this insight:

She was always either singing or listening to music. Music was going on around her. Everything is music. Music comes out of her. When she walks down the street, she leaves notes.

Pete Cavallo was her road manager. When we were up in a plane, I would go to sleep. And I'd wake up to the sound of her calling out, 'Pete, Pete!' She'd hear a song she liked. 'Pete, get the name of that. Write that down. I want it.' We added so many songs to the book that we never got a chance to do them all.

Bassist Keter Betts goes back with Ella a very long time. In 1964, Ray Brown called Keter, who had just left Charlie Byrd and was working with Bobby Timmons, to say Ella needed a bass player. Keter stayed with her for a year, then worked on and off in the trio. In December 1971, he became the permanent bassist, so this year he celebrates his 20th anniversary with Ella. "It has been excellent," he says of their relationship. "Otherwise I wouldn't have been here for 20 years. People always ask me how does it feel to be playing behind Ella Fitzgerald. Nine times out of ten, I don't even hear her, not the way they do. If I listened to her that way, I'd be in awe. I would just be holding the bass; I wouldn't be playing it." Joe Williams recalls that Ella

never lost that sweet sixteen thing in her voice, that plaintiveness that was there from the beginning. It's a gift from God. She never lost it for one thing because she worked—and still works—at it. She still always gives the very best she can. And that for years is why she always was the First

Lady. She *is* the first lady. All the girl singers back to the big band days took a page from her book. And none of them could swing with her. She still can outswing everybody.

Nancy Wilson doesn't really know how much Ella directly influenced her, noting that she

came more out of rhythm and blues—from Dinah Washington, LaVern Baker, and especially Little Jimmy Scott. But Ella had to mean something to me just because of who she is. You're a product of all you've heard. And I always thought: She is The Lady, because she's such a special person, sweet and kind. The music is a foregone conclusion. There will never be anyone who can do what she did and does. The thing people should know about her is how sweet she is. She's just an adorable person.

Bobby Durham, her drummer, began working with her on and off in 1966; they became friendly during a tour organized by Norman Granz for Ella, Oscar and Duke. By 1972, Bobby became the trio's regular drummer. "I like to play for singers," he says.

And she's the greatest, because of her temperament and warmth. If things go wrong, she turns around and smiles and says, 'Finally got you!' Other people can make a big fuss or even find fault when nothing's wrong. She's always the Lady. I don't find any faults. She's one of the guys . . . She's a musician. That's the way she thinks, and that's her secret.

She's thoughtful; on holidays, on your birthday, or if you're sick, she remembers you and your kids. She's in touch with you. When you're off, the office makes sure you're cool and can go back to work. She notices you. She might say something about your shirt—'Oh that's a nice shirt—I've seen it before'—and then you turn around and she's giving you a new shirt . . . Everything about her is interesting and touching. I love her.

Mel Torme does a tribute to Ella in concert; recasting "Lady Be Good," he originally called her "the first lady of song". "But now I call her the 'High Priestess of Song'," he says.

She has been my favorite singer ever since she sang in Chick Webb's band, and it astonishes me that she retains that little girl exuberance which I perceived when she sang 'A-Tisket, A-Tasket' with Webb. My main admiration is for her enthusiasm for singing after all these decades. When she sings a ballad, it's full-bodied and mature. But when she sings jazz, anything from 'Honeysuckle Rose' to 'Air Mail Special,' she still retains that young, wide-eyed, wildly enthusiastic and exuberant attitude that is extremely appealing to me. Singers such as Joe Williams, Carmen and Jon Hendricks may have the greatest appreciation of her because they know what she is doing technically and what is coming from her heart. The perception of scat singing in the hearts and minds and ears of some people is in my opinion erroneous. A lot of singers think that scat singing is merely making sounds with your mouth. Scat singing is obviously the alter ego to what instrumentalists are doing in improvising. Ella is at the top of the list of that kind of improvising—to not know within the millisecond of it actually coming out of the mouth. That to me is the essence of Ella Fitzgerald. She's a great friend, personally and professionally. I want her to go on forever.

George Wein is another unabashed fan:

She's the greatest living jazz singer. Anyone who has the opportunity to hear this First Lady of Song at any stage of her career should do so. We've been working with her since 1951. That was when she was with the Gale Agency, before she was managed by Norman Granz. She was always the consummate professional. She came to work in my club, Storyville, in Boston, with Hank Jones as her pianist. The public loved her; it always did. She was the sweetest person to deal with, always cooperative; she never caused me one moment of aggravation or anxiety in the forty years that I've known and worked with her.

Mike Wofford, who is starting his third year as Ella's pianist, adds:

There's a maturity and depth in her interpretations now that's better than ever, I think, in her approach to her material and repertoire. There's a new element in Ella that's beautiful to see and hear. That happened to Sass over the years. [Mike worked as Sarah Vaughan's accompanist in 1979 and 1983]. All the great singers, if they have continued over that many decades, become different singers than they were; they get deeper and better, with a touching quality.

Paul Smith, who preceded Wofford as Ella's accompanist and still plays for her occasionally, concludes: "From a musician's standpoint, she's the easiest person to play for, because you can play any chord changes without upsetting her. It's a very easy job for an accompanist, if you don't play too much, not nine million notes."

Some rare moments stand out in Smith's mind, too.

One time at the Hollywood Bowl, she stepped forward; luckily the pit was only a foot below the stage. She fell into the pit. 'It's one of the audiences I really fell for,' she said. She always had good lines for things like that. Another time she was playing with the Basie band, singing an uptempo song in the early 1980s. There were a lot of wires on the stage. She tripped and fell down on her fanny. Some of the saxophone section started to help her up, but she waved them away and finished the tune in a sitting position. The show must go on.

PART FIVE

Evening Star

Last Years

"When she goes into her improvisations on 'Lady Be Good,' everything she does following the opening chorus of that song is a composition . . . It's so exciting, so creative, so wonderfully melodic and swinging. It's the composition, and it just blows me away every time I hear it. . . . She has such an uncanny sense of hearing; she seems to hear every chord change there is. When she scats, she doesn't miss anything, and when she's singing something straight, it's pure. it's fantastic."
—Stuart Troup, in an interview with Benny Carter for *Newsday* on Ella's seventy-second birthday

Not until the 1980s, when her voice was a shadow of its former glory, did Ella come to believe that the public loved her. By the 1990s she won countless polls, thirteen Grammy awards, a Kennedy Center Award, the National Medal of Arts presented to her by President Ronald Reagan, and appointment as woman of the year by Harvard's Hasty Pudding Club—an honor that put her in the company of such past recipients as Presidents John Quincy Adams and Franklin D. Roosevelt, Henry Cabot Lodge, William Randolph Hearst, Elizabeth Taylor, John Wayne, Bette Midler, Paul Newman, Bob Hope, and Katharine Hepburn. Honorary music degrees came to her from many universities.

Yet, Norman Granz could recall times she had come offstage and criticized her own performances mercilessly. She had once been unable to sing for a week when she read an item in which Frank Sinatra said her phrasing wasn't very good. But when audiences filled theaters and concert halls for her and gave her standing ovations, they affirmed for her the love she had won.

In the 1980s it became apparent that an era was passing. Ella was no longer singing at the top of her powers. All artists undergo changes as they age. A writer's philosophies might shift, a painter's subjects or preferences might vary, instrumentalists may have less fire, but the voices of singers are the easiest to scrutinize. They always deepen, and other vagaries that come with age always visit and occasionally ravage the singers. As Ella's instrument became diminished by time, her genius kept her singing buoyant and swinging. Audiences' hearts went out to her, and the applause resounded.—*LG*

ELLA FITZGERALD SINGS WITH COUNT BASIE GROUP

New York Times, 1983

This review has special significance for me for I was also at the performance that Holden reviewed. I, too, noticed that Ella's vibrato had widened and that she was losing the control of her intonation, which, only a year earlier, she still had in abundance. Shocked and saddened, I clapped as usual for the legendary singer because of my potent memory of her past greatness. Then I became upset again when I read Holden's review. As a contemporary, well-known, veteran jazz and pop music critic, he was obliged to say that the empress had no clothes. In subsequent performances, Ella would still have many good and great nights, some of which Holden was on hand to review. But for me, this concert and this review constituted the last turning point in Ella's performing career.

Yet in Holden's second Times *review included here, the great diva is given her due. Approaching seventy-three, she gives the crowd what they have come to hear from the First Lady of Song.—LG*

There are few sights more unsettling than watching a great performer begin to falter in old age. When that artist is a musical Rock of Gibraltar like Ella Fitzgerald, one is reminded that all things, including even our most cherished symbols of permanence, must indeed pass.

Miss Fitzgerald, who headlined the Pablo Jazz Festival on Friday at Avery Fisher Hall, along with Count Basie and Oscar Peterson, is by no

The Ella Fitzgerald Companion
160

means finished as a singer. But many of her celebrated vocal trademarks—perfect pitch, an apparently effortless facility at negotiating the trickiest intervals and modulations, and an ability to unleash torrential passages of aggressive, exquisitely embellished scat singing—have crumbled. And her serene, achingly lovely soprano has acquired a wide, wobbly vibrato.

Performing with the Paul Smith Trio and with Count Basie's Orchestra, Miss Fitzgerald sang a challenging program that included "As Time Goes By," "Good Morning, Heartache" and a medley of "The Man I Love," "Body and Soul" and "I Loves You Porgy."

Not so long ago, the singer could have handled the rapid key changes, dizzying leaps and difficult melismas with aplomb. But while she scored many small technical victories, her singing was fraught with a continuous sense of struggle. If Miss Fitzgerald's best musical instincts were intact, missing—sometimes painfully so—were the physical resources to carry them out.

The same gap between intuition and execution held back Count Basie and his 17-piece orchestra. In those few moments that Mr. Basie touched the keyboard, one marveled at the economy of his pianism and the way so few notes could imply so much rhythm. But the delirious, bluesy swinging that was implied, alas, remained undelivered.

STEPHEN HOLDEN
ELLA FITZGERALD'S PLAYFULNESS RIPENS WITH TIME'S PASSAGE
New York Times, 1991

"This is the first time I've sung in six months," said Ella Fitzgerald following the opening number of her sold-out Radio City Music Hall concert on Saturday evening. That first song, an uptempo rendition of "Sweet Georgia Brown," in which Miss Fitzgerald swung out with the Louie Bellson orchestra, set the exuberant tone for a concert that found the singer in high spirits and in unusually fine voice.

It wasn't so long ago when "the first lady of song," with her seemingly inexhaustible stamina, stood like an ageless Rock of Gibraltar of pop-jazz solidity. But time and illness have taken their toll. The singer, who will turn 73 on April 25, commands an undiminished rhythmic inventiveness, but her voice has developed a wobble that makes her ability to sustain notes somewhat uncertain. But ever the resourceful technician, she has learned how to work around her vocal seams, and there are moments she even uses them to expressive advantage.

At Saturday's concert Miss Fitzgerald divided her time between singing with Mr. Bellson's 15-member orchestra and working with a trio that included Mike Wofford (piano), Bobby Durham (drums) and Keter Betts (bass). The show's most crowd-pleasing moments were those Fitzgerald staples, like "Mr. Paganini," "It's All Right With Me" and "Teach Me Tonight," that featured her matchless scat singing. Others may command improvisational techniques that are fancier than Miss Fitzgerald's, but none have ever found such a perfect balance between a steam enginelike rhythmic propulsion and an ethereal playfulness. Accenting that playfulness were sudden unexpected high notes and vocal punctuation that has become more emphatic in recent years.

In the show's more pensive moments Miss Fitzgerald made effective use of a glowing lower register. "A House Is Not a Home" (with interpolated fragments of "It's So Nice to Have a Man Around the House") and Billie Holiday's signature song, "Morning Heartache," were drenched in the emotional quality that has always characterized Miss Fitzgerald's torch singing, a mood of sweet forgiveness.

CHIP DEFFAA
ELLA FITZGERALD
From Jazz Veterans: A Portrait Gallery, 1996

Chip Deffaa, who writes about jazz for the New York Post *and leading jazz periodicals, has received an ASCAP-Deems/Taylor Award and has published eight books about music. Here he recaps Ella's early career, quotes admiring fellow singers, and recaptures one of her last great performances at Carnegie Hall on June 25, 1988.—LG*

Ella Fitzgerald, a mature concert artist at the height of her powers, has long been an important contributor. But her deep roots in the Swing Era should not be overlooked.

Even on her very early recordings, made in the 1930s as a vocalist with Chick Webb and his Orchestra (when she was not yet out of her teens), the elements that would eventually make her the most widely-beloved of jazz singers are already present. The listener is struck by the warmth, purity and honesty of young Fitzgerald's sound. Above all, we hear the unfailing—and unsurpassed—sense of swing. On an infectious number like "A Little Bit Later On," she and the musicians get into a groove that makes you want to dance. At once a star and an ideal team player, Fitzgerald swings along with the musicians as if she were one of them.

In the 1930s, she was not scatting with the freedom, inventiveness, and masterly sense of construction she would later develop. (No one was, back then.) In her occasional early recorded forays into scat singing, she doesn't go out too far. But overall, her early records represent about as satisfying a set of debut performances I've ever heard.

Originally, Fitzgerald says she didn't want to become a singer at all, but rather a dancer. As a teenager in Yonkers, New York, she used to dance in the street for donations from passers-by. In 1934, when she was 16, she decided to enter the Apollo Theatre amateur contest as a dancer; her hope then was that if she won it, maybe she'd eventually get a job as an Apollo chorus girl. But when she got out on stage and saw the audience, she was too nervous to dance.

Prodded by an Apollo staffer to do something, she began singing a current pop song, trying to sing like her then-idol, Connee Boswell (who was also cited as a major early influence by Maxine Sullivan). Fitzgerald's rhythmic, innocently girlish voice won her that contest, as well as a subsequent one at the Harlem Opera House.

Charles Linton, vocalist with Chick Webb's band, urged his boss to hire her. But Webb, Linton says, didn't see the need for Fitzgerald. Webb already had an excellent band, immensely popular with the dancers at Harlem's famed Savoy Ballroom, its base. Webb's records, with the likes of Linton, Taft Jordan and Sandy Williams, were doing all right. And if he were going to hire a girl singer, he added, he wanted someone who looked great. Linton insists he then went over Webb's head, urging the man who ran the Savoy Ballroom to give Fitzgerald a tryout. "And Mr. Buchanan told me he'd let her sing for two weeks: 'If the public likes her, we'll keep her. If not, out—no pay!' And in the same key as he said 'no pay,' I said, 'okay!'"

Fitzgerald was a smash with the savvy Savoy crowd. Webb began featuring her on most of his records, which meant less exposure for Linton and everyone else in the band. It was rare, in the mid '30s, for a bandleader to focus so much attention on a singer, but the crowd at the Savoy recognized her as a star. According to Linton, when the band traveled farther away from New York, Fitzgerald's jazzy vocal style initially did not go over as well. His recollection is that on one-nighters out of town, he got a better reception singing ballads in a straightforward, older style, than newcomer Fitzgerald. But in time, she far eclipsed every other member of the band in popularity. Linton still occasionally performs today. The last time Linton ran into Fitzgerald, he says, she gave no sign of recalling that he had once helped her.

Fitzgerald honed her rhythmic sense, singing frequently at the Savoy Ballroom, backed by Webb's superbly swinging band. She and the band were performing for enthusiastic fans who came to dance—not just listen—and those dancers influenced how she sang. Some of the spirit of the Savoy, which permeates her early recordings, is present wherever Fitzgerald sings today.

Among her successes with Webb's band were "Sing Me a Swing Song" in 1936, "Hallelujah" in 1937 (she stretched the word "hallelujah" at one point, rising and falling with it the way as jazz trumpeter might have), and her blockbuster, "A-tisket A-tasket," in 1939. After Webb's death in 1939, she fronted his band for a couple of years, then went on her own with smaller groups.

Fitzgerald became a prime scat singer when bebop came up in the mid '40s (she really learned to scat from hearing Dizzy Gillespie do it in clubs, she has said). She might actually have been the first on record to use the term rebop (as bebop or bop was sometimes called early on), when she ended her 1939 recording of "'Tain't What You Do" with that word. In the mid '50s, for producers Norman Granz and Buddy Bregman, she began recording a series of composer songbook albums (the songs of Irving Berlin, Cole Porter, the Gershwins, and so on) that have become classics. Billed as "The First Lady of Song," she attained the status of an icon.

No living female singer is more respected by other singers than Fitzgerald today. Why?

"Because what she does is impossible!" declares Annie Ross. Ross is one of a number of jazz singers who cite Fitzgerald as their first influence. "Like Charlie Parker, Ella can think it and execute it. Her musicality is beyond belief. That joyfulness and youthfulness in her voice will never go away. The sweetness of tone projects the sweet lady that she is today."

That assessment is echoed by Jon Hendricks, one of today's pre-eminent male vocalists and also, like Ross, an alumnus of the pace-setting 1950s vocal group Lambert, Hendrick, and Ross. He says of Fitzgerald: "She's the warmest soul in the world. When you put that much warmth with that beautiful an instrument, then you get an Ella Fitzgerald. A lot of female singers have beautiful instruments but don't have that warmth. It's like Toscanini said of Marian Anderson: 'A voice like that comes once in a lifetime.' Ella's a one-in-a-lifetimer."

"The first time I heard Ella, in 1937, I said, 'That is the girl. That's the champion—the Queen of Jazz,'" says Anita O'Day, herself among the all-time top song stylists. O'Day points out that Fitzgerald's exceptional vocal flights of fancy require exceptional physical attributes. "Notes and words are sung on air; you take air in and sing until you run out of air. Ella has an unusually large lung capacity." And she's made unforgettable use of her gifts, adds O'Day, who sings for me over the telephone—her voice sure and supple—the first Fitzgerald record she ever heard: "You showed me the way, when I was someone in distress. . . ."

The mention of Fitzgerald's name prompts Ruth Brown to sing samples of the first two Fitzgerald recordings she heard—"Have Mercy" and "I'm Up a Tree"—also the very first recordings ever played in Brown's Virginia home, when Brown was just 10 years old in 1938. "We didn't own a record player. My uncle bought one, and bought this record of Ella's from New York City. . . . Anyone who professes to be a singer has got to deal with Ella Fitzgerald." Brown explains her own reluctance to indulge in scat singing: "Once you've heard Ella, you've heard the best—why mess with the rest?"

Fitzgerald is still influencing upcoming artists. Cassandra Wilson, perhaps the brightest light among today's emerging jazz singers, notes that "the first recollection of vocal improvisation that I have is hearing the Ella in Berlin album when I was maybe four years old. Ella is the quintessential vocal musician. I love her!"

Fitzgerald lives quietly in retirement today. She stopped giving concerts in the early 1990s. Her voice, in her final years as a performer, may not have had the power and flexibility it once had, but she still projected an appealing generosity of spirit, naturalness, and joie de vivre. She also had an unmatched gift for phrasing, and an unerring sense of construction. All of these assets were on display in a 22-song concert she gave June 25, 1988 at Carnegie Hall. When she scatted upon "Stompin' at the Savoy"—offering a fantasy upon the melody—her phrases may have appeared random to casual listeners, but they built toward climaxes, no less than Louis Armstrong's best trumpet solos did. She created the illusion of utter spontaneity, even though parts of her intricate routine—as recordings show—had been perfected and "set" 30 years ago.

She broke things up with a raspy Armstrong vocal imitation on "I Can't Give You Anything but Love." She gave "'Tain't Nobody's Bizness" a surprising—and effective—rock touch. And she had everyone clapping on "Mack the Knife." In the 1980s, frail health limited her public appearances, and her vocal control was not always secure. But she had plenty of verve that night and seemed to grow stronger as the concert wore on.

She told the audience at the end: "You have really been medicine for me." I'm sure many were thinking, as I was, "And vice versa, Miss Fitzgerald."

JOHN ROCKWELL
HALF A CENTURY OF SONG WITH THE GREAT "ELLA"
New York Times, 1986

Rockwell, who writes about pop and jazz for the Times, *puts Ella's accomplishments into perspective and supplies an interesting, brief discography that provides a taste of honey.—LG*

Last month, Ella Fitzgerald, the serene classicist of American song, was awarded an honorary doctorate of music by Yale University, "Not bad," she said with her typically modest good humor a few days later in a Chicago hotel room, "for someone who only studied music to get that half credit in high school."

Yale's doctorate was something like her seventh, joining others on her wall from Dartmouth, Washington University in St. Louis, the University of Maryland and several more. This is a woman who's collaborated with the best, from Duke Ellington and Count Basie to Nelson Riddle to Frank Sinatra, Sarah Vaughan and Louis Armstrong. She's won every award she might have aspired to, from endless listener's polls as favorite jazz and pop singer to Grammies to a Kennedy Center Award. "I never knew how good our songs were," Ira Gershwin once said to George T. Simon, "until I heard Ella Fitzgerald sing them."

Yet Yale was special, and not just because it's Yale. In 1935 a painfully shy teen-ager entered a talent contest at the Apollo Theater in Harlem. She had meant to dance, but stage fright diverted her into imitating her idol, the woman whom today she still refers to with a big smile as "Miss Connee Boswell."

Miss Fitzgerald won the contest, but more importantly she attracted the interest of the bandleader Chick Webb, who eventually became her legal guardian. Webb took her up to a college date at Yale, and told her if she pleased the college audience, he'd hire her. She did, and he did, and the now 51-year-old legend of Ella, America's incontestably greatest woman jazz-pop singer, was born.

The latest installment in that legend is scheduled for Friday, the opening night of the JVC (formerly Kool, formerly Newport) Jazz Festival, when Miss Fitzgerald is to sing at Avery Fisher Hall. George Wein's festivals often seem over-weighted in the direction of nostalgia. But in this case, her accomplishments are so immense and long-standing, and the love felt for her by jazz fans, pop fans and the general public so enormous, that no one would dare object.

Ella Fitzgerald owes her eminence in American music to a constellation of talents. There are her musical gifts, but what may come first of all is the way her genuinely lovable personality shines through her singing. Seated on a couch in her Chicago hotel suite—she was in the city to sing for an advertising convention—she looked frail at first. Miss Fitzgerald used to be a big woman; now she seems almost drawn, with prim attire, thick glasses and a worried look.

But first impressions aren't always accurate. She began talking almost formally, polite but shy. As her apprehensions eased into smiles, she spoke alertly and frankly, without ever denigrating a soul (her most frequent interjection, whenever she spoke of a deceased collaborator, was "God bless the dead").

An example of her lack of pretense came with a no doubt embarrassing question about what it felt like to be a legend, and just when she noticed a change in people's response to her, from affection to veneration. She didn't duck the question, or hide behind fluttery platitudes.

"I don't think I noticed it at first," she answered. "But when Norman Granz and I began recording the 'songbook' series in the mid-50's, it just seemed that more people began to like my singing. The awards I started winning didn't make me feel important, but they made me realize people loved me. And then when kids started calling me 'Ella'—half of them never even mentioned 'Ella Fitzgerald'—just 'Ella.'"

Behind her personality lurk a multitude of specifically musical gifts. First but not necessarily foremost, there's her voice itself. She has a silvery, almost girlish instrument that manages to achieve the key technical goal of opera singers—the smooth passage from the mid-register up into the vibrant upper soprano register—without taking on the fruity roundness of tone non-opera fans object to with opera singing. Miss Fitzgerald's upper register might best be called a falsetto, rather than a true soprano extension. Yet she avoids the pale fragility of a really undeveloped falsetto, and she keeps her mid-range light and flexible to balance with the rest of her voice.

A voice—any voice—per se means little unless it's linked with musicality and style. Miss Fitzgerald has a sense of pitch and rhythm, and most crucially a sense of harmony, that make her the envy of skilled jazz instrumentalists. She can not only hit whatever note she wishes, bending it and coloring it at will, but she knows just the *right* note to select from the dizzying possibilities flying past her in the heat of a jazz improvisation. The way she can shade a pitch, or slither up or down a chromatic scale, or pick out the most piquantly expressive note in a chord, reveals a consummate musician, however informal her training.

But voice and musicianship are still lost without style. From her note-to-note inflections and embellishments to her overall sure sense of herself as a singer, Miss Fitzgerald makes a complete and telling statement as a vocal artist, managing to project that charm and charity into vocal performances that are always balanced and generous. She has a remarkable stylistic range, from bop and scat to pop balladry, from classic American songwriters to innocently trashy Tin Pan Alley types of the 1940's to such selected contemporary songwriters as Paul Williams and Stevie Wonder to improvisations with the great names of modern jazz. Yet she ties all those threads together into a statement about herself and about American popular music that few have come close to matching.

Her diversity has led some who care about such matters to worry about whether she should be called a jazz singer or a pop singer. The truth is, she's both, and we are the better for it. She emerged in the late 1930's with Webb's dance band, which may have been considered a jazz outfit the time but which purveyed the kind of innocent popsy tunes that aspire to the charts in those years. Her first hit (and Webb's, too) came in 1938 with a ditty co-composed by her called "A-Tisket A-Tasket."

For a while, she seemed locked into attempts to repeat that novelty success, but fate and her own instincts dictated otherwise. Webb died in 1939, and after a brief effort to lead his band herself (she was only 21 years only when he died), she went out on her own as a solo singer.

Although her record company, Decca, continued to stress pop ballads and novelties, she found herself working more and more with jazz musicians. Indeed, her scatting with Dizzy Gillespie is said to have coalesced the very notion of "bop." By 1946, she had hooked up with Mr. Granz's Jazz at the Philharmonic tours. He became her manager and, in 1955, brought her over to his record company, Verve, thereby revitalizing her recording career.

What Mr. Granz did was effect a fusion at a higher level of accomplishment of her pop and jazz instincts. Under his auspices she embarked on a series of "songbook" albums, with separate disks devoted to the classic American composers and lyricists—Ellington, the Gershwins, Berlin, Kern, Rodgers and more—and bringing her together with classic arrangers (Nelson Riddle above all) and jazz musicians. Mr. Granz also opened up for her the whole field of symphonic dates, engagements in which Miss Fitzgerald could sing American popular songs and even jazz with the backing of full symphony orchestras. "It was like a whole new beginning for me," she recalled.

The lines between jazz and pop have been polemically blurred. Pop at its worst is banal, simplistic and calculatedly commercial. But jazz, too, can devolve into mere facile virtuosity, or formless displays of ego. At its best, pop represents a cleanlined, modernist formalism, while jazz introduces wit, subtlety and expressive ornament. Miss Fitzgerald is the easy master of the improvisatory aspects of jazz. Yet unlike so many jazz singers, she has clung to the natural, conversational directness of 1930's crooning. For a younger generation, jazz singing could sound mannered and flashy. Like Frank Sinatra, Miss Fitzgerald attained a remarkable level of artful simplicity, letting her jazz enrich pop's simplicity without subverting it.

She herself sees her pop and jazz repertories as providing needed respite from potential routine. "You can get bored doing the same thing every night," she said. "I try to do a little of each. I love lyrics. I love ballads. But if I was to sing all ballads, I'd get bored. I'd feel I wasn't learning anything. When I do the improvisations, they teach my ear. I *learned* when someone like Tommy Flanagan, would throw those chords under me. That was my lesson in music."

But there's more to it than that. Miss Fitzgerald doesn't so much alternate between pop and jazz as combine the two, and she's done so from the very beginning: listen to the sly inflections in her phrasing of "A-Tisket A-Tasket" from nearly 50 years ago for proof of that. With her blending of styles, she brings together the major influences that have shaped American popular music in this century. Her style is not just a combination of pop and jazz, but of white and black, girl and woman, voice and instrument.

She herself doesn't feel comfortable talking in terms of race. But from the first, she sang with both black and white musicians, and appealed to audiences of all races. It's no accident that her idol (and one of her mother's favorites, too), was Connee Boswell, a white singer who could swing pop tunes. Miss Fitzgerald has never been a true blues singer; her vocal inflections and ingenue manners have always kept her close to the white mainstream, just as American music itself is a complex but amazingly fertile cross-pollination of Jewish songwriting, black blues and improvisation, Appalachian folk music, country twanging, Italian vocalism and indeed every ethnic impulse in our polyglot national personality.

It is Miss Fitzgerald's lack of affinity with the blues, and that whole vein of oppressed passion that black music epitomizes—especially to some white intellectuals—that may have led a few critics to complain about her lack of depth. She has her limits, areas into which she will not venture. But in her case it seems more accurate to perceive her limits as the clear, precisely focused definition of her artistic personality. For her to push still farther, into areas of confessional Romanticism in which she felt uneasy, would be to shatter her image without substituting anything valuable in its place.

For what she may lack in womanly passion, she more than makes up in ebullient charm—what the jazz critic Martin Williams has called "the stuff of joy." And if she refuses to plumb her own darkest depths, that hardly means she's skirting the truth when she says, "I sing what I feel." She's a determined, self-made optimist, a person who can even make emotional repression sound like an affirmation:

"I used to be very self-conscious," she remarked. "I used to wish I was pretty. My cousin Georgiana always taught me that if you smile, people will like you. Sometimes people will say something you don't like, and you get angry a bit, but you just smile. You let it go by, even if you really would like to choke 'em. By smiling, I think I've made more friends than if I was the other way."

Ella Fitzgerald has been before the public for more than a half century, but in recent years she's had her troubles with health. In the early 1970's it was cataracts. She built her schedule back up to some 42 weeks of performing a year. But last summer she collapsed and had to be hospitalized, and on the advice of her doctors and Mr. Granz she's cut back her touring again. In addition, her less sure breath control these days has led her to collaborate more in concert with instrumentalists, thus sparing her energies, and to emphasize her scat singing, which lessens the need for the long-held notes of ballads.

Miss Fitzgerald has a big, sustaining family, and enjoys her home in Los Angeles, where she's lived for many years. She is thrilled, too, by her first grandchild, born nine months ago. "She was my Easter bunny, when she came to visit this spring from Alaska," she said happily.

But if retirement comes, it won't be voluntary. "They say, even iron wears out," Miss Fitzgerald said in her Chicago hotel room, her lake view shaded by drawn curtains. "I think if I ever just had to sit down, I'd say to myself, 'What am I going to do now?' If I ever get to the place where people don't want to hear me, or if I ever just can't do it . . . But I hope that doesn't happen. I *love* to sing."

An Ella Fitzgerald Discography

The following albums, all in print and available at well-stocked record stores, provide a selective overview of Ella Fitzgerald's career from 1938 to 1977. A surprising number have long been available as generously configured compact disks, a tribute to her continued appeal:

The Best of Ella Fitzgerald. MCA2-4047 (two LP's; no cassettes or CD's; format availability as listed in the Schwann catalogue). A selection of her work on the Decca label from 1938 to the early 1950's, with some sappy pop arrangements but fine singing from the first.

Ella Sings Gershwin. MCA 215E (LP only). Solo piano accompaniment (Ellis Larkins) as opposed to the lusher arrangements of the *Songbook* series.

Lady Be Good! 1957. Verve 825098-1 (LP and cassette). Examples of her singing and the backing she received during her years with Norman Granz's Jazz at the Philharmonic organization.

The Verve Songbook series. Classic vocal performances in mostly Nelson Riddle arrangements, although the Ellington records represent her finest fusion of pop-jazz singing and classical-jazz composition. George and Ira Gershwin: 2615063 (five LP's); 825024-2 (three CD's); cassettes separately available. Jerome Kern: 825669 (LP, CD and cassette). Irving Berlin: 2683027 (LP only; English import). Cole Porter, vols. 1 and 2: 821989-2 and 821990-2 (CD's only). Duke Ellington, vols. 1 and 2: VE2-2535 and 2540 (LP's and cassettes). Rodgers and Hart, vols. 1 and 2: VE2-2519 (two LP's and cassettes); 821579-2 and 580-2 (two CD's). Harold Arlen: 817526-1 (two LP's and cassettes). Johnny Mercer: 823247 (LP, CD and cassette).

Ella and Louis. Verve 2V6S-811 (LP); 825373-2 (CD). Miss Fitzgerald and Louis Armstrong made a strange but affectionate and effective vocal pairing.

Ella and Basie. Verve 2304049-1 (LP only). Along with Ellington, her other great bandleader collaborator on records.

Montreux '77. Pablo (Mr. Granz's label after Verve) L.2308206 (LP only). Latter-day work, with Tommy Flanagan.

ELLA FITZGERALD AND BENNY CARTER AT THE HOLLYWOOD BOWL
Jazz Forum, 1992

Here is an example of the respectful, laudatory reviews that abounded for Ella in her last performances. Levin, a senior member of the Jazz Journalists Association, as several writers collected in this book are, wrote this piece for the Polish magazine, Jazz Forum, *which used to have an English-language version. Levin has won many awards for his jazz writing, specializing in early jazz through the swing era.—LG*

Jazz historians of the future will envy me . . . and the other 16,011 delighted fans who attended this Hollywood Bowl performance by two of jazzdom's most respected legends, Ella Fitzgerald and Benny Carter.

Ella's Bowl concerts are eagerly anticipated by her fans. This, her 12th appearance in the prestigious amphitheater, was another triumph for the 74-year-old songstress. As expected, Ella "Bowled" 'em over, again!

She very slowly made the long trek from the wings to center stage on Benny Carter's arm. Once seated on her stool, Ella greeted the audience warmly, and began to sing—and as the lyrics said, "she knocked 'em dead—with 'Sweet Georgia Brown!'"

Accompanied impeccably by Benny Carter's 16 piece orchestra, led by pianist Mike Wofford, the familiar Fitzgerald favorites followed for almost an hour. "This is an all request program,"—she giggled, "Some I know, some I don't."

But she knew them all—so did her audience. Their warm applause and cheering hoots greeted the initial strains of almost every classic Fitzgerald tune. "It's All Right with Me," preceded by 16 bars of "Big Noise from Winnetka" by Keter Betts' bass, recalled her recorded *Cole Porter Song Book*.

The varied program included an Ellington medley ("Do Nothin' 'Till You Hear from Me/I Got It Bad" and "That Ain't Good"), and a sincere tribute to Billie Holiday ("Good Morning Heartache"). Her scat version of Dizzy Gillespie's Latin-tinged anthem of the bebop era, "A Night in Tunisia," evoked enthusiastic response.

Although a slight quaver occasionally appears on a ballad, Ella can still shape a melody with her recognizable timber, resonance, and depth of feeling. Her high notes retain the clarity we have admired for years.

After an intermission, Benny Carter ambled energetically to mid-stage to lead his orchestra. Opening with "How High the Moon," he announced that it was ". . . just to confirm that this is an all-star group." The rousing roundelay of solos by every member of the band firmly established the virtuoso qualities of his sidemen.

The outstanding soloists, far too many to recognize properly, included Don Radar on fluegelhorn, Ira Nepus' stirring trombone, Bill Green's alto sax, and drummer Jeff Hamilton holding it all together.

The sanguine ballad, "Evening Star," most appropriate in the warm outdoor setting, featured the leader on alto saxophone. His super-sophisticated melodic lines flowed with nonchalant brilliance. Throughout the evening, we were aware of his uncanny sense of sonic architecture that produced soaring improvisations.

"Pure Ella" was introduced as ". . . variations on a theme—Ella Fitzgerald's improvisational gifts. Subtitle it "Lady Be Good!" Carter led his orchestra in Billy Byers's triumphant transcription of "Ella's on-the-spot-compositions." Except for the improvised solos, all the music was orchestrally voiced references to her many extemporaneous phrases.

The great lady returned to the stage for a few memorable closing numbers with Carter. The two giants collaborated on "What Will I Tell My Heart" and "Mack the Knife." After their poignant duet, "How Long Has This Been Going On," the lyrics became a reality, there were chills up my spine!

The memory of this year's Hollywood Bowl appearance by these two giants will linger in the hearts of the 16,012 of us who were fortunate to have been there.

The concert, almost on the eve of his 85th birthday, was a triumphant acclamation of Benny Carter's lofty contribution to the jazz world. For almost six decades he has set the pace as an instrumentalist, composer, arranger, and bandleader. None of these considerable skills have diminished over the years.

And, Ella—the beautiful Mack Gordon lyrics you sang were most prophetic. . . "There will never ever be another you!"

MARGO JEFFERSON
ELLA IN WONDERLAND
New York Times, 1996

Margo Jefferson, a cultural critic for the paper—not a jazz critic or historian, but an intellectual and a fan of Fitzgerald's—praises Ella

*for prevailing and triumphing against all the odds as a supremely
gifted singer and as an individualist. Ella was chosen for a special
magazine section in the* Times *lionizing the most prominent people
who died in 1996.—LG*

1917–1996

Called the First Lady of Song, Fitzgerald practically invented scat and
helped establish the popular standard as an art form.

She performed into the 1990s despite the diabetes that would take her
eyesight, both legs below the knees and eventually her life.

Ever since I found out about the horrors of Ella Fitzgerald's youth, I've
wanted to protect her from the scrutiny of critics and fans like myself, who
have always inflected the pleasure we took in her singing with patroniza-
tion. Sweet Ella, we said when she was alive, she's wonderful, but she has
no emotional depth. Poor Ella, we say now: she *did* suffer but she denied
it—banished it from her life so she could dwell in a pristine musical wonderland.

That voice never did give us intimations of the stepfather who abused
her when her mother was dead; of the aunt who rescued her, then had no
time or money to care for her; of Ella herself as a teen-age truant who did
time in a New York State reformatory for girls, where discipline was
instilled through beatings and solitary confinement. When she ran away
she went from wayward girl to urchin, shuffling alone through the streets
of Harlem, singing and dancing for small change, sleeping wherever she
could find a night's bed and board.

It was this grimy little urchin who got herself onto the stages of the
Apollo Theater and the Harlem Opera House, won their amateur singing
contests, then almost stumbled back into oblivion because she lacked
glamour or sex appeal. Big-band girl singers were fresh bait in those days,
dangled in front of audiences to soothe their souls and stir their hormones.
Fletcher Henderson wouldn't hire her. Chick Webb's band rose to new
heights of popularity after she joined, but at first he didn't want her either.
Too ugly, said the band leader with the tubercular spine that had made
him a hunchback. Was he afraid that the sight of two plain people on
stage, one malformed, the other dowdy and gawky, presumed too much
on the good will of his audience?

But he did hire the brown-skinned girl in the raggedy clothes, and Ella
Fitzgerald rewarded him three years later with "A-Tisket, A-Tasket," her
own version of a little-girl-lost nursery rhyme, meant to make you swing

joyously, not sleep peacefully. She was beginning to spin autobiographical straw into musical gold.

Thank God for the radio and the phonograph: they gave a singer like Ella Fitzgerald the same advantage—invisibility—that letters gave Cyrano de Bergerac. And thank God for jazz. It gave black women what film and theater gave white women: a well-lighted space where they could play with roles and styles, conduct esthetic experiments and win money and praise. Ella Fitzgerald had a voice any romantic-comedy heroine would kill for: can you imagine her trying to fit her persona into one of those bossy, sassy or doggedly stoic movie maid's roles patented for hefty women of color? Can you see her in "Imitation of Life" or "I'm No Angel"; in "Alice Adams" or "Gone With the Wind"?

Actually, her looks and manner always reminded me of certain quiet, well-spoken librarians and music teachers in the Negro neighborhoods of my youth. She had been a good student, but she didn't want to tend books or teach scales. She wanted to sing, dance and be famous.

Ella Fitzgerald fit no available or desirable cultural type. She wasn't a lusty, tragic blues diva and she wasn't a sultry, melancholy torch singer. People didn't fantasize about her love life; they didn't want to be her or have her. And so she turned herself into a force of music: music as it releases us from the dramas of our lives and lets us experience something more airy and other-worldly. She became Ella in Wonderland, where rhythm, harmony and melody ruled.

Ah, but a singer must make the lyrics matter, you say. Well, she found ways to make the lyrics sing, and that matters just as much. Anyway, this was a question of strategy as well as temperament. If you're stuck with the 32-bar banalities she was so often handed, especially in the early years, you're a fool to take them to heart or ask your listeners to. Ella eluded banalities with her buoyant phrasing and supple time sense; her melodic revisions and interpolations. Her scatting is a jazz form of nonsense poetry. And there's her love of mimicry too: an infusion of Louis Armstrong here and of Connee Boswell there; some serious Dizzy Gillespie pyrotechnics and line readings fit for Shirley Temple or Marilyn Monroe.

By the 1960s she was singing wonderful songs. But she was never a dramatist. She doesn't really interpret songs; she distills them. She gives us pure gaiety and clarity. Pure rue and longing too: listen to her sing Gershwin ballads, especially accompanied by Ellis Larkins; listen to her sing "You Turned the Tables on Me," "Something to Live For," "Can't We Be Friends?" or "Angel Eyes," especially that wistful final line: "Excuse me while I disappear."

Sadness is an emotion recollected in tranquillity. Despair is absent from the work and (so it seems) from the life: how else could she have invented herself, then sustained the invention for so long? There was a core of fierceness, though, which her invincible musicality let her deploy with cunning. Popular music is one endless love song that, I suspect, the basically solitary Ella Fitzgerald approached much as the basically solitary Marianne Moore approached poetry: reading it with a certain contempt for it, Moore said, you could find a place in it for the genuine. Think of contempt as a self-protective code word here: We are talking about the refusal to write or sing in any voice but the one you know to be your own.

LEONARD FEATHER
ELLA FITZGERALD
Jazz Times, 1994

As he had done before, Leonard Feather writes an exceptionally well-informed piece about Ella. He conveys an intimate knowledge of his subject. He was able to do so, in part, because he had known her for so long and because she had trusted him enough to confide in him over the years. He was clearly very fond of her, accentuated all her positive qualities, and effectively explained away criticisms that were sometimes leveled at her. It's unlikely that he is absolutely accurate in his complete defense, but he is committed to his loyal and tasteful point of view about Ella. She inspired him.

He confirms that Stuart Nicholson's book had great value in bringing to light hitherto hidden facts about Ella's childhood and adolescence. And he had the insight to ascribe a mysteriousness that Ella maintained about herself to her forgetfulness as well as to her desire to keep certain less glorious events—over which she had been able to exercise little choice as an adolescent—hidden from the public and banished from her own conscious, mature life.

Jazz critic for the Los Angeles Times *for many decades, Feather brings together in one article many of the facts and milestones of Ella's life and career. Among them, he includes her adopted son Ray Brown Jr.'s rare, interesting public reflections about his mother, with whom his relationship improved as time went on.*

Feather brings Ella to life on the printed page and makes clear why her voice, style, and heroic ebullience captivated the hearts of millions. That's more than many writers can do with a subject in an entire book. Feather draws on his wealth of information about Ella gleaned from years of writing about her and throws in such bits of legend and trivia as Ella's passion for cookbooks, her avoidance of cigarettes and an only occasional indulgence in a glass of wine, and her practice of never eating before going onstage, because a heavy meal interfered with her breath control.

Often she had told reporters that she loved all the singers. To Feather, she said she particularly liked Phoebe Snow and the pianist-singer Shirley Horn among the newer singers at the time he interviewed her.

Feather broached the subject of Ella writing her own book. She told him, "I've had some wonderful love affairs and some that didn't work out. I don't want to dwell on that and I don't want to put people down, but I think all the fabulous places I've been, the wonderful things that happened for me, the great people I've met—that ought to make a story."

Leonard Feather was a few years older than Ella Fitzgerald. At the time he revamped his earlier piece for Jazz Times *she was ill, and he was well. But suddenly he had to weather a disaster in his house in Sherman Oaks, California. Many of his valuable papers and possessions were destroyed by flooding. He became ill and went to the hospital, suffering from pneumonia. He had always seemed to be lean and hardy, a survivor of a long and fascinating career filled with many of the same thrilling moments and successes—and stresses and travel hazards—that musicians faced. Unexpectedly, he died before Ella did.—LG*

The Guinness Book of Records may be unsure of it, but Ella Fitzgerald is now qualified for admission into its pages. She made her first record ("Love and Kisses" with the Chick Webb band) on June 12, 1935, and her last (according to Mary Jane Outwater at Ella's office) two years ago. This would give her a longer ongoing career as a featured recording artist than anyone else in music.

That, of course, is merely a statistical achievement. What she accomplished during those years is staggering in its immensity, its diversity and its creative consistency. Given her personalized treatment, trivial songs have become timeless—not the least of which was "A Tisket, A Tasket," her nursery rhyme adaptation that elevated her stature as Chick Webb's band vocalist to a point where she became more popular than the band itself.

Trivia aside, she has left a legacy of recordings by the thousands that displays her talent for beautifying a ballad, bringing spontaneity and humor to her scat masterpieces ("Flying Home," "Lady Be Good," "How High The Moon," "Air Mail Special") and her ear of languages (she has recorded in Portuguese, German and Italian). The achievement that did most for her burgeoning career in the 1950s and early '60s was the "Songbook" series in which she brought new life to the works of Porter, Berlin, Rodgers & Hart, Ellington and others.

Leafing through Phil Schaap's admirable discography section of the newly released and splendidly researched biography, Ella Fitzgerald, you cannot fail to be amazed at the quantity (and remind yourself of the quality) that marked her life; in the studios (and at the many venues where some of her greatest live performances were documented).

The past tense is needed here because, quiet as it has been kept, Ella Fitzgerald has been in total retirement since Norman Granz, her manager for 40 years, announced that he would accept no more work offers for her. She would be reluctant to admit this, for singing has been her entire life. Husbands or boyfriends have come and gone, but music has been her enduring passion. She played her last gig in December 1992.

For more than 20 years she has had to deal with a series of health problems. She was hospitalized in 1965 suffering from fatigue; in 1971 she went to a Paris hospital, and then to an infirmary in Boston, for the removal of a cataract in her right eye and treatment of a hemorrhage in her left eye, supposedly caused by diabetes.

Intermittently thereafter she took leaves of absence, sometimes triggered by an over-hectic work schedule. She underwent heart bypass surgery and took several months off in 1987 when diabetic complications led to the amputation of a toe.

During the past two years there has been surgery of an even graver nature; Ella now gets around in a wheelchair.

What amazes those closest to her is the apparent equanimity with which she has handled these crises. Mary Jane Outwater, still running the Salle Productions office (Ella's spelled backward), says: "I've never known anyone like her. She never gets depressed, never complains; she just accepts what happens. The chauffeur takes her out every day, sometimes with her son Raymond, and they may have lunch out. Her spirits are good; it's truly incredible."

Ray Brown Jr., who was adopted by Ella in 1949 (his birth mother was Ella's half sister) said recently: "My mother is the most resilient woman I know. She's very independent and doesn't want to feel she's a burden to anyone. She has always been a person of extreme class. I really think when they made her they broke the mold."

In her sumptuous home in Beverly Hills, Ella watches television. "At dinner," says Ray, "we listen to records. Tommy Flanagan, who was her pianist for so many years, sent her his current CD, *Dedicated to Ella*, and she absolutely loves it. There was a Scott Hamilton CD that she really liked too, and albums by Lee Ritenour, Jimmy Rowles, Ray Brown.

"Ella continues to enjoy life. We have a beautiful home and after so many years of doing the work of 15 people, it's nice for her to be able to have this time. And the phone keeps reminding her how many friends she has, all over the world."

Ella has always been a private person. Even those who have known her over long periods, such as Mel Tormé and Benny Carter, admit that a real intimacy has never been achieved. The shyness she has evinced before every show (which vanishes the moment she steps onstage) has a parallel in her personal life. Her half-sister, to whom she was close, died in the 1960s. Her first marriage was a disaster, ending after a few months when an annulment was arranged. The second, to Ray Brown (1948–52) went well for a while until their careers—Ray was busy with Oscar Peterson— drew them apart.

The basic facts of her life have been subjected to a number of distortions, some of which are due to Ella's forgetfulness, others simply because there are certain aspects of her past she would rather not remember.

Stuart Nicholson's research revealed that even her birthdate has been wrong in every reference book. She was born Ella Jane Fitzgerald April 25, 1917, not 1918. Her parents were Tempie Williams and William Fitzgerald; the latter left home in 1920 and Ella has no recollection of him. She was raised by her mother and a Portuguese stepfather; in the early 1920s they moved from Newport News, VA to Yonkers, NY.

"I never considered myself a singer," she once told me. "My real ambition was to dance, and I idolized Snakehips Tucker. But mother had a lot of records—Mamie Smith, the Mills Brothers, the Boswell Sisters—and

Connee Boswell became my favorite." (Louis Armstrong, whom she imitated often in her act, also became an early influence.)

"I had a warm family life. Growing up in a mixed neighborhood I had mostly Italian friends. First time I ran into a prejudice thing, a boy came in from another school and called me a nigger. Well, I pushed him, he fell down and the other kids thought I had hit him—so I became a heroine at the school! They made him apologize, and after that everyone looked up to me, thought I was real bad, I was about 11."

Ella studied piano for a while, but the lessons were stopped when her mother, realizing she was in a rut, decided that $5 a shot was a poor investment. But Ella did learn to read music, albeit slowly.

As for the "warm family life," this was possibly true up to 1932, when her mother died suddenly. There may have been abusive treatment by her stepfather, as Nicholson implies; at one point Ella's aunt stepped in and took Ella into her own family. But the true breaking point came when Ella, taking an intense dislike to a physician who had charge of her at the Riverdale Children's Association, decided to run away in late 1934. For several months her whereabouts were unknown even to her aunt; Ella was almost literally living on the streets, dancing for tips, sleeping in movie theatres. (None of this was ever mentioned in any interview given by Ella.)

The vogue for amateur nights in Harlem was taking hold. Ella entered one at the Apollo as a dancer, but on finding she was on the same show with a highly skilled dancing duo, she changed her mind and decided to enter as a singer.

Nervous at first, she cracked a note, then took control and went on to win. She was supposed to win a prize of one week's work, but never received it, supposedly because she was poorly dressed and had no home address.

Benny Carter, who heard the show, was duly impressed and called John Hammond, who was helping Fletcher Henderson reorganize his band. Carter and Hammond took Ella to Fletcher's apartment. To his surprise, both Henderson and his wife were unimpressed—and so was John Hammond! For Ella it meant a return to the street life, and another disappointment when, in an amateur night at the Lafayette, she was booed off the stage. Finally, a third effort, at the Harlem Opera House, did earn her a week's work; she was booked, along with the Tiny Bradshaw band, in February of 1935.

Certain alleged facts around this time are in dispute. According to Nicholson, the chance to sing on the Arthur Tracy radio show, supposedly killed because her mother had died and there was nobody to sign for her, simply didn't happen. As for Ella's entry into the Chick Webb band, every story to date has placed it at a Yale concert where she tried out. However, Charles Linton, who was singing in the Webb band and who gave Nicholson several unpleasantly derogatory stories about Ella, claims he was entirely responsible for getting her the job, and at the Savoy Ballroom rather than Yale (Linton may have had reason to resent Ella's subsequent success, which resulted in his near-eclipse as she took over most of the vocals.)

Another Fitzgerald myth is that Chick Webb adopted her. He allowed the publicity to imply this, but it never happened. In a sense Ella was adopted by the band. "They called me 'Sis' and used to heckle me, tried to make a lady out of me," Ella says. "We'd go up to Boston, I'd get out of the bus and the first thing I wanted to do was play baseball. Later on I tried to play the accordion, but the fellers in the band got tired of lugging it around, so that was the end of that."

Ella's voice at this early stage already had developed most of the characteristics that would take her through decades of triumph: a pure sound, perfect intonation, easy phrasing, and a little-girl quality that has never quite left her.

Ella's first few records were not spectacularly successful, but her ode to "Mr. Paganini," with its touches of scat, made an impression. Webb's band swung hard with the leader driving from the drums and Beverly Peer supplying a firm undercurrent on bass (he's still around, having been with Bobby Short for years). After sharing honors on sessions with Louis Jordan, the Mills Brothers and others, Ella finally broke through when "A Tisket" (recorded May 2, 1938) was released. Ella's salary, originally $12.50 a week, had edged up to $50. Jimmie Lunceford now offered her $75 to join his band, whereupon Chick upped the ante to $125. Benny Goodman, after Ella had made a record date and a radio appearance with him, offered Webb $5,000 to buy out her contract—without success, of course.

Always physically infirm, Webb suffered several relapses in 1938 and part of '39 until, on June 16, 1939, he died in Johns Hopkins Hospital in Baltimore. With Ella now as nominal leader and Skin Beaton taking over on drums, the band continued, but conditions were difficult. First trumpeter Taft Jordan, then saxophonists Teddy McRae and Eddie Barefield did the actual leading, but the men were underpaid and unhappy, the band's arrangements were not too well suited to Ella, and by July of 1942 the Webb band struggled to a halt. Meanwhile, a few months earlier Ella had a small part in a forgettable Abbott and Costello movie, "Ride 'Em Cowboy."

Sadly, Ella's entire movie career was confined to what were mainly cameo roles, the best of which had her playing a nightclub singer in the 1955 "Pete Kelly's Blues." But "St. Louis Blues," with a ludicrous script and Nat Cole playing W. C. Handy, and "Let No Man Write My Epitaph," which bombed in 1960, gave her no chance to realize her potential.

Her recorded output also was hampered when the American Federation of Musicians ban went into effect. During the next year or two Ella teamed with the Four Keys, the Ink Spots, the Delta Rhythm Boys and various studio groups. Milt Gabler, in charge of her sessions for Decca, tried to maintain a balance between what he felt would sell and the superior songs that seemed more in character; however, Ella herself seemed to take joy in such material as "Hello Ma! I Done It Again" and "Stone Cold Dead In De Market."

A significant influence on Ella was her close association with Dizzy Gillespie, who joined her band in 1941 and later was booked as a package with his big band and Ella. They both took part in a concert I coproduced at Carnegie Hall in September of 1947. It was a Carnegie first for both of them, as it was for Charlie Parker; the concert sold out and established beyond question Ella's sympathy for and understanding of bebop.

In 1948, when Ella visited Carnegie to see her boyfriend Ray Brown along with Norman Granz's "Jazz At The Philharmonic," she was lured onstage, created a sensation and by 1950 was touring with Granz regularly. It was the start of an association that lasted for the rest of Ella's career, and it began with a major problem: she was still under contract to Decca and Norman couldn't include her part of the taped concert albums he was putting out on his own label. Finally a deal was worked out, Ella ended her Decca days and soon afterward began the legendary Songbook series for Granz's new Verve label.

By 1954 Granz, who had been handling Ella's affairs informally (her previous manager seemed to have no conception of her esthetic and creative potential), now became her official manager. Granz had/has an irascible side, but Ella told me she soon learned to live with it. "The idea was to get him to do the talking for me and I'd do the singing. I needed that. Sometimes we'd argue and wouldn't speak for weeks on end, but now I accept him as he is, or I may just speak my mind."

Granz did not interfere with Ella's private liaisons, which in the post-Ray Brown years involved occasional romances. She seemed to be attracted to Scandinavians. In July of 1957 the New York Post quoted a Reuter's report that she had been secretly married to a Norwegian impresario, Thor Einar Larsen. Ella at first confirmed and later denied it, but the transatlantic affair apparently continued for a couple of years.

In 1961 Ella began a romance with a Danish airline employee. This time it was serious enough for her to decide to take an apartment in Copenhagen. "I had to learn Danish, to do my shopping," she recalled. Granz confirmed that "Ella loves Denmark, and it is her intention to stay here in Copenhagen between her many tours." She kept the new home for three years, but by 1963 the affair was long gone and she took her expensive Danish furniture back to her Los Angeles home base. Since then, more often than not, she seems to have been unattached.

If Granz did not become involved with Ella's love life, there was another aspect in which he played an invaluable role: he made every effort to shield her, and the other JATP artists, from any encounter with racism. It didn't always work: in 1955 in Houston, then a notoriously segregated city, Ella and Granz were picked up, along with several others who had been found committing the sin of watching a dice game between Dizzy Gillespie and Illinois Jacquet.

The charges were eventually dismissed, but not against Dizzy and Jacquet; it cost Granz $2,000 to dismiss their charges and recover the $20 they had posted for bail bonds. Ella laughed at it all later on: "I was just sitting there eating pie; they took us down to the police station, and when we got there they had the nerve to ask for an autograph."

During the decades after Granz's assumption of managerial duties, she was able to reduce her nightclub work while expanding into the great concert halls of the world. In many theatres and luxury cabarets she would be the first black artist to have played there. It is not known exactly when she became a millionaire, but that milestone surely was passed many years ago and at no cost to her artistic integrity. Ella became a member of the informal Granz family, artists with whom he had an official or unofficial interest: as a result, Oscar Peterson and Joe Pass, later the Basie and Ellington orchestras, assumed important roles in her personal appearances and recordings.

By the 1970s her career had taken on a valuable new dimension as she started to perform with symphony orchestras. This began through Arthur Fiedler, who Ella says, "Heard my version of Cole Porter's 'Too Darn Hot' and said he would like to get the lady who sang that song, and have her do it with the Boston Pops." By late 1973 Ella had sung with the Pittsburgh, New Jersey, Cincinnati, St. Louis and Oklahoma Symphonies, and eventually there were at least 50 other such recitals. Ella enjoyed the opportunity to work with lush strings and horns, the kinds of settings that had rarely been available to her.

Over the years Ella was accompanied by a series of consistently sympathetic pianists, several of whom joined and rejoined her two or three times. Tommy Flanagan had a couple of long stints, as did Paul Smith. Lou Levy, Hank Jones, Jimmy Jones and Jimmy Rowles also had mutually satisfying tours with her, and of course Oscar Peterson became a regular part of the JATP unit.

Along with the constant tours, the annual poll victories and countless Grammy and other awards, Ella managed to maintain the admiration of singers who had been her contemporaries—Peggy Lee, Anita O'Day and others roughly in her age range while attracting similar enthusiasm among vocalists, both female and male, who came up in later decades.

Tony Bennett once told me: "You know how I got to hear Ella? Through my mother. She had a birthday coming up and I asked her what she'd like for a present. She said, 'Take me to Birdland to hear Ella. She's my favorite.' And when I met her she complimented me on my record of 'Blue Velvet,' which really flipped me."

Fitzgerald and Bennett clearly were mutual admirers; in many other cases, mainly among women, the admiration extended to inspiration. "I think she influenced me more than any other singer," says Nnenna Freelon. "When I was a very little girl, what struck me was the clarity of her sound—like a bell. I know her from records, and I found that if you want to learn a standard tune and can't get hold of a lead sheet, just get Ella's record and she will give you an accurate reading. Other singers will give you their own interpretation.

"There's also a certain little-girl quality inside that voice, a youthful, joyful quality that she retained even in some of her later albums."

Dianne Reeves has similar recollections. "I saw her when I was in the 11th grade, in Denver. The first song I ever heard her do was Duke's "I Like the Sunrise." Sure she influenced me, in the sense that this was the first time I'd ever seen a singer as a musician—that was something I really wanted to be like. She communicated with her musicians and had total control over the audience; and she really knew how to build a show.

"I met her backstage afterward—this was in 1973, I was 16—and I remember her offering me kindly words of encouragement. I recall looking up at her and thinking how her talent and musicianship made her truly great."

Though most singers evaluate Ella in terms of her earlier recorded work, there has been relatively little criticism of her supposedly diminished powers in later years. While it is true that her vibrato widened and her range narrowed, as late as August 1991 I was able to report, reviewing her at the Hollywood Bowl: "She has retained the qualities that established her more than a half century ago as the definitive jazz and pop singer . . . she can still swoop through two octaves (upward or downward) within an eight bar stanza."

Ella's final professional years were, in fact, marked by a series of triumphs and tributes. In 1989 the Los Angeles-based Society of Singers instituted its annual "Ella" award for lifetime achievement, the first award going to Ella herself. Bill Cosby hosted the affair, at which Mel Tormé, George Shearing, Joe Williams, Patti Austin, Kay Starr, Martha Tilton and many others performed. The following year, when Frank Sinatra received the Ella award, they sang together.

Meanwhile New York had staged its own celebration: in February of 1990 the "Hearts for Ella" was presented, cohosted by Lena Horne and Itzhak Perlman. The wildly assorted program included Perlman duetting with Bobby McFerrin's scatting, and later joining Oscar Peterson for a poignant "Summertime." Ella herself, who had been sitting in the audience, was finally brought onstage by Joe Williams and wound up trading scat-libs with Williams and Clark Terry to what I described as "an ovation bordering on levitation."

It's all over now, I suppose, but the memories are very precious. Looking back, I can still see Ella on the bandstand at the Savoy with Chick, Edgar Sampson introducing her to me, and the many gestures of friendship and appreciation every time I wrote something that pleased her. She was and is, as Mary Jane Outwater and Ray Brown, Jr. attested, truly one of a kind.

"MAMA JAZZ" BOWS OUT
New York Times, June 18, 1996

Relatively few geniuses in any art or discipline have rated an editorial in the New York Times *to honor them. This tribute bestows upon Ella, usually called the First Lady of Song, a new sobriquet, Mama Jazz, that I never heard ascribed to her before. To a degree it captures the spirit of the warmth of her singing style and makes a fitting way to say good-bye to a woman whose music was as comforting as sunshine and laughter.—LG*

Jazz is a distinctly American art form, and the great jazz singers are among its foremost interpreters, transforming lyrics as Picasso and Cézanne transformed visual life. Betty Carter, Billie Holiday and Sarah Vaughan come quickly to mind. But no jazz singer has burned so spectacularly, and found such universal acceptance, as Ella Fitzgerald, who died last week at 79.

Miss Fitzgerald (she disliked being called "Ella" by strangers) started out singing for change on Harlem sidewalks. Her career spanned seven decades. She moved from big-band swing in the 1930's to Charlie Parker's bebop improvisations in the 1940's. In the 1950's and 60's, she explored, memorably, the works of Cole Porter, Irving Berlin, Duke Ellington and the Gershwin brothers. Her stage and orchestral performances in the 70's and 80's were equally magical.

Given her inexhaustible inventiveness, and a range of nearly three octaves, she moved easily from a bluesy growl up into the stratosphere— with astounding clarity all the way. Ira Gershwin spoke for many composers when he said: "I never knew how good our songs were until I heard Ella Fitzgerald sing them." Her famous *Songbook* recordings of Gershwin, Porter, Kern and Rodgers and Hart are masterworks. Having excelled in nearly every noteworthy period of the modern jazz era, Miss Fitzgerald set a timeless standard. Young fans in Italy named her "Mama Jazz." That she was.

Selected Discography

Ella Fitzgerald's recording career can be divided roughly into four parts: the Decca years, beginning in 1935 when she made her first record with the Chick Webb band; the Verve years, beginning in 1955 when she signed with Norman Granz, and in those years she was in her prime; between 1966 and 1971, when Ella recorded for several labels, among them Capitol, Verve, Columbia, and Reprise; and finally, the Pablo years with Norman Granz's new label, beginning in 1971.

In 1997, in Tower Records, the MUZE machine that lists recordings had information for more than one hundred and fifty CDs for Ella, plus several recordings on cassettes only.

Stuart Nicholson's *Ella Fitzgerald: A Biography of the First Lady of Jazz,* has a lengthy, highly praised discography by jazz historian Phil Schaap. *The Ella Fitzgerald Companion* offers choice selections from Fitzgerald's discography to help readers sample her recordings, all of them reissues on compact disks, and most of them done when she was in her prime.

Among the most popular of all her recordings is *The George and Ira Gershwin Songbook,* done in 1959 on Verve. If you cannot find it in the stores, you can have a taste of it on *Ella Fitzgerald Love Songs: Best of the Verve Songbooks* (Verve, 1996), which contains some Gershwin selections. So does *Ella Fitzgerald: The Best of the Songbooks* (Verve, 1993), a CD of selections taken from a 16-CD box set.

Another Gershwin album, *Ella Sings Gershwin,* done with pianist Ellis Larkins in September 1950 and produced by Milt Gabler, is probably her best work on the Decca label. Not available on a CD in the stores as of early 1997, it is listed as available on cassette only—it is highly recommended. Other excellent selections, available in the stores in early 1997, are the following:

> *The Best of Ella Fitzgerald* (Decca, 1996), including Ella with Chick Webb's band, the Ink Spots, Louis Armstrong, Louis Jordan, Sy Oliver, the Song Spinners, and others, and includes her songs "A Tisket, A Tasket," "Stone Cold Dead in the Market," and "Oh, Lady Be Good." The first song gained her fame; the second numbered among her novelty hits for Decca; and she was very well known throughout her career for the third song.
>
> *The Early Years, Parts 1 and 2,* with Chick Webb, has both "A-Tisket, A-Tasket" and "I Found My Yellow Basket."
>
> *Clap Hands, Here Comes Charlie* (Verve, 1989), compilation.
>
> *The Cole Porter Songbook, Vols. 1 and 2* (Verve, recorded and released 1956).
>
> *The Rodgers and Hart Songbook* (Verve, recorded and released 1956).
>
> *Compact Jazz* (Verve, recorded in 1957), Ella Fitzgerald and Louis Armstrong with Oscar Peterson, Ray Brown, Herb Ellis, Buddy Rich, and Louis Bellson.
>
> *Day Dream: The Best of the Duke Ellington Songbook* (Verve, recorded 1957, reissued 1995).
>
> *Ella Fitzgerald and Jazz at the Philharmonic* (Tax, recorded live 1957).
>
> *Ella Fitzgerald at the Opera House* (Verve, recorded and released 1957), with Lester Young, Roy Eldridge, Coleman Hawkins, Oscar Peterson, and Stan Getz.
>
> *Ella in Rome: The Birthday Concert* (Verve, recorded 1958, released 1988), with Lou Levy (pianist), Max Bennett (bassist), Gus Johnson (drummer), and the Oscar Peterson Trio.
>
> *The Irving Berlin Songbook, Vols. 1 and 2* (Verve, recorded and released 1958).
>
> *The Complete Ella in Berlin: "Mack the Knife"* (Verve, 1960) with the subtitle tune and "How High the Moon," among other songs for which she is famous.

The Harold Arlen Songbook, Vols. 1 and 2 (Verve, 1961).

Ella Returns to Berlin (Verve, recorded 1961, first release 1991).

The Jerome Kern Songbook (Verve, 1963).

Ella Fitzgerald with the Tommy Flanagan Trio (Laserlight). Flanagan, one of the great accompanists for Ella, recorded with her between the years 1964 and 1977.

Live at the Newport Jazz Festival (Legacy, recorded live July 5, 1973, at Carnegie Hall).

Easy Living (Pablo, 1987), Ella Fitzgerald with Joe Pass.

Ella Fitzgerald: The Concert Years (Pablo, released 1994), a two-disc collection spanning the years from 1953 to 1983.

Bibliography

Arnaud, Gerald, and Jacques Chesnel. "Vocal Jazz." In *Masters of Jazz.* New York: W & R Chambers Ltd., 1991.

Bach, Bob. "The First Lady of Song." *Metronome*, November 1947.

Balliett, Whitney. "Close but No Cigar." In *The Sound of Surprise*. New York: E. P. Dutton & Co., Inc., 1961.

———. "First Lady of Song." *The New Yorker*, April 26, 1993.

Bernstein, Nina. "The Gap in Ella Fitzgerald's Life." *New York Times*, June 23, 1996.

Bussang, Marion. "Ella Fitzgerald—Chick Webb." *New York Post*, 1939.

Cooper, Ralph, with Steve Dougherty. *Amateur Night at the Apollo*. New York: HarperCollins, 1990.

Coss, Bill. "Ella." *Metronome*, October 1953.

Dahl, Linda. "The Canaries." In *Stormy Weather*. New York: Limelight Editions, 1984.

Dance, Stanley. "Four to Keep." *Jazz Journal* (London, England), 1952–54.

Davis, Francis. *Outcats: Jazz Composers, Instrumentalist, and Singers*. New York: Oxford University Press, 1990. ("An 'outcat' is an outcast and a far-out cat combined."—pianist Paul Knopf, 1959)

———. *In the Moment: Jazz in the 1980s*. New York: Oxford University Press, 1986.

Deffaa, Chip. *Blue Rhythms: Six Lives in Rhythm and Blues and Traditionalists and Revivalists in Jazz*. Urbana, Ill.: University of Illinois Press, 1996.

————. *In the Mainstream: Eighteen Portraits in Jazz.* Metuchen, N.J.: Scarecrow Press, 1992.

————. "Ella Fitzgerald." In *Jazz Veterans: A Portrait Gallery.* Fort Bragg, Calif.: Cypress House, 1996.

Doyle, Dic (R.J.D.). "It's Recorded: Ella Sings the Duke and It's a Treasure." *Globe and Mail* (Toronto), June 14, 1958.

Dunbar, Ernest. "Ella Sings Just This Side of the Angels." *New York Times* (Arts and Leisure section), November 24, 1974.

"Ella May Quit as Leader." *Music and Rhythm,* 1941.

Feather, Leonard. "Ella Gives Carmen, Peggy, Hackett 5 [Blindfold Test]," *Down Beat,* October 5, 1955.

————. "Ella Fitzgerald—Lonely at the Top" in "Jazz Beat" column. *New York Post,* October 19, 1965.

————. "Ella." In *From Satchmo to Miles.* New York: Da Capo, 1972, reprinted 1984.

————. *The Book of Jazz. From Then till Now. A Guide to the Entire Field.* New York: Horizon Press, 1957; reprint, 1965.

————. "Ella Fitzgerald." *Jazz Times,* September 1994.

Fidelman, Geoffrey Mark. *First Lady of Song: Ella Fitzgerald for the Record.* New York: Citadel Press, 1995.

Fields, Sidney. "Only Human." *Daily Mirror* (New York).

————. "Songbird Is Missing a Note" in "Only Human" [column]. *New York Mirror,* June 21, 1957.

Fox, Ted. *Showtime at the Apollo.* New York: Holt, Rinehart and Winston, 1983.

Freedman, Bob. "The Audience Loved Ella's Evening" in "The Jazz Scene" [column]. *Boston Traveler,* October 20, 1959.

Friedwald, Will. "Lady Day and Lady Time." In *Jazz Singing,* edited by Will Friedwald. New York: Charles Scribner's Sons, 1990.

Giddins, Gary. "Chilled Classics and the Real Thing." In *Rhythm-a-ning: Jazz Tradition & Innovation in the '80s.* New York: Oxford University Press, 1985.

————. "First Lady." *Village Voice,* December 1976. Reprinted in *Faces in the Crowd,* New York: Oxford University Press, 1992.

———. *Celebrating Bird*. New York: William Morrow, 1986.

———. *Rhythm-a-ning: Jazz Tradition & Innovation in the '80s*. New York: Oxford University Press, 1985.

———. *Satchmo*. New York: Doubleday, 1988.

Gleason, Ralph J. "Rhythm Section." *Beacon* (Wichita, Kan.), November 30, 1958.

———. *Celebrating The Duke and Louis, Bessie, Billie, Bird, Carmen, Miles, Dizzy and Other Heroes*. Boston: Little Brown, 1975.

Gourse, Leslie. "The Time of Ella Fitzgerald." In *Louis' Children: American Jazz Singers*. New York: William Morrow and Company, 1984.

———. "Celebrating Ella." *Jazz Times* (Silver Spring, Md.), September 1991.

Greene, Bob. "The Sky's the Limit" in the "American Beat" section. *Esquire*, May 1983.

Harman, Carter. "Ella Has a Way with a Song." *New York Times*, September 1951.

Haskins, Jim. *Ella Fitzgerald: A Life through Jazz*. London: New English Library, 1991.

Hasse, John Edward. "Essential Ellington, 1956–1965." In *Beyond Category: The Life and Genius of Duke Ellington*. New York: Simon & Schuster, 1993.

Hentoff, Nat. "Ella Tells of Trouble in Mind Concerning Disks, Television." *Down Beat*, February 23, 1955.

———. *The Jazz Life*. New York: Dial Press, 1961; reprint, Da Capo Press, 1978.

———. *Jazz Is*. New York: Random House, 1976.

———. *Listen to the Stories: Nat Hentoff on Jazz and Country Music*. New York: HarperCollins, 1995.

Hentoff, Nat, and Nat Shapiro. *Hear Me Talkin' to Ya: The Story of Jazz by the Men Who Made It*. New York: Rinehart and Company, 1955; reprint, Dover, 1966.

Holden, Stephen. "Jazz: Ella Fitzgerald Sings with Count Basie Group." *New York Times*, November 27, 1983.

———. "Ella Fitzgerald's Playfulness Ripens with Time's Passage." *New York Times*, April 15, 1991.

Jackson, Reuben. "Ella Fitzgerald." In *Black Women in America: An Historical Encyclopedia*, ed. Darlene Clark Hines. Brooklyn, N.Y.: Carlson Publishing, 1993.

Jefferson, Margo. "Ella in Wonderland." *New York Times*, December 29, 1996.

Jeske, Lee. "Ask Norman." *Jazziz* (Gainesville, Fla.), November 1996.

Johnson, Malcolm. "Cafe Life in New York." [unidentified New York daily], October 30, 1940.

Kempton, Murray. "She." *New York Post*, June 1954.

———. "The Americans." *New York Post*, June 25, 1959.

Kennedy, Frank. "Ella Fitzgerald: A Supreme Moment." *Daily Star* (Toronto), May 13, 1966.

Kliment, Bud. "Two Stages." In *Ella Fitzgerald*. New York: Chelsea House, 1988.

Kolodin, Irving. "Rodgers and Hart, Ella and Ellington." *Saturday Review*, March 16, 1957.

Levin, Floyd. "Ella Fitzgerald and Benny Carter at the Hollywood Bowl." *Jazz Forum*, May 6, 1992.

Luce, Betsy. "Someday Ella'll Buy." *New York Post*, 1943.

Lyons, Len. *The Great Jazz Pianists*. New York: Quill, 1983.

———. "Bebop and Modern Jazz (The Early Styles)." In *The 101 Best Jazz Albums: A History of Jazz on Records*. New York: William Morrow and Company, Inc., 1980.

"Mama Jazz Bows Out." *New York Times* [editorial], June 18, 1996.

Murphy, Mark. "Tisket, Tasket, It's Rhythm." *New York Post*, February 20, 1941.

Nicholson, Stuart. *Ella Fitzgerald: A Biography of the First Lady of Jazz*. New York: Charles Scribner's Sons, 1994. A reprint of a British edition from the previous year.

Okon, May. "She Still Gets Stage Fright." *Sunday News* (New York), September 8, 1957.

Pleasants, Henry. "Ella." In *The Great American Popular Singers*. New York: Simon & Schuster, 1985. A reprint of the British edition of 1974.

Rockwell, John. "Half a Century of Song with the Great 'Ella.'" *New York Times*, June 15, 1986.

"Shakeup Hits Ella's Band: Bob Stark Out." *Down Beat*, November 11, 1941.

Siegel, Joel. "Ella at 65." *Washington Post* [in an abridged form]. Reprinted in *Jazz Times* (Silver Spring, Md.), November 1983.

"She Who Is Ella." *Time*, November 27, 1964.

Simon, George T. *The Big Bands*. New York: Schirmer Books, 1981.

Smith, Jessie Carney, ed. *Notable Black American Women*. Detroit, Mich.: Gale Research, Inc., 1993.

"Tales from Ella's Fellas." *Down Beat*, September 1995.

Taylor, Angela. "Ella Fitzgerald, in Tune at Her Own Party." *New York Times*, October 10, 1980.

Troup, Stuart. "A Reunion of Jazz Giants." *Newsday* (Long Island, N.Y.), April 25, 1990.

Tynan, John. "It Took a Hit Album to Make Miss F. a Class Nitery Attraction." *Down Beat*, November 28, 1956.

"The Visual Arts." In *Women of Achievement: Thirty-five Centuries of History*. New York: Harmony Books, 1981.

Watt, Douglas. "Miss Ella" ["Popular Records" section]. *Show*, October 1961.

Wilmer, Valerie. *Jazz People*. New York: Da Capo, 1977.

Wilson, John S. "'Angel Eyes' Is Triumph for Ella Fitzgerald." *New York Times*, June 26, 1978.

Wilson, Earl. "A Tisket, A Tasket, the Wrong Colored Basket." *New York Post*, August 15, 1938.

Permissions and Credits

Introduction
Jim Haskins. *Ella Fitzgerald: A Life through Jazz,* chapter 1. London: New English Library, 1991. Reprinted by permission.

Part One: Spring Is Here
Earl Wilson. "A Tisket, A Tasket, the Wrong Colored Basket." *New York Post,* August 15, 1938. Reprinted with permission from the New York Post. Copyright 1938 NYP Holdings, Inc.

Nina Bernstein. "The Gap in Ella Fitzgerald's Life." *New York Times,* June 23, 1996. Copyright © by the New York Times Company. Reprinted by permission.

Ralph Cooper, with Steve Dougherty. *Amateur Night at the Apollo.* New York: HarperCollins, 1990. Copyright © 1990 by Ralph Cooper Literary, Inc. Reprinted by permission of International Creative Management, Inc.

Part Two: How High the Moon
Whitney Balliett. "The First Lady of Song." Copyright © Whitney Balliett. Originally published in the *New Yorker,* April 26, 1993. All rights reserved. Reprinted by permission.

Carter Harman. "Ella Has a Way with a Song." *New York Times,* September 1951. Copyright © 1951 by the New York Times Company. Reprinted by permission.

Stanley Dance. "Four to Keep," excerpt from "Lightly & Politely" [column]. *Jazz Journal* (London: England), 1952–54. Reprinted by permission.

Bill Coss. "Ella." *Metronome*, October 1953. Copyright © R. Scott Asen, Metronome Archive.

Nat Hentoff. "Ella Tells of Trouble in Mind Concerning Discs, Television." *Down Beat*, February 23, 1955. Reprinted by permission of the author.

Dom Cerulli. "Ella Fitzgerald: The Criterion of Innocence for Popular Singers." *The Jazz Horn* album liner notes. Reprinted by permission of the author.

Bob Bach. "The First Lady of Song." *Metronome*. Copyright © R. Scott Asen, Metronome Archive.

Leonard Feather. "Ella Gives Carmen, Peggy, Hackett 5." *Down Beat*, October 5, 1955. Reprinted by permission of the author.

Part Three: Everything I've Got

R. J. D.(Dic Doyle). "Ella Sings the Duke and It's a Treasure." *Globe and Mail* (Toronto), June 14, 1958. Reprinted with permission from the *Globe and Mail.*

John Edward Hasse. "Essential Ellington, 1956–1965." In *Beyond Category: The Life and Genius of Duke Ellington.* New York: Simon & Schuster, 1993.

Leonard Feather. "Ella." In *From Satchmo to Miles.* New York: Da Capo, 1972; reprinted 1984. Reprinted by permission of the author.

Bob Freedman. "The Audience Loved Ella's Evening" in "The Jazz Scene" [column]. *Boston Traveler,* October 20, 1959. Reproduced courtesy of the *Boston Herald.*

Ralph J. Gleason. "Rhythm Section." *Beacon* (Wichita, Kan.), November 30, 1958. Reprinted by permission of The Estate of Ralph J. Gleason and Jazz Casual Prod., Inc. All rights reserved. © Jazz Casual Prod., Inc.

Douglas Watt. "Miss Ella" in "Popular Records" [column]. *Show*, October 1961. Reprinted by permission of the author.

Unsigned. "She Who Is Ella." *Time*, November 27, 1964. © 1964 Time Inc. Reprinted by permission.

Lee Jeske. "Ask Norman." *Jazziz* (Gainesville, Fla.), November 1996. Reprinted by permission of the author.

Francis Davis. "Ella." In *Outcats: Jazz Composers, Instrumentalists, and Singers,* by Francis Davis. New York: Oxford University Press, 1990. Reprinted by permission of Oxford University Press.

Leonard Feather. "Ella Fitzgerald—Lonely at the Top" in "Jazz Beat" [column]. *New York Post,* October 19, 1965. Reprinted by permission of the author.

Will Friedwald. "Lady Day and Lady Time." In *Jazz Singing,* edited by Will Friedwald, New York: Da Capo Press, 1996. Copyright © 1990, 1992 by Will Friedwald. Used by permission of the author.

Leslie Gourse. "The Time of Ella Fitzgerald." In *Louis' Children,* edited by Leslie Gourse. New York: William Morrow and Company, Inc., 1984. Reprinted by permission of William Morrow & Company, Inc.

Part Four: How Long Has This Been Going On?

Frank Kennedy. "Ella Fitzgerald: A Supreme Moment." *Daily Star* (Toronto), May 13, 1966. Reprinted with permission—the Toronto Star Syndicate.

Henry Pleasants. "Ella." In *The Great American Popular Singers.* New York: Simon & Schuster, 1974. Reprinted by permission of the author.

Ernest Dunbar. "Ella Still Sings Just This Side of the Angels." *New York Times,* arts and leisure section, November 24, 1974. Copyright © by the New York Times Company. Reprinted by permission.

John S. Wilson. "'Angel Eyes' Is Triumph for Ella Fitzgerald." *New York Times,* June 26, 1978. Copyright © by the New York Times Company. Reprinted by permission.

Angela Taylor. "Ella Fitzgerald, in Tune at Her Own Party." *New York Times,* October 10, 1980. Copyright © by the New York Times Company. Reprinted by permission.

Len Lyons. "Bebop and Modern Jazz: The Early Styles." In *The 101 Best Jazz Albums.* New York: William Morrow & Co., 1980. Copyright © 1980 by Len Lyons. Reprinted by permission of William Morrow & Company, Inc.

Gary Giddins. "First Lady." In *Faces in the Crowd.* New York: Oxford University Press, 1992. Reprinted by permission of Oxford University Press.

Joel E. Siegel. "Ella at 65." *Jazz Times* (Silver Spring, Md.), November 1983. Reprinted by permission of the author.

Leslie Gourse. "Tales of Mel Lewis and Walter Gil Fuller." Reprinted courtesy of the author.

Ted Fox. *Showtime at the Apollo.* New York: Da Capo Press, 1983. Copyright © 1983 Ted Fox.

Giddins, Gary. "Chilled Classics and the Real Thing." In *Rhythm-a-ning: Jazz Tradition & Innovation in the '80s.* New York: 1985. Reprinted courtesy of Oxford University Press.

Gourse, Leslie. "Celebrating Ella." *Jazz Times* (Silver Spring, Md.), September 1991. Reprinted courtesy of the author.

Part Five: Evening Star

Stephen Holden. "Jazz: Ella Fitzgerald Sings with Count Basie Group." *New York Times,* November 27, 1983. Copyright © by the New York Times Company. Reprinted by permission.

———. "Ella Fitzgerald's Playfulness Ripens with Time's Passage." *New York Times,* April 15, 1991. Copyright © by the New York Times Company. Reprinted by permission.

Chip Deffaa. "Ella Fitzgerald." In *Jazz Veterans: A Portrait Gallery.* Fort Bragg, Calif.: Cypress House, 1996. Copyright © 1996 by Chip Deffaa. Reprinted by permission of the author.

John Rockwell. "Half a Century of Song with the Great 'Ella.'" *New York Times,* June 15, 1986. Copyright © by the New York Times Company. Reprinted by permission.

Floyd Levin. "Ella Fitzgerald and Benny Carter at the Hollywood Bowl." *Jazz Forum,* May 6, 1992. Reprinted courtesy of the author.

Margo Jefferson. "Ella in Wonderland." *New York Times,* December 29, 1996. Copyright © by the New York Times Company. Reprinted by permission.

Leonard Feather. "Ella Fitzgerald." *Jazz Times,* September 1994. Reprinted by permission of the author.

"'Mama Jazz' Bows Out" [editorial]. *New York Times,* June 18, 1996. Copyright © by the New York Times Company. Reprinted by permission.

Every effort has been made to identify the sources of publication of these essays and make full acknowledgments of their use. If any error or omission has occurred, it will be rectified in future editions, provided the appropriate notification is submitted in writing to the publisher or editor.

Index